EYE ON CAVETT

Also by
Dick Cavett and Christopher Porterfield
CAVETT

EYE ON CAVETT

by
Dick Cavett
and
Christopher Porterfield

ARBOR HOUSE
New York

Parts of Eye on Cavett have appeared in a different form in
the New York Times [© 1977 the New York Times Company. Reprinted by
permission.] the New Republic and Film Comment.

The authors wish to thank St. Martin's Press for permission
to exerpt material from the foreword of By George, by George
S. Kaufman. © 1979 Anne Kaufman Schneider.

CONTENTS

À LA RECHERCHE DE NEBRASKA

"My God, it's you!"

"We heard you were coming but didn't know whether to believe it."

"Hey, you look fan-tastic!"

"Well, you've certainly gone places since the last time we saw you."

"This is just incredible. I can't believe it!"

"Make me a hero by saying hello to my wife, would you? It'd be such a thrill for her."

I NEVER LOOKED FORWARD to anything more than to my twentieth high school reunion. I couldn't *wait* for it. I was like a kid checking off the days on the calendar until Christmas. From the moment I decided to attend I was in a state of breathless emotional enthusiasm that I still find puzzling. I'm not sure what I expected to happen there or why it took on such significance, but whatever it was it went deep.

I thought about taking a camera crew to Nebraska with me and making a TV special about the festivities, but I knew what would happen. My favorite scientific principle, and almost the only one I know, is the Heisenberg Uncertainty Principle. It describes the way some phenomena are changed by the very process of observing them. I didn't want the Heisenberg Principle distorting the reunion, or turning it into a public event. I wanted this moment to be all mine.

Scanning the list of classmates who had made reservations, I let the names carry me back nostalgically to scenes in Lincoln High School. One of the people who was coming was the girl who beat me out for the first chair in the second clarinet section of the band. And the guy *I* beat out for first place on the pommel horse in the state gymnastics meet—he would be there too. Also the girl with whom I declined to sing "Abba Dabba Honeymoon" at Joy Night. (The annual school variety show; not, as it sounds, a drug party. The times then were innocent.)

I wondered if I would see the less-than-brilliant but sexy brunette from French class—the one at whose firm and fully packed purple cashmere sweater I used to steal longing glances; the one who, after almost a year of French, came to the word *voilà* while reading aloud, hesitated, and said quizzically, "Voyla?" It was a word we had (presumably) learned from day one, and my ear-splitting shriek of laughter brought a warning of expulsion from Miss Grone.

Would Harry Hammond be there, and would I still feel animosity toward him for ratting on me and Tom Keene the night the three of us broke someone's front window with a pop bottle, and lied to the cops about it?

Or Miss Hall, the teacher who was the student council advisor and to whom I owed an apology for acting mean to her?

I had a full set of anticipatory images that I took out mentally and fondled like childhood baseball cards. I imagined the mini-conversations I would have with people, impressing and flattering them by recalling things they had said or done, creating glowing moments for them and me. I amused myself by mentally telling various female classmates how I had yearned for them, and I savored in advance how this would tantalize them with the thought of the opportunities they had lost, poor dears.

I especially fancied the idea of not letting anyone know for sure whether I was coming, or even in town, until my sudden appearance sent waves of electricity through the throng. At one point, I confess blushingly, I even considered saying I was definitely *not* coming in order to heighten the impact of a surprise entrance.

Meanwhile the days dragged by more torpidly than they do for the kid who has secretly discovered he is to get a bike for Christmas.

The plain truth, only dimly sensed by me at the time, was that I was already living a fantasy of the reunion, one in which, strangely, I was even more hypnotized by my celebrity than I wanted my classmates to be.

One particularly vivid vision stays with me still, the way a bright object burns an afterimage onto the TV screen. I am sitting at a table full of classmates in a large hotel ballroom, merry as a grig, the cynosure of every eye. I am sporting a golden suntan and—the sort of dream detail you tell your analyst—wearing a white dinner jacket. (All the other men are dressed in suits.)

Since nobody would want to be the only one at anything in a white dinner jacket, this detail puzzles me and must have some unconscious meaning. Am I Gatsby? Robert Redford as Gatsby? Golden Boy?

Whatever else I am in this vision, I am a Big Star. The One Who Made It. The Cosmopolite among the Yokels. I have had my Own Show, won Emmy Awards, been on the cover of Time, Life and TV Guide, been to the White House, and now I'm back and sitting down with my classmates and being envied and wanted and admired.

I know, I know; it's revolting. But let me hasten to say that these are not my true feelings. I don't think of my friends or of the Midwest as yokeldom, and surely I have outgrown the adolescent fantasy of coming back to the home town on the back seat of an open car, nodding and strewing flowers to hoi polloi who stayed behind. At least consciously.

This sort of thing would make more sense if I had been an anonymous, acne-infested wallflower in high school, the sort who repaired radios as a hobby and whose social life consisted of going alone to football games, haunting the edges of sock-hops, playing with younger kids and jerking off in the garage. Oddly enough, I felt like one of those guys, and to some degree I did all of the above, or virtually all. (Nobody wants to admit to repairing radios.)

But in fact I was president of the student council, the perennial lead in the school play, a witty emcee at football banquets and quite a sizable frog in the pond in which I dwelt.

The paradox was that I still was not in the inner circle, not a member of that debonair group of "neat people" who dated and danced and who maybe, in those pre-liberated days, had some s-e-x. I could, even in those days, ad lib from a nightclub stage like a seasoned pro, yet I felt socially awkward. I got into scalding sweats just talking to a girl, and at the end of a date either took long enough saying goodnight to read the *Aeneid* (aloud) or else went for a compulsive peck on the mouth which, had I held it for a count of two, would've caused me to spontaneously combust.

Ah well, all that would be behind me when I made my triumphal return. (Wouldn't it?)

I flew to the Omaha airport and drove on to Lincoln in a rented car in which, before even informing my parents of my arrival, I prowled the town under cover of darkness, feeling like a spy on assignment in a once-familiar city. Driving the shadowy streets, I felt a tingle of excitement as I rolled past familiar haunts, toying with the idea of ringing a doorbell at random and hearing some reaction like, "Martha, guess who's standing on *our* porch!"

I had made other visits to Lincoln over the years, of course, but the emotion this time was different. I passed the houses of former friends, resenting the absence of a remembered tree or the presence of a new *paved* driveway. These impertinent changes altered my affectionate image of the settings of recalled pranks and fond romantic memories. How dare they tamper with them!

I drove the route of my old walk to school, convinced that it had been severely shortened and that what in my mind's eye were wide avenues had been narrowed and somehow made prosaic.

An abundance of buried memories and names and faces swam to the surface—things I couldn't for the life of me have recalled without the stimulus of a familiar hedge or street sign. Even voices came back to me as I passed a place where I had heard a particularly pungent dirty joke or planned an evening's mischief.

After an hour or more of this nostalgic cruising I pulled into the Cavett driveway as if arriving straight from the airport. Before going to bed I got out my old yearbook and let the fresh-faced portraits bring back still more memories and half-forgotten names.

*   *   *

Against all odds, the day itself finally dawns, the kind of sunny and warm May morning that used to make me long to have nothing more to do with school. It occurs to me that the reunion will soon happen *and soon be over.* That brings a premonitory letdown, a slightly sour reflection that things looked forward to are often less exciting in fact than in anticipation.

Trying not to think about that, I lay out my clothes hours ahead of time: an expensive, off-ivory suit (the white dinner jacket?) and a dark shirt whose open neck once caused a woman to say enticingly, "I didn't realize you were *hairy.*"

With a few hours to kill, I sit for a while in my parents' backyard to tan my face a bit (Golden Boy?), savoring the coming event as I recline half-dreamingly in a lawn chair, enjoying the forgotten total quiet of a midwestern afternoon.

I have let a few people know I'm in town. June Schorr, a date from bygone days, now married to another classmate who is a successful local businessman, has called to invite me to a pre-reunion cocktail party. And there, in the sumptuously furnished library of the home of one of the "big wheel" crowd from the class, the evening begins.

Over the hors d'oeuvres, I am impressed with what a cosmopolitan looking group we are—certainly not the easterner's image of "the sticks." The ladies look handsome, the men prosperous. There is bright chitchat and a mild dash of gossip, such as the tale of the couple who came perilously close to divorce over the last reunion: the husband succumbed to his wife's demands that they purchase an ill-afforded sleek new station wagon to park prominently at the entrance, but when they arrived they found to their chagrin that all the spaces were taken.

Although I'm enjoying this glossy little gathering, it is not among my preconceived images. My thoughts keep pressing ahead to the reunion itself. I begin to worry that we will be late, at the same time chiding myself for the awareness that I want to get there and start dazzling my other classmates.

The first of my assumptions is dismantled, though, when I learn that the venue is not to be the hotel ballroom I pictured myself in, but the Legion Club, a place I don't know at all.

When we finally pull up there, the low, cinder-block building seems too small to hold the event I've been thinking of. Nevertheless, crossing its still sunny parking lot, I almost have to restrain myself from breaking into a run to get inside and get it all going.

Inside—amidst a decor that a condescending observer might call knotty-pine-roadhouse-tacky—there is already a thick throng, which I scan quickly for familiar faces. The girl taking names at the door is (was) Karen Bahr, who had been my assistant in my Joy Night magic act. As I give her a peck on the cheek I spot a guy from the gym team, then a fellow band member, and memories begin to swarm and collide.

I push on in among banquet tables set around an open dance area, aware of sentences stopped in mid-word as people tell others to turn around and look, and an overlapping murmur of "there he is." One guy does a take, grins and darts deeper into the crowd, presumably to spread the word. A woman I don't recognize stops speaking when she sees me, puts her hands to the sides of her head and appears to emit a silent "eeeeeek!"

Would Redford have an even greater effect? I ask myself.

"Dick!" another lady says to me. "I bet you don't recognize my curly head."

"Nor your curly hair," I start to reply, but instead say, "Don't be silly." She seems inordinately pleased by this.

As I begin circulating, shaking hands, kissing, hugging on all sides, I'm struck by the effect it has on people when I address them by name. At one point I recognize a face a few yards away in the crowd and throw a greeting to the guy by forming his first name with my lips. He nearly comes apart, nodding so eagerly in confirmation that it's touching, with a delighted look that says, "Ohjesuschristheknowsmyname!"

I should be embarrassed, I guess, but I confess that the effect is so enjoyable that I resolve to make a special effort for the rest of the evening to come up with everyone's moniker, and when I'm at a loss I will try to have someone at my elbow prompting me.

At this point I have my first authentic vivid impression. The apparent age range is startling. By definition we're all the same age, of course, yet as I look around, this could be, in show biz terms, a casting call for people from twenty-five to—so help me—sixty.

One fellow who confronts me, announcing his name, appears to be about the age of Robert Young as Marcus Welby. How nice of Bill, I think, to bring his father to the reunion. "I certainly remember—" your son, I was going to say, but I catch myself. It is almost like seeing an actor friend in character makeup, his features emerging, on close inspection, from behind the drooping mustache, creased flesh and gray hair. I realize that my expression must register the unspoken question: "What happened?"

What indeed? I have to remind myself that some of these folks have children who are as old as I *feel* I am.

By and large it's the men who have let themselves go. Dropouts from sports (including, perhaps, all but intramural sex), frazzled by their respective rat races, so many of them seem to have grayed and spread and sagged. The women have tried harder to stay in trim and project a little youthful spark, sometimes with all too obvious help from makeup, undergarments and goodly stretches at what I once heard a Southern maid call "the hair presser." I see several attractive women whom I don't recognize from high school. They must be cases not so much of careful preservation as of belated blossoming over the years.

There are exceptions, though. As an apparently late middle-aged lady approaches a knot of people I'm in, someone says, "You remember L—." She hasn't reached us yet and I have time to say, "What did she teach?" She didn't. She is one of us. She looks about the same age as the handful of L.H.S. teachers—thoughtfully invited by the planning committee—who are seated around a special table somewhat on the periphery.

They, strangely, look to be exactly the same age as when I "had them." For the first time it hits me that, in my adolescence, teachers I loosely guessed to be on the verge of retirement were actually in their thirties or early forties, staggering as it is to realize. That was the callow time of life when, hearing it lamented that someone had died at fifty-one, I thought, "What are they complaining about? That's more than *thirty years* from now—almost two lifetimes longer than mine to date."

Gradually, penetrating the disguises of two decades, I discern again the outlines of our class with its (probably universal) gallery of types: leaders, sissies, brains, nerds, jocks, hoods, sexpots and wall flora.

Fragments of their biographies filter through the greetings and banter. ". . . made sales manager last year" ". . . two lovely daughters" ". . . her second divorce" ". . . think they're somewhere out in California." One guy from the class, incredibly, is unmarried and still living at home.

At the pre-reunion cocktail party I was stunned to learn that one of the beautiful Swanson twins, who also assisted me in my magic act, is dead. Now, spookily, that news flashes again to mind just *before* someone tells me that the girl who played Emily in the class production of *Our Town* died several years ago. This jolts me for a moment, and I recall Emily's line in the play: "Do any human beings ever realize life while they're living it?—every, every minute?" No time to think about that now.

I begin to sense the absence of others, people who ought to be here because I imagined they would be. Where is sleek and funny Dick Bond, who could shake (sic) his eyeballs? And David Kingsbury, the tough urchin who liked to grab other boys' pectorals in the locker room and give them a "blue tit"? Don't they realize I wanted them here?

I feel out of touch and shocked when June Schorr whispers to me that some of the class couldn't afford the, to me, negligible fee—even some living in Lincoln. In a moment of ego I wish she had told me their names so I could have paid their way in a combination of *noblesse oblige* and *grande largesse*.

Suddenly something happens that I hadn't pictured. Someone asks for my autograph. In a phrase almost extinct nowadays, it blows my mind. You don't sign autographs for your own classmates! But I sign, of course, and it distances me in some way I regret. I wanted them to see me as a star, but when they do it in this way it seems to cut me off from something else I hungered for in all this, some fusion with them.

One request touches off several more, and then a whole series. I feel the psychological current reversing. Instead of basking in the intimate glow of remember-when conversations, we might as well be at a stage door.

I get the star treatment, too, in their excessive and artificial reaction to my every nod in the direction of humor.

"Dick," says one guy to me, "you put us all to shame doing that thing on the parallel bars on your show last week. You're supposed to have a gut like me, but you're still built like a brick shithouse."

"Some people think that's exactly what I *am,*" I retort. Gleeful hilarity ensues.

Another chap says, "Hey, Dick, remember me?"

"Vividly." (Boffo.)

"Tell me, how come my wife stays up to watch your show after I go to bed?"

"Probably horny." (Pandemonium.) I am Bob Hope, stepping out of the carriage into the admiring throng, saying, "I wonder what the dull people are doing?"

Occasionally an undertone of resentment—could it be more common than I realize?—impinges on all the fussing and fawning over me. After I am finally seated for dinner (at what someone refers to as "the chic table") and chatting over the grapefruit appetizer, a fellow abruptly asks me, "How come you don't have children?"

I respond with a glib and frivolous answer—something like, "I guess so far I'm the blessed event in our household." But it is clear that his question was intended to show he isn't afraid to challenge or even irritate the famous guest. There is noticeable eye-averting and disapproval from others at the table, which *does* embarrass me. An unexpected, awkward moment.

A little later it is followed by another one. A guy looms up at the table with a glass of scotch and says, in a voice that reveals he's had quite a few himself, "Here, I bought you a drink."

I tell him a few sips of wine are my limit, thank him, and set the scotch aside.

"Oh, come on. You gotta have a drink on a great occasion like this."

"I'll work on it later," I say, sensing tension.

"Whatsamatter? Too good to have a drink with me?" Before it gets worse, his wife leads him away with a pained smile.

I am quickly surrounded by more cheerfully avid classmates. Too surrounded. Too avid. I can scarcely eat my dinner for signing autographs. One particularly exuberant girl has slid in next to me, if not on me, and is nattering and nibbling at me in a way that draws looks of scorn and a couple of suggestions to "cool it," which she ignores.

My head is beginning to swim. It's all happening too fast. Every encounter, instead of being what it is, to be enjoyed for its own sake, seems a distraction from something else. I yearn to cover more of the room, to be democratic and mingle with the unknowns who are too shy to come over. I don't feel that I'm taking the event in, but being taken in *by* it instead.

Even without lights and cameras, the Heisenberg Principle is taking its toll.

A manager of the Legion Club, apparently having spotted my discomfort from a distance, comes over and offers me his office as a momentary retreat. I accept.

The silence and privacy are a blessing. After I've sat alone for a few minutes trying to get my bearings, there's a tap at the door and one of the few females from our class who is unaccompanied tonight asks if she can come in.

She joins me on a red leather couch and gives me a quick fill-in on her life since L.H.S.: a divorce, a career in another midwestern city, a drift away from much that the scene outside the door represents.

Although in high school she was not among the top six, say, in my mental pin-up of desirable and therefore unattainable girls, she was easily in the second rank, and because tall, out of the question for me. Now I note that she is more attractive than she was back then—one of the late bloomers—and I am aware of an undercurrent of sexuality. I begin to lose my focus on what she is saying and I interrupt her to suggest (but only in my mind), "Let's get undressed and have it off right here on the couch with the reunion going on outside."

What keeps me from saying it in fact is a version of the same inhibition I felt way back then—a fear of getting back something like, "Are you crazy? I thought you liked me for myself, and now *this!* You're no better than all the rest."

But even deeper down, I can't help suspecting that she might have accepted the offer with enthusiasm, and we both might have been better people for it. I make a mental note to tell this to a psychiatrist if I ever get one.

Emerging from the office (hoping maybe someone will think we *did* have it off), I find that the formal part of the evening's program is about to begin. Everybody takes seats, and my school buddy Tom Keene, the emcee, steps up—not on the glamorously spotlit ballroom stage I had pictured, but on a simple wooden riser along the wall.

Tom is a polished and lively speaker, and I reflect that he probably could have had a career as an actor or entertainer. It comes back to me that when we were kids I was irked that he started his own magic act (copying me, as I saw it), and I feared that he might encroach on my turf and even (horrors!) go farther than I in show biz.

This prompts me to wonder what would have happened if I weren't the only star at the reunion. What if Sandy Dennis, for example, had been in our class instead of a year or two behind? An Oscar winner! Would I have even showed up tonight?

Before I can pursue the thought, Tom introduces me. I stand up in front of this group as I so often used to do, years ago. In fact, as I go through my pleasantries, get off a few jokes and begin taking questions from the floor, time telescopes: I'm back emceeing the football banquet or the honors assembly, getting laughs just like a professional comic.

Standing here now actually feels no different from those earlier occasions, just as hosting the Emmy Awards and appearing at the White House, I've discovered, feels no different from them either. The truth of the matter is that I *felt* as famous after wowing them in the ninth grade assembly as I ever have since. You might well ask, then, why I still care so much about it after all these years.

Well, why?

A partial answer occurs to me as I gaze out at my classmates' faces, which at this point run the gamut from beaming, adoring looks to booze-sodden indifference. It is clear now. Getting up on stage has always been my device for separating myself from them, for feeling superior to them. However, the feeling of superiority can't quite compensate—not now, any more than it could in high school—for the simultaneous longing to be out there with them in some sense, to be one of them, to be in their houses and at their parties and part of the fabric of their lives.

I flash back to the feeling of packing up my magic-act props after absolutely killing the student audience at some function, and then, before going home alone, looking back longingly at the dancing couples. They had enjoyed me but by now—who knows?—perhaps had forgotten all about me as they swayed together, looking forward to private parties afterward, and maybe to s- -, or at least to (does the phrase still exist?) heavy petting.

As an adolescent, I had the notion that if I could cause the kind of stir that real celebrities did when they entered a restaurant, if I could move through a crowd the way I'd seen Hope do, leaving awed whispers of "There he goes!" in his wake—if I could do these things, then all my other problems and desires would be resolved. Just give me that, O genie, and you can keep all the rest.

A wild non sequitur is involved here. It goes: if I could be the most envied one, then I would also be the best and happiest one; fame will make my more basic, if obscure, longings and inadequacies pale by comparison.

The notion is crazy, of course; in the case of some people, tragically so. But it is potent and has a lot to do with why people go into show business or seek fame for its own sake.

Unfortunately, one's own fame doesn't seem like fame, if for no other reason than that you can't feel the effect you're having on others. In order to get the charge you always wanted from it, you have to keep trying to rekindle your original juvenile image of it, or find that image reflected in people's feelings toward you.

It must be what I'm trying to do here tonight.

I close off the question period, stepping down to a roar of applause that should please me more than it does.

A hubbub forms around me again, but I realize the evening is winding down. Instamatics come out and snap me with other guys' wives, our arms around each other. Addresses are exchanged. There is a drift toward the door.

I feel a mild panic. I want to say, "Wait—don't go! There are so many things that haven't happened for me yet!"

I have a sudden and too late urge to throw a picnic for everybody tomorrow, as a way of prolonging the reunion and giving myself another chance to move around and have all those richly intimate encounters I never quite got to.

But it's no good: the reunion is ending.

Later, perplexed and a bit dispirited, I lie in bed at my parents' house and ask myself over and over what this pathological appetite is that I thought the evening would appease. I try to figure out what mysterious satisfaction I both wanted more of and knew I could never really get. I can't fathom it. (Much later, two years of psychoanalysis won't provide the answer either.)

In the days after the reunion I take out the guest list and muse yet again over the names. I can't remember seeing some of the people there. But I want to, so badly that I can clearly picture the meetings and hear imagined conversations.

Soon I begin revising scenes that actually did occur, until eventually the whole event reshapes itself once more into a set of anticipatory images, with all their tantalizing glitter and excitement intact.

These scenes haven't happened, and yet they haven't gone away. My old appetite for them persists. I'm still looking forward, in my imagination, to the reunion.

* * *

For years before my reunion, I used to have a recurrent dream about going back to high school and attending my old classes. This was a real dream, not a waking fantasy like my ballroom appearance in a white dinner jacket.

I went from room to room in the guise of a student but, at the same time, in one of those dream incongruities, I was also my grown-up self, a TV host, a celebrity. Disappointingly, my friends and classmates didn't recognize me for what I had become—or if they did, they apparently weren't impressed. I still wasn't envied and admired in a way that would make up for all those youthful years of feeling inept and frustrated, of being left out of the social world of my smoother, more confident contemporaries.

The dream always ended with me sadly wondering, "Why don't they react more? What good has it all done me?"

Memory and desire, mixed together just as my fellow midwesterner T. S. Eliot said they were.

My thoughts go back often to those childhood friends and school-mates. In recent years, quite apart from the promptings of the reunion, I've taken to looking up or phoning many of them out of the blue, some of whom I haven't been in touch with since graduation.

Why? Partly it has to do with the urge I felt again so piercingly at the reunion—to fuse with them, to become them. I have such a strong awareness that they've led the lives I never led and now never can.

In this part of middle age? A sense just beneath the surface that haunts us all to some extent? That whatever we have done with our lives is the wrong thing and we are stuck with it?

I remind myself, whenever I feel this way, that everybody's life has to have some pleasures and rewards that mine lacks, even though mine has plenty of both. But I can feel horribly deprived at having only one life. I wish I could know the heady existence of a symphony conductor or the simple rounds of a mailman, complete with pipe, slippers and a small vegetable garden. Calling my old playmate and childhood neighbor Hugh McKnight on an impulse one night, I suddenly crave to live on a hill in Indianapolis and work for the Eli Lilly Company, as he does.

Then again I don't, of course. But I find it strange that I can succumb to this hemorrhaging feeling that whatever the other person has is clearly what I not only ought to have but want with every fiber of my being.

What, after all, *does* the other person have? And what, from his or her point of view, do I have? This is the sort of thing I had hoped to explore at the Legion Club, in all those satisfying tête-à-têtes that never happened. Now, lingering in Lincoln for a couple of weeks after the event, I find myself tending to seek answers elsewhere, from other intriguing figures in my past.

I begin with a classmate who didn't come to the reunion: Wilma the Wolf.

The zoological sobriquet, derived from her real name of Wilma Wolfe and bestowed probably sometime in grade school, had relegated her permanently to the joke category. Wilma in no way resembled a wolf, but she was an eccentric little girl, given to exaggerated gestures and histrionic remarks. By sixth grade she had the speech patterns and mannerisms of a full-grown literary lady. I imagined her sitting in her bedroom in a long scarf or boa and practicing sweeps of her arm with a long cigarette holder, or having tea with whoever her friends were in a grotesque parody of a book club meeting.

In the eighth grade it was whispered that Wilma had written a novel. Because the most popular people in class never actually did *anything*, this automatically put her out of the mainstream and made her an object of scorn. We covered our uneasiness about how to appraise her by ridiculing her. "Carolyn Carter go out with you? You're kidding. You'd be lucky to get a date with Wilma Wolfe."

She acted too. I remember thinking she was quite good in some one-act school play, but it was dismissed as no great accomplishment because "she was only playing herself"—a common misconception about what it takes to give a convincing performance. Anyway, unlike our schoolmate Sandy Dennis, Wilma was not taken seriously as an actress.

There were rumors that she and her circle put on plays privately, and even wrote their own scripts. Secretly—very secretly—I was envious. I thought it would be fun to be in on that, if it could be done so that none of the "neat" people would catch me associating with oddball Wilma. But the fear of being found out was too great.

How do I find Wilma today? I've heard that she's still living in Lincoln, but is she an old maid, sour, gone to fat? The sort who gets her doorbell rung by neighborhood urchins who then hide in the lilac bushes and make rude noises at her?

With a little detective work I track her down under a different last name. Wilma married! On the phone her voice is melodious and full of varied emphases, not the droning flat twang that is often the aural curse of this part of the country.

I make an appointment to come to her house. She seems to hesitate because her husband won't be home at the time. Does she consider it improper, in this day and age, for me to be there when he isn't? She refers to him as an "Army sharpshooter." A warning, perhaps?

Next day I ring her bell. A teenage boy appears on the other side of the screen door. He has the manner of someone who just woke up, but it is probably congenital.

"You Dick Cavett?"

I admit it.

"What you doin' *here?*"

Wrong house.

I move two doors down, trying to saunter casually but feeling the kid's eyes on the back of my neck. Wilma's house is an old stucco structure with slightly overgrown grass and shrubs. It reminds me of one of those midwestern houses from which reclusive old ladies totter to chase dogs from their yards with a broom. I have a sudden image of Wilma living here with a senile mother and a jingoist hothead of a husband who cleans and fondles guns all day and threatens to let her have both barrels if she "gets out of line."

The door is opened by a slender, attractive woman in a white pants suit. "Well, it really *is* you," Wilma says. We embrace somewhat theatrically in a way that we probably both realize is out of proportion to our scant acquaintance in school.

After the glaring sunshine her living room is dark, cool, with over-stuffed chairs and a clutter of carved clocks and other knickknacks that reminds me pleasantly of the homes of my old German relatives. Against this background, Wilma's white outfit sets her off effectively.

"You caused quite a lot of consternation by calling here last night," she says. I wonder if her immaculate hair is the result of rushing out to the beauty parlor this morning.

If she is flustered she doesn't show it. In fact, as we reminisce, I realize that she still has all her childhood mannerisms but they have been refined into an impression of real style. What in those days seemed ludicrous suits her now. As she gestures there is a glint of bracelets, an elegant weaving of forearms that brings to mind, say, a young Agnes Moorhead.

I tell her that she has always been a striking figure to me, a figure of charisma, and that if I hadn't been so constricted by my sense of who the "right" people were in school we would have been friends.

"Me?" she exclaims. "My God, this is wonderful for my ego. No one would believe this."

Interestingly, she is more impressed by my compliment than by my retroactive snobbery. As for those "right" people, she merely shrugs. "I didn't need them," she says. I know she's right and I wish I could say the same.

When I ask about her acting, I learn that she actually did, as we used to say, try the big time. After college her mother had taken her to New York, where she had her teeth straightened and did some modeling; then on to the West Coast, where she appeared in showcase productions at the Pasadena Playhouse.

The mention of her mother triggers a memory from high school days. It was after a touring actor gave a one-man evening of Shakespeare at the University of Nebraska. I went backstage to introduce myself, as I always did whenever there was even a quasi-celebrity in town. But my carefully prepared opening gambit was shattered by a middle-aged woman who nudged me aside, seized the man's attention and directed it to a flock of teenage girls she had in tow, with Wilma in the lead.

"I want to tell you, this Shakespeare business!" the woman said. "These girls have put on their own productions and gotten a great deal of publicity out of it."

She invited the actor to see the girls strut and fret, an invitation he deflected with practiced weariness: "These one-night stands, you know. One must move on."

I remember mentally grumbling to myself, "This girl with her mother pushing her will probably get into the theater and I won't."

But it turned out otherwise.

"I didn't have the tenacious quality Sandy had," Wilma explains. "She hung on." A pause. "Oh, maybe I was a home child. . . ."

Certainly there was a strong attachment to her mother, of whom Wilma says, "She was quite a fantastic woman." It was her mother who, after Wilma's career failed to take fire on either coast, urged her to return to Nebraska and qualify as a teacher. Wilma complied by getting a master's degree: "I wanted to give it to her." An M.A. for Ma.

I ask if she envies Sandy.

"Of course. But I'm very, *very* happy." She underlines the second "very" with an emphasis that a good director might've suggested omitting.

I tell her that I see Sandy from time to time, and that she too seems happy.

"Perhaps she is. Of course, she lost her child over some movie. I've thought of that. I have my daughter and she doesn't."

She tells me that over the years she watched my show often, but just as often made a point of not watching. I ask why, expecting to hear an objection to my politics, a common Nebraska complaint.

"Because you were *there* and I wasn't."

"Would you change places with me, Wilma?"

"Of course." Then she adds, "If I could have everything I have now." My eye is caught by an arsenal of rifle shells stacked in boxes in a corner, and a portrait of her husband in his uniform. A good-looking man.

"How often do you think about going back and trying it again?"

"Oh, whenever I'm cleaning the cupboards."

I wonder whether she's done any acting around Lincoln, in community theaters and the like, or whether, out of some all-or-nothing attitude, she has deliberately eschewed it, being unwilling to "come down to" or "settle for" the amateur level.

But before I can ask, Wilma's daughter, a ten-year-old dervish named Holly, explodes into the room, miraculously not spilling a drop of the brimming glass of punch she is bringing me. Evidently Holly was rendered hyperkinetic by my call the previous night, and ever since has been conducting a phone marathon with her friends, all of whom want my autograph. I duly sign several pages of a notepad.

Wilma, with some of the irritation of one whose scene has been interrupted by a younger actress, suggests that Holly leave us alone again, which she does with a plaster-cracking slam of the door.

I ask Wilma about her writing. It's all poetry now, she tells me. Evidently it has earned her a lifetime membership in a midwestern literary society whose name I don't quite catch. "My one claim to fame," she says with more than a hint of self-mockery.

She keeps coming back to how amazed and flattered she is by my visit. "Why me? Why not—" and she mentions a couple of our classmates who have done well for themselves. "They're wealthy and influential, people more on a par with you."

I object politely to the implication that Wilma is not on a par with me.

She shakes her head and then says something that affects me deeply. "I could've lived my entire life and never known."

What is it that she feels I have let her know? My interest in her now naturally carries a certain weight that it wouldn't have in high school. Should it? What does this say about my younger self, ungraced by celebrity?

On the other hand, does belated praise from me now change the way Wilma views *her* younger self? Does it make her feel she may have had what it takes after all, that like Sandy she should have hung on in New York or California and ended up with an Oscar on her mantel?

When I try to put these questions into words, Wilma withdraws from my probing. "Who was it," she says, lifting her chin and giving a smile-through-it-all smile, "who said, 'Hell is what you make of what might have been'?"

I don't know who said it. We subside into pleasantries. Though the conversation leaves me vaguely frustrated, I reflect that Wilma is probably right. Trying to make something other than a hell out of might-have-beens is probably a luxury I can afford better than she.

As I get up to leave she repeats how good this has all been and we embrace again, partly because we did before, but partly, too, because she is a genuinely appealing woman.

Stepping out of the dark, cool house into the blindingly brilliant day is like coming out of a movie theater. A last wave, and I drive off with three equally pleasant thoughts: that I'm glad I went; that I hope Wilma *is* happy; and that now, as never before, I will miss her.

* * *

"I suppose you've *heard* about Karen."

This, with varying degrees of emphasis on "heard," comes from all sides during my stay in Lincoln. Sometimes the tone is sympathetic, sometimes lip-smacking, sometimes shocked, but invariably disapproving. It is beyond question that what Karen has done is not the behavior of a nice person.

Oh, yes. I've heard about Karen.

When I knew Karen in school, she was smart, pretty and energetic, an "activities girl" who was always on committees and probably edited the yearbook and served as a cheerleader. She even sang in the choir of the church we both attended. I remember that as she marched past my pew during the processional, head aloft, looking earnest but very fetching in her black robe, I used to wonder if I could make her snicker if our eyes met.

We never dated, because Karen was two years older than I. For a boy to date an older girl was unthinkable, although girls dated older boys and nobody ever questioned the inconsistency.

Her folks and mine were friends, though, and our two households often visited back and forth. They struck me as a warm, solid family, and Karen and her attractive brother and sister seemed destined to fulfill a cozy scenario of middle-class success.

True, Karen had a wry, slightly willful streak, a hint of something up her sleeve. There were even rumors that she had once engaged in you-know-what with a member of the track team. After she went on to the University of Nebraska she shook everybody up by insisting on marrying, against much advice and her parents' wishes, a Catholic. That was still an act of rebellion in Protestant circles of the Midwest in the 1950s. But at least the fellow was a frat man and a lawyer.

Once the crisis of their wedding was past, Karen and he settled

reassuringly into the conventional pattern of a nice house, three kids
and the country club, and I wouldn't have been surprised if Norman
Rockwell had painted their portrait. They were Mr. and Mrs. Bour-
geois Respectability if anyone was.

So it is surprising, I have to admit, to hear that Karen is now
separated from her husband and living with—yes, a black man. Openly.

In New York or Los Angeles, of course, if I heard that some actress
of my acquaintance was doing the same thing it wouldn't raise a ripple,
particularly in this age of no-holds-barred liberation and self-realization.
But among my former schoolmates Karen's is a deed of flaming infamy,
and in case I don't realize it there are plenty of concerned moralists
to remind me.

She is sunk in depravity, as far as I can make out from even the
milder accounts. "You wouldn't know her if you ran into her," I am
told. She has her children with her but has lost all interest in them, let
them "go wild"; in some versions the kids are into drugs and God
knows what. Her husband and parents are in a state of shock. It can
only end, a few extremists suggest, with Karen found dead of an
overdose someday, a note beside her apologizing for all the misery she
has caused.

I decide I must see her. Driving through the downtown area one
evening, I stop on an impulse at a phone booth outside a drugstore.
While looking up Karen's address in the book, I become aware of a
woman who is standing on the sidewalk about two feet in front of me
and cocking her head first to one side and then the other. I brace myself
for the recognition bit.

"Well," says the woman, "I certainly know who *you* are, don't I?"

I explain that I'm looking for a friend and tell her the address.

"Oh, that's a new addition." In Nebraskanese this refers to a new
part of town. It occurs to me that since one never hears of an old
addition the term must be redundant, like the ad game's "an added
plus."

I thank the woman for her help, realizing as I leave that she hasn't given me any and that I can still get disconcerted at being recognized in public.

Pulling into Karen's driveway, I notice two men eyeing me from a neighboring yard and imagine I can see one of them mouthing the words, "At least this one is white." What will I find here? An orgy with half-stoned kids asleep on the floor? Will I be told by a ravaged Karen, "I'm sorry, I don't know anybody from my past"? I begin to wish I hadn't come.

However, the teenager who comes to the door is alert and friendly. After telling me Karen is home he suddenly recognizes me and says, "Oh wow, just a minute!"

Fortunately he has turned and gone before he can hear me say, "Are you her daughter?" I mean son, of course, and cannot account for such a stupid slip except that I must be rattled in some way. Famous and smooth of tongue, supposedly, and I can't handle myself at a front door in Lincoln.

The house, while sparsely furnished and obviously not tended by a maid, is presentable. The front room is dominated by an elaborate drum set.

Karen emerges, saying, "I don't believe it," and we embrace warmly and slightly self-consciously. She looks a bit thin and tired and isn't quite the Karen I remember—how could she be?—but she certainly isn't the junkie gone in the teeth that the gossips evoked either. Still attractive, well scrubbed, brimming with vitality and, to me, bearing an almost startling resemblance to her mother that was never apparent before.

She leads me out to sit on the front steps. Does she hope the neighbors will see who has come to call? In a quirk that I sometimes notice in myself, I'm suddenly exceedingly diffident about the very thing I came here to find out, so the only fragments I glean about her new life are the ones she lets drop as we chat.

The drums in the front room belong to her current beau, who is indeed black and who, according to Karen, has run afoul of the law in

Omaha because of some imbroglio that I never quite get straight. So there is more than a suspicion of scandal here after all. Karen, the breadwinner of this unusual ménage, is working a bit improbably as YWCA director at the university.

I tell her I'm looking up old friends, thinking of writing something about the changes in all our lives, and I ask her to try to recall some things that might be helpful. We agree to meet again before my return to New York and I drive off.

Two days later, in Karen's office, I'm struck again by the disparity between the tarnished soul who has been consigned to perdition by my old circle and the brisk, responsible woman sitting across from me. She hands me two typed pages of notes about high school days that are clearly the product of an active and fertile mind.

It seems obvious that, whatever the motive for Karen's separation, it was no aimless or impulsive action but a conscious, deliberate decision on her part to rip asunder the Rockwell portrait and strive seriously toward—what?

Later, in a banquette of a thickly carpeted, romantically lit restaurant that a New Yorker would consider surprisingly sophisticated for Lincoln, she tries to explain.

From childhood on, she says, she and her brother and sister were pushed relentlessly by their parents to assert themselves, to cultivate the right people and get ahead, to *be* somebody. She describes her father in particular was almost obsessive about his ambitions for them all. He endlessly admonished them to exploit those who could be helpful. "The finest people," he intoned, "play their connections."

The children did it, but they felt oppressed, resentful. The more success they enjoyed over the years the more they felt trapped in a game in which they did nothing for its own sake.

In the end, by Karen's account, they all had their revenge, at great cost. Her brother, instead of pursuing his promise in tennis or art—flighty activities that didn't measure up to the family values?—dropped out of college, chucked everything and took off for New Orleans, where he remains. Her less vivacious but attractive sister recently divorced her dull husband, another blow. And now Karen is carrying out the most flagrant revolt of all.

Her parents are in equal parts appalled, furious and heartsick. Karen implies that their recent move to California was a retreat from what they took to be the collapse of their children's lives, in particular hers. Yet she claims to feel no guilt whatsoever.

Her mother has been ill, and for a while it appeared to be terminal. Karen says she had hoped the ordeal might "teach" her parents something but it hasn't. When I ask if she didn't feel sorry for them when they were sweating that out, her answer shocks me. "They deserve whatever they get," she says grimly.

As we sit there, it seems that every employee of the restaurant finds an excuse to pass by the table for a peek at the "television personality" (nauseating phrase); and Karen is quick to notice that some of the well-heeled customers who come over to say hello wouldn't spit on her (or might) if they met her on the street.

I enjoy this and in a juvenile way hope they imagine that Karen and I are having a brief, passionate affair.

Over cocktails—or under them, in my case—she talks some more about her attempts to break away from the tedium and constraints of her old life, about the need for sensitivity and openness to new experience. All painful and real for her, of course, but as I listen I get the uneasy feeling that any minute she will tell me she digs Kahlil Gibran. She does.

This makes me wonder whether the black boyfriend represents something more than a personal attachment to Karen, something more, even, than a way to outrage her parents. Maybe she is one of those liberal white women who, by entering into a compromising relationship with a black man, feel they are somehow expiating the racial guilt of their people.

There's a touch of this, at any rate, in the way Karen makes an issue of race. She laments, for example, the fact that there were few "minority" students in prominent positions at our high school. I refrain from pointing out that there were few minority students at our high school at all.

While nodding and murmuring sympathetically, I ask myself how I feel about Karen's quest, if that's what it is. Does it take nerve or callousness to do what she has done? Was one of the reasons I got out of Lincoln to avoid the kind of questions she's agonizing over?

Despite her enthusiasm for Gibran, I can't deny that I admire her rebellion. I believe that if I had remained in town and felt the same pressures she did, I probably would have succumbed to them. I certainly would *never* have had the guts to shock the home folks as dramatically as she has.

Thinking back on Karen's family, on those evenings when the room would quake with laughter as her father and mine clowned, cavorted, told dirty jokes and did dialects, I realize it's not so much a question of focusing my image of them all as of deciding what that image really is—as if it were one of those illusionist drawings that suddenly reverses perspective after you stare at it for a while.

When we had dinner at her folks' house they seemed an ideally happy family, and I assumed that the attractive and accomplished kids were as amused by their robustly funny father as I was. I wish I could see a film of it now. Would the concealed tensions all show subtly, as in an Ingmar Bergman movie? Might they even be obvious to my now more "sophisticated" eye?

Karen tells me I used to make her furious because I seemed to know how to come across as cute, law-abiding, talented little Dickie Cavett who got elected to student council and said the right things at assemblies, always managing to tread the fine line between being respectable and landing in the shit. "I always knew you were a spy," Karen says, "but nobody else did."

It occurs to me how much I must have been thrown up to her as an example of someone who knew how to make the right moves and get ahead. When my folks and I waved goodnight and the porch light was turned off, did her parents fall to bickering and chiding the children? ("How could you say that in front of the Cavetts? Why didn't you assert yourself more so Dick will remember you when he gets back East?")

These are beginning to seem like treacherous speculations, and I end the evening not only uncertain of how to measure Karen's and my present against the past, but no longer so sure that she and I share the same past.

She recalls vividly one encounter that I don't remember at all. Home on vacation from Yale, I visited her in the hospital just after she had a baby. After saying I had expected childbirth to leave her looking haggard and ruined I never mentioned her or the baby again, according to her, but launched into an endless name-dropping monologue about all the famous people I had met back East.

Cringing, I ask her if she ever held against me a more serious conversation we had a year or so before that. It was the time I earnestly entreated her, child of the Bible Belt that I was, to consider what she was doing by marrying a Catholic. I used Dostoevski's Grand Inquisitor to illustrate my thesis of lost freedom, plying my arguments with all the callow enthusiasm of a freshman, which I was, who has just had his first philosophy course, which I had.

I expect Karen to say either, "You were so full of shit that night, not to mention presumption . . ." or, "I said to myself that night, 'Here is one brilliant young man—why aren't I marrying him?' "

But she has absolutely no recollection of it.

                    *   *   *

One can reevaluate the past or refocus an image of it, but it's a mistake to tamper with it—to try to go back to it or wrench it into the present. Why don't I bear that in mind as I drive past my old grade school and suddenly remember Tommy Crane?

I haven't thought of Tom in years. He was the school cripple, the only one, a polio victim. He was a scrawny kid with curly hair and thick glasses, and he got around by sort of pivoting on his toes and swinging his rigidly braced legs in wide, stiff arcs. He fell frequently, and the knees of his trousers were always torn. Willfully he would join in baseball games, at least the batting halves of the innings. Squinting and swiveling awkwardly, he occasionally managed to hit a slow pitch; then he would stand there and watch while somebody ran for him.

A repressed memory swims up—would it have come if I weren't in front of the school?—of bounding down a stairway one day while delivering a message for a teacher. Tom, who was allowed to leave each class early so he could arrive on time for the next, was working his way up the same stairs, and we collided.

He glared at me. "You damn teacher's pet!"

Stung, because I was sensitive to this particular accusation, I said (and I wince to recall this), "I'm not going to say anything back to you because you're crippled."

He looked a little stunned. "I'm *not* crippled."

I couldn't say anything, and he resumed his laborious climb.

Remembering this scene more than thirty years later I break out in a sweat. Or is it just the heat? It *is* one of those murderously hot Nebraska days that one forgets about back East, with box elder bugs swarming and a parked car so stifling when you return to it that you can scarcely breathe or stand to touch the steering wheel.

Time and again on this trip I've been struck by the impact of my visits on old acquaintances. "You have no idea what this has meant," they will say. After the reunion one woman said about her husband, "The fact that Dick Cavett spent time talking with Henry has done more for him than two years of psychiatry." Alas, with a slight air of lordly beneficence I decide to bestow some of the same balm on poor Tom.

His apartment building turns out to be next door to the first one I lived in after moving to Lincoln. I recall a mulberry tree out front that I used to climb, usually emerging with my clothes teeming with fuzzy caterpillars. It saddens me to find the tree gone.

In the lobby of Tom's building, once elegant perhaps, but now bleak, two old women in worn wing chairs stare blankly at a game show on TV. I pause for a moment, giving them a chance to recognize me. They don't, and I ascend in an old-fashioned wire cage elevator. Tom presumably will have a bachelor apartment, and maybe a hobby that we can talk about.

The long corridor is baking hot. For air conditioning there is only a dusty window raised at each end. I knock on Tom's door, my insides churning with a curious kind of stage fright over whatever is about to happen.

No answer. I knock again, and finally a muffled female voice says, "Yes?"

"Tom Crane?"

"Who is it?"

"Dick Cavett." My name sounds preposterous.

Several moments pass. Maybe the voice was from another apartment. Had I scared them? Were they calling the cops to deal with this crank imposter outside their door? I fervently wish I were at Little Dix Bay swimming in the Caribbean right now, although as I stand here the notion of such faraway things, or of me as a boy from Nebraska who does such things, hardly seems credible.

The door opens far enough to reveal a plump, middle-aged woman in a smock, no makeup, her hair in a towel.

"Is Tom here? I'm—" I can't say my name again. "I went to school with him."

She pulls the door all the way open and steps aside demurely. I am in a small, dark, suffocatingly hot room, redolent of humanity. Most of what space there is to my left is occupied by the woman; to my right, by a rumpled bed. Ahead, facing away from me, is a high-backed, overstuffed chair with a man in it. At his feet is a black-and-white TV set on which the movie "Desert Song" is just beginning. There is a portable window fan on the floor that doesn't seem to be helping.

The man turns and I realize I'm in the wrong place. He is fat, with a round moon face and some sparse remnants of hair combed flat on his head. It is, however, Tom.

He greets me with, "When my wife said you said, 'It's Dick Cavett,' I said, 'What would a big star like that be doing in our building?' "

I'm beginning to wonder myself.

I'm hardly aware of how the next few minutes pass. Tom and I converse after a fashion, fumbling for subjects and names that we can hold in common, however briefly. He tells me that his father, whom I remember as one of my teachers in junior high school, is dead. Tom had a job with the railroad for a few years, but had to quit "because of my disability." I note the euphemism.

I gather that now, except for government benefits, he is supported by his wife, the woman in the towel, who hangs back in the shadows of the room while we talk.

I regret coming, but stubbornly I feel that it's been good for Tom somehow to have my intrusion into his life, into this room, even into "Desert Song" on TV.

Impelled by I don't know what—guilt? an urge to dramatize the moment?—I ask if he remembers me in grade school.

"I sure do, Dick."

There is an awkward pause, and I decide to go right for it.

"Tom, I have to apologize for something." And I relate the incident on the stairs. It pours out in one long sentence and near the end my voice cracks as I become moved by it. I feel tight in the throat and my temples throb with a combination of embarrassment and exhilaration that it's finally out. I finish with a raw appeal to Tom. "It's bothered me for a long time and I hope you haven't held it against me all these years."

He sits impassive and immobile, blinking nearsightedly, his face and globelike scalp beaded with sweat. "How are your folks?" he says.

Oh Christ, now I've ruined it. He had forgotten the whole thing, and now that I've brought it up he realizes that I've always thought of him as pathetic. If I'd left it alone he could've said to his wife after I left, "See? I don't think Dick even remembers me as disabled." On the other hand, maybe the fact that I've worried about it, had him in my mind all this time, is flattering to him. Who the hell knows? I'm having trouble breathing in here, not entirely because of the heat and lack of air.

But I can't drop it. "You didn't hold it against me, then, Tom? I guess I've owed you this apology for a long time."

"Oh, heck no."

Soon (but not soon enough), after a few more attempts at reminiscence, we make our goodbyes. Tom turns back to his TV and I, drenched, aching for the air conditioning in my car, escape to the wire cage elevator, feeling less like an angel of mercy than a fool. I vow, as one does at such times, never to complain about anything in my own life again.

The old women in the lobby eye me uncertainly. I decide to speak to them so they'll be sure it's me, and at the same time to make a parting stab at redeeming myself by giving Tom some status in the building.

"Do you know Tom Crane?" I ask them.

"No."

* * *

Sometimes, though, when you're not straining for it or fussing over it, it just comes. Unbidden, some delightful part of the past will suddenly rise up and surround you like a tub filling with warm water. Like the time, after returning to New York, when I came across Jim McConnell's picture while leafing through an old Lincoln High School yearbook.

Jim was my best friend in grade school, after my family first moved to Lincoln. He lived two doors away from us on South 23rd Street. (Why is it two doors away in the Midwest and not two houses away? I picture a block of free-standing doors with no buildings attached to them.) We had great fun together for several years and then gradually drifted apart, until by high school we rarely spoke or met. I'm mildly surprised to be reminded by the "The Links" that we went to high school at the same time, even though we still lived two doors apart. (Did the Indians say two flaps apart?)

I suppose Jim was the closest thing I had to a Huck Finn in my life. He was a sunny, carefree kid who moved with natural athletic grace and had a crooked Irish smile that was totally winning and at times kind of dreamy. He always smelled vaguely of peanut butter. He could ride his bike anywhere and was never forced to eat at certain times or "come in." From him I learned dirty words, dirty jokes, a reasonably accurate idea of female anatomy and the facts of life, how to catch crawdads in Antelope Creek, the art of window-peeking, and how to smoke and hold a pool cue.

Even without knowing the half of this, my parents, like many other parents around the neighborhood, considered him not quite suitable company. Partly this was because he was a year older than I. (Playing with "someone your own age" apparently averted unnamed dangers.) Partly it was because the McConnells were not quite approved of for other reasons.

They were known to smoke, drink and swear, and—what really made them morally suspect—they were far from tidy housekeepers. Furthermore, they were thought to give their children entirely too much freedom. Polio was the dread childhood disease of the day—after all, look what happened to Tommy Crane—and during the hot weather "polio months" all us children were forbidden to mix with crowds at swimming pools and movie theaters. All, that is, except Jim, whose parents let him swim at the municipal pool and roam freely right through the summer.

I can remember people on our block forever clucking about that messy McConnell household and how they let Jim run around "un-washed." Naturally I envied him that and loved their house. In who else's living room could you find an old, probably flea-bitten cougar skin hanging by its tail near the fireplace?

I was always cheerfully welcomed by Jim's father, an Ernest Hemingway lookalike who had something to do with conservation and whom I don't recall ever seeing out of his easy chair, just as I don't recall ever seeing his mother when she wasn't puffing on a cigarette or sipping coffee that she poured from a perpetually simmering pot.

Mrs. McConnell made great candy, appropriately called Divinity. Both parents laughed often and played cards a lot. They knew they were faintly disreputable and, in an attitude as different as could be from that of Karen's parents, they didn't give a damn.

My favorite part of their house was Jim's room. Some years ago a grown-up Jim, by then a dignified businessman in Oklahoma City, visited me in New York, and I took him to an apartment in Greenwich Village belonging to a member of the cast of the musical "Hair." I remember being amused that a now fastidious Jim found the building unkempt.

Two flights up, I rang and the door was opened without inquiry by a well-built naked blond (male) with shoulder-length hair. We found ourselves in a scene of disarray, our senses assailed by rock music and an odor that seemed to combine the best qualities of sweat, urine and marijuana. Around us undraped bodies were strewn, or intertwined, on mattresses and in sleeping bags, in various states of consciousness.

As I watched Jim in that setting, impeccably groomed in a three-piece suit, glancing around uneasily, suddenly all I could think of was his old room back in Lincoln, a careless jumble of a more innocent sort to which I used to retreat for so many contented hours.

His bed—more a mattress than a bed—lay amidst piles of moldering comic books, castoff socks and empty dope bottles (the airplane paint variety, not the Greenwich Village kind). The walls, I seem to recall, sported calendar paintings of stags and mountain scenery and a saucy Varga girl. His room was everything mine would've been if I could've gotten away with it.

Despite his roughneck manner in those days, Jim was essentially a gentle soul. He was no coward, but I don't remember him ever rising to a fight. One time when I was furious with him over something, I struck out in a blind rage with what I thought was a non-telegraphed punch calculated to open his lip. Without blinking he deftly caught my arm, held it very firmly for a moment, then let go without saying anything. The catlike quickness of the move and my surprise effectively defused the violence.

His occasional dreamy air reflected a sentimental side of his nature. Once when I was sick with flu he came to the door with a bouquet of gladioli, a gesture that wouldn't have occurred to me in a million years.

Although childhood is full of daytime leisure, it was the nights that were Jim's and my favorite times, especially summer nights, when we would "play out" after supper. I've almost forgotten that expression. "Do you have to stay in, or can you play out tonight?"

Evenings had a kind of dwindling sadness about them that I somehow associated with great thirst. Not the literal thirst produced by playing baseball or "guns" violently and sweatily for hours, when you would run into the house and wolf down quarts of water and feel at first erotically satisfied, then quenched, then oafishly bloated from overdose. This thirst was a kind of yearning—sensual in its keenness, but also mixed with a poignance that I suppose came from the knowledge that the magic moments were slipping by quickly while I was still stuck inside at the supper table.

For supper did have to be gotten through first, made worse by admonishments to eat calmly, take your time, digest your food. Meanwhile, darkness had fallen and I was almost shivering with the delicious anticipation of the night's adventures.

The last half of the meal was intolerable. Somewhere out there I knew that Jim and maybe Hughie McKnight were already deciding whether tonight was to be kick-the-can, say, or window-peeking, or some form of vandalism or theft (removing the drainpipe from someone's house, plugging the exhaust pipe of their car with a potato, entering the empty house of some family that was out of town).

Finishing supper and finally being able to dart through the screen door into the enveloping darkness, I felt like a skindiver eagerly plunging overboard into the world below. The air felt wonderfully clear after the heat and haze of the day. In the stillness a faint breeze rustled the elm branches above us with a sound that could raise goosepimples on the forearms and which I still associate with nocturnal adventure.

Another such evocative sound came from what we called "locusts" —some kind of summer bugs that began a thin, hypnotic buzz around sunset and provided a sort of musical background as we prowled the deeply shadowed streets and alleys.

When an approaching car's headlights flared in the night, we felt the thrill of potential trouble. He couldn't see us but we could see him. (Jim had taught me that cop cars always had brighter headlights.)

Reveling in these memories as I muse over Jim's cheerful face in the yearbook, I feel I have to talk to him. Only by going into a psychic mini-trance can I come up with the city in the Southwest where he now lives. Then, of course, in order to find the right Jim McConnell there, I have to contend with the phone company's infuriating game-playing.

"I'm sorry, we can only give two listings at one time."

"You mean I have to hang up and dial again to get information that is sitting there right now and you're looking at it?"

"I'm afraid that's the rule."

"Fuck the phone company." (She disconnects.)

Finally I hit upon Jim's number. A young man says, "Mr. Cavett? [My sometimes maddeningly recognizable voice.] Just a moment." Already emotionally back on a best friend status with Jim, hearing the voice of a son I've never met produces an irrational twinge of jealousy (he likes his family better than he likes me).

"Hi, there." Jim's greeting is as casual and friendly as if we'd just run into each other under the elms of South 23rd Street, and the years fall away.

We immediately plunge into a mutual conjuring of old memories and incidents that make us giggle and snort with hilarity. Most of our conversation would be utterly cryptic to anyone listening in. The mere mention of the word "zapoom" sends us into stitches, and not even I am sure why until Jim jogs my recollection.

It has to do with a kid named Milton Cochell, who was sometimes permitted to join us in our rovings and mischief-making, his role chiefly being to be picked on and humiliated by the two of us.

Once, when we were transforming ourselves into comic book characters, Cochell was told to leap out of a closet and turn into Captain Marvel. Dutifully submitting to this latest humiliation, he retired behind the door. Upon reemerging, however, he couldn't think of Captain Marvel's magic word, "Shazam!" so he said "Zapoom!" instead.

Jim and I fell to the floor, doubled up in derisive laughter, while the hapless Cochell tried at least to enjoy the fact that he was amusing us, if in the wrong way.

On and on Jim and I go, for more than an hour enriching Ma Bell's wretched coffers while howling over these silly, wonderful fragments in our mental scrapbooks.

Our phone call seems to stir up my unconscious, and for days afterward I get flashes of things we did together that have been buried for years. Strangely, not a single one of them is a memory of our meeting or talking together in the halls of Lincoln High School. Our drifting apart coincided with Jim's entrance into junior high school and after that was exacerbated, I fear, by my growing self-consciousness about adopting the right style and moving with the fashionable crowd, neither of which ever concerned Jim.

During our teenage years I apparently felt I had ensconced myself on such a lofty rung of the social ladder that I couldn't acknowledge my slightly scruffy friend of yore, any more than I could bring myself to join in Wilma the Wolf's intriguing theatricales. Auld acquaintance was forgot, or at least put aside.

Brooding on this, I keep glimpsing a partial image that, perhaps because it produces a pang of guilt, remains elusive for a long time, emerging only reluctantly, bit by bit. It's like trying to recall a dream that retreats as soon as you fasten on a fragment of it—a chimney, a scarf—and when you repeat the words "chimney" or "scarf" you merely drive it further from reach.

This image is of cinder blocks. It fills out to become the cinder-block wall that was part of Jim's front yard. Then I see it all: Jim and me, sitting on the wall talking.

It was years after we'd ceased to be close, and was almost as if one of us was back on a visit, having moved away. I was bragging to Jim about what an intimate comradeship I'd struck up with one of the glamorous figures in school, a guy named Jim Kiley.

I narrated two or three things I'd done with Kiley, at least one of which was a lie. Whether consciously or not, I must've been trying to show Jim how well I could get along without him. The next few lines of dialogue I remember vividly.

Jim: "We used to hang out a lot together."

Me (deliberately misunderstanding): "Who, you and Kiley?"

Jim: "No, you and me."

Me (unable to deal with the sudden sense of poignancy and regret over the fading of our friendship): "Hm."

How happy are the supposedly happy times of our lives? How much do we enjoy them at the time? It seems we can never know, because it's only after we leave those times behind that we realize what they were. Living through them we're in a state of total unawareness—the definition of happiness, perhaps?—and then afterwards we can only recollect them through nostalgia and irony.

I can remember older folks saying to me, as far back as when Jim and I played out every night, "These are the wonderful years of your life. You have no responsibilities, no money problems, no kids to worry about. Someday you'll realize how lucky you are to be this age."

Doubtless they were right, but what did it mean to me at the time? Nothing, of course. Absolutely nothing.

THE CAVETT
ALBUM–I

HE WAS ON HORSEBACK when I met him. He swung down from the saddle in western costume—Stetson, neckerchief and six-shooter—and ambled toward me saying, "Gee, it sure is good to meet ya."

My scalp tightened. As with the Great Pyramid at Giza, nothing prepared you for John Wayne's size. Yet as he loomed over me, his easy geniality and drawling familiar voice made me instantly comfortable. I wondered how women could maintain their equilibrium in his presence.

"Why don't you stick around and watch us do this scene?" he asked.

It was an easy decision, and would have been if I'd been scheduled to address Parliament.

It had never occurred to me that I *could* meet John Wayne any more than I could meet Buffalo Bill. Rationally, I knew that he was alive and that we inhabited the same planet—even, broadly speaking, the same profession. And by that time it seemed I had met just about everybody else in show business. But somehow he was different, apart, a mythic figure existing in another realm.

It may have had something to do with the notion that one's heroes are invariably disappointing in the flesh. Perhaps I didn't want "The Duke" reduced to mortal status. After all, he was the demigod who had ranged across the screen of the Capitol Theater in Lincoln, Nebraska, as my friend Jim McConnell and I had stared up in open-mouthed admiration on Saturday afternoons. He was everything we had emulated when afterwards we played cowboys.

I was in Hollywood to tape a special for CBS about the back lots of the big movie studios. The idea was to try to capture some of the romance of Scott Fitzgerald's description, in *The Last Tycoon,* of a back lot as "thirty acres of fairyland—not because the locations really looked like African jungles and French chateaux and schooners at anchor and Broadway by night, but because they looked like the torn picture books of childhood, like fragments of stories dancing in an open fire."

Under the expert guidance of the producing team of Gary Smith and Dwight Hemion, I was sort of assembling the show as I went along, roaming the fairyland and picking up atmosphere and interviews and even musical numbers from whoever was available.

One day, as I sat in Gary Smith's office at Universal Studios, someone happened to mention that the Duke was shooting a western right there on the Universal lot.

How could anyone, knowing that he was a matter of yards away, remain calmly in the room? I was part-way out the door when Gary shouted after me, "See if you can get him for the show!"

Getting across the six blocks or so of back lot seemed to take a week. My pessimistic streak told me that I'd get there and a technician would say, "We wrapped an hour ago and Mr. Wayne left for Paris." Another voice said, "When I lay my head on the pillow tonight, my last virginity will be gone. I will have met John Wayne."

I rounded the corner of a phony Parisian street, cut through a simulated section of Central Park and there, amidst a milling throng of western dress extras in the square of an old frontier town, bestriding his steed like a Colossus, was the heroic figure in the mammoth Stetson, cracked and weathered but unmistakably the Ringo Kid from "Stage-coach."

And there was nothing between him and me but air.

We became friends. He agreed immediately to be part of my special. The next day, with the TV cameras in place, Wayne in his movie costume and I in my open-necked shirt hopped up on a buckboard that was hitched to a team of mules, which he skillfully reined in and quieted when they became fractious.

Catching sight of the two of us on a monitor screen, I wished Jim McConnell could see me now.

"How shall we start?" I said.

A giant hand took the mike from me. "I'll get us started. Are we rolling?" And with his million dollar grin, he said, "Hi, this is John Wayne interviewing Dick Cavett!"

My name never sounded so good.

For the next thirty minutes or so he talked perceptively and pungently about moving from a UCLA football field to a Hollywood sound stage, about working with John Ford, about great stunt men he had known, and about the essential dignity of the Indian civil rights movement. (I wish some of my liberal friends could have heard that. One of the lesser pains of the Vietnam war for me was having Bob Hope and John Wayne as heroes and being annoyed that friends could not separate their support of that national catastrophe from their art.)

He talked, too, about his current movie, which many people believed (rightly, as it turned out) would be his last. It was called "The Shootist" and it co-starred James Stewart and Lauren Bacall. In it, he played an aging gunfighter who had cancer, and although he brushed off the correspondences with his own life they seemed striking.

I remember a poignant moment near the end of our talk. It was late in the afternoon and I said, "Is this about the time of day you usually wrap up shooting?"

Surveying the sky, he said, "Yeah, it's gettin' a little yella." And then, more thoughtfully, "Gettin' a little yella . . ."

For the next few days I spent every available moment hanging out with Wayne on that western set, cadging a few lines of conversation when I could, watching him play scenes, musing over the torn picture book of my own childhood.

It was star worship pure and simple, and I make no apology for it. But for those who find it a little nauseating, the following may provide at least an amusing antidote, however much it may strain credulity.

A scene was being set up in the interior of a ranch house. The Duke was sitting alone at the kitchen table, waiting. I was standing in the shadows, marveling at how totally convincingly it seemed that we were in an old house in another century and not in the corner of a giant sound stage with a freeway outside.

I titillated myself by saying to an imagined Jim McConnell, "Hey, Jim, wanna see John Wayne? Look over there."

Wayne was idly drawing patterns on the dusty tabletop with his finger and humming. Recognizing the tune, I half-unconsciously began whistling it softly. He looked up slightly embarrassed, and began the following dialogue. Cross my heart.

> WAYNE: Wasn't he great?
> ME: Who?
> WAYNE: Coward.
> ME: *(realizing the tune was "Someday I'll Find You"):* You know that?
> WAYNE: Yeah, I love that song. I don't know whether I like his music or his writing more.
> ME *(verifying):* Noel Coward.
> WAYNE: Yeah. God, he could write. Remember the scene in *Private Lives* when they realize they still love each other?
> ME: Did you know there's a record of Coward and Gertrude Lawrence doing that scene?
> WAYNE: I should get that. I guess I've read most of his plays.
> ME *(still not convinced there isn't a ventriloquist in the room):* I'll send it to you.
> WAYNE: Well, thank ya. *(In upper-class British.)* "You're looking very lovely you know, in this damned moonlight."

ME: Do you know the part about China and Japan?

WAYNE *(still in accent):* "China must be very interesting." "Very big, China." "And Japan—?" "Very small." I kinda hoped I'd meet him when I was in England, but I guess I waited too long.

ME: I did a show with Coward and Alfred Lunt and Lynn Fontanne. Before Coward died. *(Brilliant, Dick.)*

WAYNE: I heard about that but I never got to see it.

ME: I'll send you a tape of it.

WAYNE: That'd be awfully nice of ya.

ME *(wishing there were a witness):* Did you ever want to do one of his plays?

WAYNE: Sure, but I don't think anybody believed—*(The spell is shattered by a staccato-voiced assistant bustling in and shouting, "Okay! Places, people, for twenty-three!")*

This conversation echoed in my head for weeks. I thought of writing it up under some title like "John Wayne Is a Fraud."

A better interpretation was Woody Allen's when I got back to New York and recounted the whole scene to him. "Sure," Woody observed calmly. "Reminds you he isn't a cowboy, he's an actor."

* * *

For several years I *was* Bob Hope.

From about the age of twelve through fifteen, when people weren't looking, I would stand in front of a mirror and do jokes from Hope's most recent TV show, shifting my weight as he did on a punch line, staring into the imaginary camera with eyes slightly widened, then shifting my weight to launch into the next line, holding my arms at my side with one foot slightly forward, looking into the wings and drawing down my upper lip while pressing the right canine against the tooth directly below it. At times I even imagined I had developed the slight scar he had on his upper lip.

At the end of a gag I would do the Hope run-on, appending without pause the words, "But I wanna tell ya . . ." or, "But I just wanna say . . ." or the by then anachronistic, "But the one I wanna tell . . ." which Hope never used after leaving radio. (He doesn't remember it, but I do.)

I could enter a room the way he did, walk down the street like him and even chew gum à la Hope. When he abandoned gum I was sorry. But I added a golf club to fill the gum gap and leaned on it in the Hope manner.

I even knew how to get into the back seat of a car the way he did. I learned by seeing him do it in Lincoln with my own eyes.

The first time I saw Rapid Robert was at 9:14 P.M. on a spring evening of, I think, 1950, on the stage of the University of Nebraska Coliseum. For weeks before this momentous event, I had pored over the ad that said, "Bob Hope, onstage, in person," trying to figure out how it could be literally true. The man I had recently seen in "Monsieur Beaucaire" for the fourth time *couldn't* actually be in the same four-wall-enclosed space I would be occupying. I knew it had to be some kind of false advertising.

When the big night finally arrived I was in the front row of the balcony with some school friends, growing ever more suspicious as act after act of a humdrum vaudeville bill rolled on. When the first half closed with a mediocre juggler, Lyle Burke and I speculated on what sort of a hoax we had been victimized by, and what sort of film or facsimile would be presented as part two.

We resumed our seats, the lights went down, the band played "Thanks for the Memory" and *he* emerged from the wings into a spotlight. I froze. Lyle gasped and said, "My God, there he is!"

From that point on, I was his. Or more accurately, I was he.

Somehow I managed to push to the front of the stage-door crowd as Hope and Marilyn Maxwell emerged and got into a Cadillac. "Fine show, Bob," I said.

"Thanks, son," he said.

I remember staring at him in the car and thinking something that I still can't make quite clear. A few weeks earlier I had watched him on the screen and now here he was, the first huge star I had ever seen.

It hit me for the first time that these figures could actually be encountered. I thought, "My God, he walks around with that face on all the time. What must that be like?"

After the car pulled away, Norman Gieseker and I ran to the Cornhusker Hotel, hoping in vain to beat the car there and see him emerge. Later we found the floor he was staying on, and then his room. I knocked on the door, petrifying Norman. An officious red-haired woman answered and informed us that Mr. Hope had retired for the evening. I caught a glimpse of him inside, fully dressed, so I knew he hadn't; but my nerve was used up by the knock.

For days afterward I couldn't concentrate on my schoolwork. Where was he now? Had it been a dream? I made a point of not missing his next program in case he mentioned Lincoln and even the kid who had spoken to him at the stage door. Apparently there wasn't time.

I often had dreams about him in which we were in an airplane together or playing in a golf tournament. A friend of mine told me about seeing him play golf once in Omaha (probably hobnobbing with the Strategic Air Command generals there). A heckler, referring to his flowered Hawaiian shirt, had yelled, "Hey, Bob, your slip is showing."

To which Hope had replied, "So is your father's."

I so envied and admired this glimpse of the Hope movie persona in action—glib, fast and a little risqué—that even now I have to remind myself that it was a friend and not I who saw it.

Twenty years later, I had the dream-come-true experience of having Hope as my sole guest for a full ninety minutes on my ABC talk show. I got *paid* for sitting next to him and talking to him. If only ABC knew how much I might've given *them* for the privilege.

I told him about knocking on the door of his hotel room in Lincoln, and jokingly said, "I thought maybe I saw Marilyn Maxwell in there with you but I couldn't be sure."

He glanced around in mock alarm. "Hey, hey, I'm a married man. If Dolores is watching, you *didn't.*"

At one point I reminded the audience that he was born in England. Feigning an unintentional double-entendre, I said to him, "Do you think of yourself as even partially English? I mean, when you hear 'God Save the Queen' does any part of you rise?"

The thunderclap laugh lifted him out of his chair, and he seemed as genuinely broken up as the audience.

Backstage later, he said, "That 'rise' line is a good one. I'm gonna use that over there." For him, a casual enough compliment to pay, but for me, a tribute that will warm my old age.

Stan Laurel once showed me a prized letter from Alec Guinness in which Sir Alec testified that he had consciously emulated and even imitated some of Laurel's mannerisms on the screen. Woody Allen freely acknowledges a similar borrowing of Hope's mannerisms; at some point in most of his movies you can see him "doing Hope." I've done the same thing on TV, making good use of all those years of practice in front of the mirror. When I'm nervous backstage, a few moments of walking like Bob magically brings back my confidence, or more accurately, fills me with his.

Every comic thinks of Hope as The King, and his realm takes in all the media. He has triumphed everywhere, on stage and radio, in films and TV.

Because of his dazzling versatility, and because in recent years he's been seen mostly on TV, the film work he did in earlier decades is in danger of being undervalued. I once asked him if he had read a review by Penelope Gilliatt in the London *Observer* that began, "Bob Hope is a fine screen actor."

His response, typically, was, "Hey, in that great?" ("In" is phonetic Hope for "isn't.")

Gilliatt was absolutely right. His screen technique doesn't analyze so well, at least by me, but it has to do with his light, graceful movement, his bright delivery and, something invariably overlooked, his remarkable diction. Take a Hope line with a lot of words in it and try saying it as brightly and quickly as he does without seeming to hurry it. And comedy aside, he handles the sentimental scenes very adroitly with "real" acting.

Among the questions I have never managed to ask him over the years are whether he got any tips on how to act for the camera, whether there were mistakes he thinks he made at first, whether he modeled himself after any screen comedians. (My guess is that his answer to the last would be no, because the only influence of any kind that he has cited is a vaudeville comic named Frank Fay.)

Does he even realize consciously what his screen technique is, or would he say, like some performers, "I guess I just do what feels right"?

I hope he has never read Cahiers du Cinéma or any of the learned film journals that tell us why Jerry Lewis is the only worthy successor to Swift and Chaplin. I am told that he reads Time and golf magazines, so my fears are no doubt baseless. I'm sure the ultra-intellectual, long-winded justifications of a variety of trivia with which these film journals are replete are as foreign to him as I wish they had remained to me. Why, for example, they aren't content simply to admit that Jerry makes them laugh is a subject for another book. (And another writer.)

When I had Woody Allen on my PBS program—having all but blackmailed him into breaking his no-TV rule to help me get the then new program off the ground—one of his more inspiring cadenzas was about Hope the screen comic. After carefully making a distinction between Hope's movies and his TV shows (and political views), Allen went on to praise him in immaculately worded encomia, allowing as how it would be fun to edit the body of his film work into excerpts illustrative of the many sides of his talent.

Not long after the show aired, I got a call from an alert member of the Lincoln Center Film Society offering Woody a chance to make good on his offer. The society was giving Hope its annual award that year, and it would be delighted to have Woody assemble the half-hour reel of highlights from Hope's cinematic career that would be shown as part of the festivities. Woody did it.

I sat in with him during some of his marathon screenings of the footage, and we howled like a couple of kids at—well, at a Bob Hope movie. "Monsieur Beaucaire," for one, looked every bit as good as it ever did at the Capitol Theater in Lincoln, Nebraska.

Later I heard that Hope was flattered and pleased by the selections, regretting only the omission of his favorite dancing sequence, the one in which he and James Cagney, playing George M. Cohan, performed on a banquet table at the Friars Club in "The Seven Little Foys."

I emceed the Lincoln Center tribute, and was able to pay Bob some compliments in front of the black-tie audience of 2,500 in Avery Fisher Hall that would've been difficult to say to his face had we been alone.

I also got a long-wished-for chance to write for him. Standing in the wings as he wound up his portion of the evening, I had a sudden inspiration that I thought might give him an ending. I borrowed a stagehand's pencil and, racing against time, composed special lyrics to his theme song, printing them in large letters on a sheet of paper. The thought that he would be sight-reading them would have deterred me under rational circumstances, but I was in love with the idea of Hope doing my material.

I joined him onstage for the goodnights and passed him the lyrics. He swung right into them and they worked, if I do say so, triumphantly.

> "Thanks for the memory
> Of Avery Fisher Hall;
> I've really had a ball
> With Woody's flick
> And dear old Dick—
> To me they're six feet tall . . ."

Hope's acceptance of the award was smooth and gracious, as always, but I couldn't tell how much of an impression my words, Woody's clips, the whole tribute made on him. His relentless schedule and his impervious professional cheerfulness kept it all on a "Hey, in that great?" level.

It left me wondering whether he really knows what a great comic artist he is, or whether he wants to know. I still wish I could think of some way of telling him how much he means to me.

FAME IS A MANY-SPLINTERED THING

IS FAME A GOOD THING or a bad? It is hard to say without further definition. Since the question, "What do Shakespeare, Elizabeth Taylor, Billy Graham, Hitler and Morris the Cat have in common?" can be answered by that single monosyllable, obviously it is not easily described as good or bad.

Leaving aside fame's loftier aspects—respect for achievement, significant influence, a place in posterity and all that—let us consider the everyday practical reality of it.

Sure, there are times when a little fame is a wonderful thing. Everybody can enjoy being fussed over and given free rides and special treatment, even in such minor instances as when the man who has just closed his store recognizes you and unlocks the door to let you in to pick up your snapshots.

There are also times when it is simply a four-letter word, as in, "I've been f---d." (This use of the word—"famed author," etc.—has been cited as an abomination invented by Time magazine, but Shakespeare and Dryden both used it this way.) It can keep you from enjoying the very things it brings you; for example, when you are waved ahead of a line to a choice table in a restaurant and then have your meal constantly interrupted by fans or autograph seekers.

This is not, of course, one of life's larger problems, and nobody can be expected to feel sorry for you if the fame you have so eagerly sought turns out to be a mixed blessing. But still.

I suppose most people have thought at some time or other, *Wouldn't it be nice to walk down a busy street and have your face recognized by everybody?* Believe me, an equally good question is, *Wouldn't it not?* Fame is like the Midas touch; it would be nice if you could also shut it off.

Let me illustrate by describing two brief encounters.

In the first, the scene is the Amtrak Metroliner between New York and Washington, D.C. A man is riding in the parlor car, trying to complete some paperwork before the journey's end.

The door from the adjoining club car opens and a woman with a drink in her hand enters unsteadily, lipstick smeared, stretch pants doing extra duty. She lurches along the aisle between the swivel arm-chairs of the parlor car, then stops when she sees someone she recognizes. It is the man working.

"Hey, there's a familiar face!" she exclaims loudly enough that heads turn and fellow passengers verify the previously unnoticed fact for themselves.

She addresses the man as "honey" and announces, or more accurately broadcasts, the information that she is his biggest fan. He accepts the compliment with civil thanks and returns to work.

She is not finished. "Where are you going, anyway?"

Considering and rejecting the obvious witty retort, "Who wants to know?", he replies, "Washington" and returns to his work again, somewhat more pointedly than before.

This information intrigues the inquirer enough to prompt her to seat herself precariously on the arm of the chair opposite his and say, "Well, well, and what are we going to be doing there?"

"I am going to rape a convent of nuns," he replies only in his mind, while wishing he could call in an air strike. Instead he confines himself to, "Working," which he utters without looking up.

"Oh, is that supposed to be a hint of some kind?"

His brief smile, again without looking up, is a cool formality, betraying no hint of the image in his mind of a woman buried up to her chin in an African red-ant hill.

"Why aren't you having a drink?" she asks. "I'm gonna buy you a drink!"

He is looking out the window now with a chilled stare, jaws clenched in an enamel-cracking mode, and he says as calmly as possible, "Look. I'm trying to work. We've spoken. Now I need to be left alone."

Then it comes. The *sine qua non* of all such encounters. "Whassamatter? Too good to have a drink with me?"

For some reason he imagines some stately nineteenth century gentleman of letters responding to the question. Henry James or someone. What might he say? "Madame, an honest answer to that question would do neither of us credit." Perhaps.

"I watch your shows," she says. "How come you won't have a drink with me?"

He is spared having to answer by a traveling companion in the next chair, a man who, having witnessed the scene so far, says to the woman, "You know, the fact that you have watched him on television does not automatically entitle you to his private life."

"Who's this, your bodyguard?" Before she can go on to tell the companion, "Why don't you butt out?" she slips and falls on hers. The man decides there *is* a God.

By now she has warranted an appearance by the conductor who, amid dialogue unfit for well-bred ears, escorts her untidily from the car.

As I said before, worse things happen to people than this, but when you multiply such an incident by the hundreds, or thousands, the wear and tear on the celebrity does mount up. If I had a nickel for every time it has happened to me (for I might as well reveal to the perhaps unsurprised reader that the man in this episode is me), the government would need to mint some more.

What became of the woman, of course, I have no idea. But I can be certain of one thing. Somewhere today she is telling someone how rude I am.

Rudeness, real and alleged, also figures in the other brief encounter. It takes place at an otherwise pleasant after-theater cocktail party in bucolic Williamstown, Massachusetts, where I am appearing in a summer play.

A woman wearing a black leather jacket accosts me. She is not dainty. A small section of her blue jeans has been sandpapered away to reveal a tattoo on her upper thigh—something like a snake being struck by lightning. You might cast her as a female bouncer in a bowling alley. She is trouble.

"Well, well, if it isn't Dickie Cavett."

"Then who is it?" I reply ill-advisedly. Something about this kind of opening makes me want to light out for the territory immediately, and also makes me want to stay and match so-called wits to amuse the onlookers. I wish I could learn to choose the former.

"Dickie Cavett. Television star. I guess I'm supposed to be impressed."

"Suit yourself."

Someone tries to steer her away as the guests nearby begin to look uneasy. She pulls her arm free and says, "Just a minute. I have a bone to pick with Mr. Television Star." With her left hand she has squeezed her beer can out of true cylindricality. I make a mental note to be alert for a possible left hook.

"Some friends of mine," she goes on, "came over to get your autograph in Howard Johnson's yesterday and you were snotty to them. I just want to know where you get off."

"I'd like to get off here." I remember the friends, but not being snotty to them.

"I guess that's supposed to be funny."

"Once or twice I've been funnier."

"All I want to hear from you is an apology."

"I'm afraid you're going to need extremely acute hearing."

There is a nervous laugh from the circle around us.

"Very funny. I didn't realize you were so fucking short."

"Do I detect a hint of insult in your voice? How do you know I'm not sensitive about it?"

"Where's your cute little Barbie Doll wife? Bet you wish she was here to defend you." This is said with an enigmatic smile, revealing teeth that look as if they have been used to open oysters.

"Wow! Beauty *and* wit. You're delightful." Anger, adrenaline and rapid heartbeat have brought me near the flash point. "Look, sis. If I was nasty to your friends, assuming you have some, I shouldn't have been. Since I wasn't, it would be pointless to apologize. You have a chip on your shoulder the size of your head and all I want to know from you is, where have you been all my life? And how quickly can you get back there?"

I shall now draw a curtain of charity across the remainder of the scene, the almost-flung beer, the scuffling as two other guests hustle her off to the kitchen, the exit by me into the cool night, temples pounding, to head for my car and try to sort out some turbulently mixed emotions.

There is something pathetic about someone like that and I do feel sorry for her. I also feel sorry for myself, in that I missed the opportunity either to help her with her problems or to knee her in the groin. Does this make me a bad person? I can't be sure.

*   *   *

On the other hand, fame does have its uses. Among them, I discovered once, is that it can help to spare a poor working girl from getting busted.

The girl was a black call girl whom I encountered in a place called something like Jolly Joe's on Bourbon Street in New Orleans. The venue seemed appropriate, for I had always thought that Jolly Joe's would make a perfect movie set for a turn-of-the-century house of pleasure, the kind with a winding stairway, crystal chandeliers and plush red furnishings.

In actuality it is only a restaurant. I was there with my wife and some friends. While waiting for our order, I left them seated in the dining room and wandered into the piano bar. There I struck up a conversation with the girl and sort of interviewed her about the tricks of her trade. She was bright and fun, and our conversation went on for maybe twenty minutes.

When I started to get up and rejoin my party she put her hand urgently on my arm. "Could you leave with me?" she asked.

I explained that I had friends waiting and wasn't really in a position to be a customer, and said I hoped I hadn't wasted her time.

"Oh, that's okay. I enjoyed talking to someone intelligent for a change," she said. "It's just that after we've been sitting here this long, and everybody's seen us, if you don't leave with me—even if you just go around the block and come back in a few minutes—I'll sort of . . . . lose my status, if you know what I mean."

After such an appeal to gallantry, how could I refuse? I went into the dining room and took pleasure in half explaining to my wife and friends, "I have to leave with a hooker. I'll be back shortly."

Then I returned to the piano bar and collected the girl with sufficient openness that her status was retained (if not particularly enhanced).

Outside the restaurant, we had only walked a few blocks when a cop approached us purposefully. "Shit," said my companion. "That sonofabitch is going to bust me."

"Meaning what?" I asked nervously.

"Nothing, except that it's a hundred dollars down the drain. They just do it to us every so often. They know we'll be right back out and at it."

The cop confronted us. "Okay, honey," he said, pushing his cap back with his ballpoint and starting to write out a summons. He glanced at me and said, "Is this lady with you?"

I could already picture the salacious gossip column item that might result from this, at the very least, but I decided to play it cool. "Yes, officer. She's my psychiatrist."

He recognized my voice, and cocked his head in order to peer more closely under the cap I was wearing. "Well, Mr. Cavett. This is a surprise. Your psychiatrist, huh?"

His chuckle sounded friendly, so I went on. "I, of course, lied about her being my psychiatrist. She's my decorator."

With this he laughed outright and flipped his book shut. But before moving on, he retained some integrity by warning my friend that there would be a next time.

The near-miss prompted her to knock off for the night. She kissed me on the forehead and said, "It was sweet what you did." Then she left me, saying she lived nearby and could manage alone, and I turned and retraced my steps along Bourbon Street.

No one back at Jolly Joe's believed my story.

* * *

Fame can make you a target of certain kinds of criminals and nut cases but, oddly, it seems to be a shield against others. At least it was for an actor friend of mine, Louis Edmonds.

Louis plays the elegant con man Langley Wallingford on the vastly popular TV soap opera, "All My Children." As with every role he plays, he does it with utter conviction and authenticity, right down to the professor's English accent. Like another actor friend, Remak Ramsay, Louis has the gift of counterfeiting English accents so perfectly that the Queen herself would be fooled. I doubt if Shaw's Henry Higgins could detect that Louis was actually "raised up" in Baton Rouge, Louisiana. When he and I played together in *Otherwise Engaged* on Broadway, it always amused me that Britishers would come backstage and say, "We know Mr. Edmonds is English, but who else in the cast is?"

One evening Louis—ill-advisedly, as he now admits—was walking his bike through a more remote precinct of Central Park than it is wise to be in at dusk. A young black man approached from the shadows and suggested that Louis unburden himself of his cash. He had with him a small, shiny firearm to emphasize the urgency of the request.

Louis was remarkably calm. He heard himself say, "How much do you need?" Had you or I tried this line—unless you are as mellow and soothing of tone as Louis is—we might quickly have resembled swiss cheese.

"Ten dollars," came the reply from the apparently neophyte highwayman. He didn't even mention the bike.

"Well, I think I can manage that," said Louis, reaching into his running sock for the sawbuck.

At this point the would-be cutpurse took a closer look at the Edmonds visage and said, *sotto voce* at first, "Omigod . . . Oh my god! You—you on my story! You on my *story!* Go on, man . . . go! You okay, man . . . I'm sorry . . . I don't want your money. Just go! Go!"

There is something touching about this incident that I can't put my finger on. Did Louis owe his escape to the fact that he plays a charlatan on the show so stylishly? I think so—that, plus the total reality the soaps have for their addicted viewers, who never think of the actors as anyone but the characters they play anyway.

I like to imagine the dialogue a few days after the incident as the holdup man and a friend are watching "All My Children."

"See that cat?"

"Perfesser Langley?"

"Yeah. I stuck him up the other day in Central Park."

"You so full o' shit." And so on.

Perhaps the answer to the crime problem is to put everybody on soaps. But then the casting would be a problem. For example, if Louis had happened to play a racist southern sheriff on his show he might now be, at the very least, ten dollars poorer.

* * *

Lola (Mrs. Robert) Redford once told me about an experience of her father's in which a connection with fame provided, if not a shield against a mugging, at least a sort of lifeline afterwards.

Her father was out walking on a city street and got "coshed," as the British say, suffering a partial concussion. He was relieved of his billfold and his memory in the attack (the latter for only a few hours, fortunately). The police tried to determine who he was, but he could not recall his or any of his family's names. All he could remember was that his *son-in-law* was Robert Redford.

The police, of course, assumed that this was a temporary delusion.

* * *

For a brief, vivid illustration of irony, you cannot beat the example devised by my comedy-writer friend David Lloyd: the fire alarm system that develops a short in its wiring and burns the house down.

Fame itself is an ironic condition, and its accouterments, much like the fire alarm system, only compound the irony. Among the relatively harmless examples of this, my favorites are those involving conveniences and luxuries that turn out not to be. For instance, the limousine.

Whenever I hear the words, "You don't have to worry about transportation; we'll send a limousine," anxiety sets in. First of all, limousines are embarrassing. Aside from the fact that they are unwieldy, voracious guzzlers of fuel and notoriously faulty mechanically, in a presumably democratic country and especially during hard times it is a tiny bit humiliating to be seen getting into and out of from twenty to seventy thousand dollars' worth of unnecessary chrome, glass and steel.

It gives me a bilious attack to read the line in print, "Cavett then stepped into his limousine and sped away." Whenever I do enter one at some unfortunately chosen location like a bus stop in the rain, and fourteen pairs of eyes watch me step in with a driver-held umbrella over me for the few seconds when I might be exposed to raindrops, it is all I can do to keep from either inviting those in the line into the shiny monster or assuring them that I don't own it and don't usually ride in one and have waited for many buses myself. (Someone said, probably rightly, that the problem with the Reagan administration is that no one in it ever waited for a bus in the rain.)

Because of my limophobia, I have sometimes asked drivers to let me off around the corner from my destination so that I could arrive like just folks. At other times, presumably during periods of mental imbalance, I have had fantasies of revolution in which I imagined that the pedestrians my driver was honking out of the way would rock and burn the twenty feet of Lincoln Continental I was being transported in.

In addition to the ill will they create by appearing to be appurtenances of aristocracy, seemingly calculated to remind onlookers, "I am better than you are," limousines create other problems for their users.

The drivers frequently don't know where they are going, and get you there later than if you had taken a humble taxi or bus. The vehicles are usually ill-assembled and therefore drafty; the privacy and quarantine they allow from the mob so that you can, theoretically, write or work is vitiated by the fact that the reading light often burns out and the temperature controls have two settings, Arctic and Inferno.

But my worst experience with a limousine surpassed all of these difficulties, and surpassed anything that I've ever heard of happening to anybody else.

It was, for once, an occasion when I was undemocratically glad they were "sending a car." ("Car" is the reverse-snobbery euphemism for limousine, as if to suggest, "What other kind of car is there?") It was late on a cold Friday night after a hard week. I had one hundred and thirty miles to traverse from Manhattan to my house at the end of Long Island, and important chores to do the next morning. I had two dogs and assorted baggage with me. Best of all, I would be picked up where perhaps not even one person would see me get in.

It was about eleven P.M. when I boarded the overgrown Black Maria with my two canine companions. They were a comic pair; a black poodle so big that it looked like a man in a dog suit, and a golden Yorkshire-type so small that it looked like a dustmop without a handle. My plan was to nap for about thirty minutes, then spend the remaining two and a half hours or so getting through some paperwork. It was not to be.

I did nod off somewhere in the middle of the Triboro Bridge, but was awakened by the sensation of the car stopping. Amusingly, as it turned out, I thought for a moment that I had overslept and the journey was finished. Instead, we were at a gas station on the Grand Central Parkway just outside the city; the driver had to respond to a call of nature.

A few seconds after he left the car, I decided to let the poodle heed nature too. The dog anointed some juniper bushes next to the gas station, then tugged me a few feet around the corner of the building. I noticed that I could no longer see the car and thought, "Wouldn't it be funny if the driver came back, pulled out and, upon noticing that I was missing, had to take the next exit and come back for me?"

Well, you can see what's coming, or in this case going. After the dog finished its second bit of business, I retraced the three steps that had taken me out of sight of the car just in time to see its taillights merge with those of the stream of traffic.

The station attendant realized what had happened, laughed and said, "Make yourself comfortable, Mr. Cavett." He and his assistant decided to bet on how long it would take the driver to notice and return. The assistant, calculating the distance to the next exit, said five minutes. The attendant said ten because traffic was heavy. To be funny, I said twenty minutes.

We all lost.

The initial humor of the situation, already greater to my two observers than to me, began to wear very thin after the twenty-minute mark came and went.

Since there were no chairs, my hosts offered me a small storeroom in which there were stacked-up cartons of motor oil that I could sit on. The storeroom was also marginally warmer than the rest of the unheated establishment, owing to the presence of a hanging bare light bulb, by whose eye-watering glare I might have done some of my work had it not been in the car.

Thirty minutes passed. Even if the driver reappeared right now, it would be at least two-thirty A.M. before I reached my house. The opened carton of oil cans on which I was enthroned had an uneven surface that forced me to keep shifting my position, thereby imprinting a slightly different pattern of rings on my buttocks. I looked for a scrap of newspaper, a road atlas, the Yellow Pages, *something* to read other than the word Pennzoil, which stared me in the face a thousandfold.

Forty-five minutes. I began to speculate that the driver was dead. He had piled up just around the next curve. No, that was unlikely. He *wanted* to leave me. That must be it—he was stealing the car. I hoped he would be kind to the small dog. It came down to this: if he knew I was not in the car, then we were in trouble; if he didn't know—but that was impossible.

I was fairly sure he had seen me get out. But if not, the interior of the car would have lit up when he opened the door to get back in; wouldn't he have glanced in the back seat? And in any case his natural impulse would have been to say something, to apologize for the delay or just make conversation. If he got no response, wouldn't he check to see if I was asleep?

I closed my eyes and a choreographed array of Pennzoils danced in my head. I began to think about fame, success, glamor—all the things I presumably had at that moment—and of the poor workaday devils with no access to luxuries like limousines who had braved the Long Island Railroad and were now home and tucked snugly in their beds. Even my poodle was sleeping contentedly on the dirty concrete floor.

I will omit a recital of the various stages of puzzlement, rage and despair I went through as another hour passed, while in the meantime the station attendants' hard-to-conceal amusement grew in geometric increments.

Finally, I somehow recalled the name of the small limo company that had dispatched my car, got the number from Information and called it. No answer. Thirty minutes later I tried again and, by the sheerest luck, caught the boss just as he was returning exhausted from a funeral job in Philadelphia.

I told him my story. In a groggy voice laced with fury, he said, "I'll come get you." Still another hour later he arrived, collected me and the poodle and away we went.

As we sped east on the expressway, the boss kept repeating that he couldn't understand how his driver could have done such a thing. After about the seventy-third restatement of this I began to feel nostalgic for the Pennzoil cans.

Suddenly we spotted the original limo coming toward us in the westbound lane. After much blinking of headlights and frantic hand signaling, the other driver managed to get off the highway and pull up alongside us in the parking lot of a diner.

The boss got out and went around to speak to him, but I felt incapable of moving. Blankly, somewhat brain damaged, I watched through the thick-tinted window a sort of pantomime titled, "One Man Chews Out Another with Violent Gestures and Swearing."

The boss, still livid, transferred the small dog and luggage and climbed back in to finish my trip while the other driver headed for the garage. "I told him that the first rule of limousine driving is to be sure your passenger is in the car," the boss said with a straight face.

It seemed that the hapless other fellow had not seen me get out of the car and had assumed all along that I was asleep. When he pulled up in front of my house, hopped out, opened the back door and saw only a small sleeping dog, he nearly fainted. He thought the poodle and I had fallen out.

Horrified, he made his way back down the now dark and nearly deserted highway, looking anxiously along the roadside for the mangled bodies of a boy and his dog.

I do not know what he is doing today, but I hope he is able to bring as much originality to his new calling as he did to chauffeuring.

As the boss drove on toward the end of the island, I finally had to insist that the preceding hour and twenty minutes of apology were a sufficiency and that I was now going to try to nap. About the time I dozed off in what I swore would be the last limo I would ever be dragged into, we arrived.

It was, I suppose, a lovely sunrise that was gleaming over the Atlantic. And I still had well over an hour and a half before I had to be up.

IS ENGLISH A DYING LANGUAGE?

A JOURNALIST I KNOW once had the temerity to correct a colleague's misuse of the word "infer." He pointed out that the proper word in the context should have been "imply."

The affronted colleague made it clear that he had little patience with such niceties. "What are you," he growled back, "one of those word prigs?"

Inspired by that little faceoff, I have decided to take this occasion to declare myself, to come out of the linguistic closet and stand before the world in my true colors. Yes. I too am one of those word prigs.

I may not go around stopping people in the street to correct their usage, or pulling out a Magic Marker on the bus to edit the ad for the National Urban League that says, "Everybody deserves to have their chance."

But I do care about these things. I care when people mistakenly use "disinterested" for "uninterested," or "fortuitous" for "fortunate," or "flout" for "flaunt." I cringe when people try for refinement by saying, "Between you and I," as if they were raising their pinkies over teacups.

I'm perplexed when people adopt the modish abbreviation "Ms.," which doesn't abbreviate anything except common sense.

I take to heart the strictures of Safire, Newman and Simon, earnestly try to stamp out dangling modifiers and would happily pay taxes for a new Environmental Protection Agency to fight language pollution and verbal smog. Such an agency could begin by correcting the "No Smoking" signs in elevators all over New York City, on which "environmental" is misspelled "enviromental."

I often find the newspapers painful reading, not only for what they say but for the way they say it. A senator has to run the "gamut" of protesters to enter his office. Can there really have been one of every kind in order?

Mary McCarthy's love of country is impugned when she is described as an "ex-patriot," now living in Paris.

The New York *Times* has the President "appraised" of the situation in Central America. The *Times* makes this mistake so often that it has become the newspaper of stuck record.

I wish blurb writers would learn that it is not possible to receive *many* kudos from the critics or anyone else. Kudos is not plural. It means glory. A single instance of kudos is not a kudo any more than a single instance of pathos is a patho.

I once received kudos from a critic for my way with an "anticdote." This sounds like something you take to counteract clowning.

And I'm weary of seeing my friends and companions identified in picture captions as "cohorts." You cannot be my cohort no matter how hard you try, unless you are an army in which case I apologize. If I am a host you can be my co-host, but I will not be a hort for anyone.

I've been this (slightly insufferable) way for years, ever since the fourth grade, at least, when I used to correct the spelling errors that my teacher, Miss Fuchs, made on the blackboard.

Back when the critic Edmund Wilson used to fulminate against the misuse of words like "massive" and "jejune" I raced faithfully to the Webster's Third International Unabridged Dictionary in order to purge myself of these offenses. And then, when the late Dwight Macdonald reviewed Webster's Third in The New Yorker, showing how, in comparison with Webster's Second, it failed to make vital distinctions between words and how it followed common usage instead of trying to lead it, I flung my copy straight into the fireplace.

(Actually, I didn't own a copy at the time, any more than I had a fireplace, but I was deeply impressed by a gesture of that kind in one of Rex Stout's novels. Archie Goodwin, assistant to the brilliant detective Nero Wolfe, comes into the office one day to find his employer methodically tearing one page after another out of the new Webster's Third and tossing it into the fire. Wolfe explains himself with a single outraged sentence. "Contact," he says, "is not a verb under this roof.")

To me, being concerned about such things is not merely a matter of correctness or propriety. That makes it sound too prim. Even we word prigs realize there are times when it's best to loosen up and indulge a mistake. In this, too, I'm with Dwight Macdonald, who said he had his own opinion of people who, when asked to identify themselves outside a door, answer, "It is I."

Nor am I talking about language as an ornament. I don't believe in developing a good prose style in the spirit that you might develop, say, a good backhand. So many attempts at a high-toned, cultured effect end up achieving the opposite anyway (a basic principle of comedy).

In venturing into foreign phrases, the pitfalls and landmines cluster. It amuses me when someone thinks he is being French by saying "vichy-*swah*" or "coup de *grah*," and on the other hand saying "pâté de foie *grahss*." A majority of Americans and all Englishmen seem to think "masseuse" (mispronounced "massoose") is French for masseur. Especially when they describe "him" by saying, "I'd like the masseuse with the crewcut and the anchor tattoo."

My late friend, the writer Jean Stafford, once called me in one of her hilarious rages, claiming to have just removed a large tuft of her own hair manually upon receiving a startling piece of information. "Have you *heard?*" she snarled. "The next edition of the American Heritage Dictionary is going to allow *chaise lounge!*" This particularly irksome illiteracy depends on misreading the French adjective "longue" and contorting it into an inaccurate noun. Perhaps a little ditty would help: "How long will you lounge on the *chaise longue* in the lounge?"

What is at stake in all this is everyday logic, not to mention the cardinal virtues of clarity and precision and, on good days, simplicity, vigor and grace.

Consider the expression, "I could care less." Its actual meaning is precisely the opposite of what people intend to say when they use it. If you could care less, then you *do* care. But people use the expression as a corruption of "I *couldn't* care less," which apparently is now too much trouble to say. (When something is too trivial to fool with, do we say, "I *could* be bothered"?)

The woman who says to me, "I could care less," is willing to use a hand-me-down phrase without examining it first. She simply isn't thinking about what she's saying and I judge her accordingly, even if she *is* my wife.

The man who says, "I literally exploded with anger" isn't thinking about what he's saying either, even if he *is* me sometimes (nobody's perfect). He is using "literally" as a heightening word, to give emphasis, but he is using it figuratively. Had he literally exploded with anger, he not only would have created a nasty mess on the carpet but wouldn't be here to tell the tale.

It bugs me that all my life I've been saying something that means what it *doesn't* say. For example, "I can't seem to get this lid off." When we use this construction, do we mean the desirable thing would be to *seem* to get the lid off, or actually to get it off? What we mean is, "I seem to can't get this lid off," which is impossibly awkward. "I seem unable to get this lid off" almost works, but still implies that seeming able to get it off would be just as good as getting it off. Is it too blunt, too crude, too humiliating to say, "I can't get this lid off?"

Richness and diversity are at stake, too. When people confuse a pair of similar words like "nauseous" and "nauseated," they are taking two distinct, useful meanings and blurring them into a single, useless smudge. Every time it happens the language shrinks a little.

In fact, why not take a little test right now? How many times have you used "lay" when you meant "lie"? "Adverse to" when you meant "averse to," or "comprised of" when you meant "composed of"? "Loathe to" when you meant "loath to"? "Enormity" when you meant something like "vastness"? "Masterful" when you meant "masterly"? "Precipitous" when you meant "precipitate"? "Fortuitous" when you meant "fortunate"? "Momentarily" when you meant "in a moment"? Rate yourself on a piece of paper and send it, enclosing a stamped, self-addressed envelope, to Howard Cosell, with my compliments.

"Ours is a precarious language," James Thurber once wrote, "in which the merest shadow line often separates affirmation from negation, sense from nonsense, and one sex from another." In his later years, when he was blind, Thurber took in the world mostly through his hearing, and what he heard, acutely, was the sound of people stumbling over the shadow line.

He wrote often about "The Spreading You-Know" and other blights that he wished would pass "from the lingo into limbo." (I wish he were alive today to deal with teenagers' penchant for pasting their syntax together with the word "like," as in, "I wish you would, like, like me.") Even the sound and the fury, Thurber said, had become the unsound and the fuzzy.

He told a story about talking at a party with an actress he knew (not my wife). She was telling him about a female friend whose apartment had been broken into so many times that she finally had to have it "burglarized." Thurber thought about that for a moment. Then he said, "Wouldn't it have been simpler for her to just have it alarmed?"

As usual with Thurber, the story was amusing but the underlying point was serious. Thurber was, in fact, one of a long line of people who have confirmed what George Orwell wrote four decades ago in his invaluable essay, "Politics and the English Language"—that "most people who bother about the matter at all would admit that the English language is in a bad way." We can confirm it ourselves, every day.

We can confirm it when we take a plane trip and the pilot says he anticipates experiencing considerable turbulence (expects a bumpy ride); or when we read in the papers that a government agency is undergoing a budget shortfall situation (going broke); or when we hear policemen on the TV news relating that the alleged perpetrator exited the vehicle (the suspect got out of the car).

We can confirm it when we find ourselves within the parameters of viable, meaningful and prioritized buzz words; for example, "input," "interface" and "thrust," which, as somebody said, shouldn't be used in public but might be all right in private among consenting adults.

Those of us with steady nerves can confirm it by glancing at student essays, perhaps those of our own children. Not having children (or students) of my own, I have to rely on second-hand reports like one in the *Wall Street Journal* a couple of years ago. It quoted the employment manager of the Continental Illinois Bank & Trust Company in Chicago saying, "More and more of the applicants we're seeing straight out of school can't write a complete sentence." I think I've received résumés from some of those applicants myself.

Yale, which seemed an empyrean of literacy when a fellow student named Bart Giamatti and I were there in the 1950s, went into something of a decline in that area after I left (caused, let's face it, as much by the neo-primitivist student rebellions of the 1960s as by my departure). Bart stayed on to do what he could, which eventually included becoming president of the university.

During the 1970s, when he was still a professor of English and Comparative Literature, Bart wrote an article declaring that undergraduates had "lost touch with the language." To them, it was the final repressive institution to be overthrown, and they succeeded to such an extent, according to Bart, that "young people today can't write, can't shape themselves through words."

By then, of course, I had taken up professional residence in television, which is one of the designated disaster areas of language. (Just think of sports coverage, for example, or game shows, or commercials.) In my years of talking on the tube, I've probably been an accessory to, or committed myself, all the known violations. I shouldn't even discuss this subject unless I'm granted complete immunity.

Television is, among other things, a machine for turning nouns into verbs. When I had my interview series on public television, I "hosted" a show. It was "aired" by PBS and "funded" in part by the Chubb Corporation. Naturally I always hoped that it would be "successed."

Yes, heaven help us, the language *is* in a bad way. There is a famous phrase characterizing the Broadway theater as a fabulous invalid. To me that's exactly what the language has become. Jean Stafford once described its symptoms in wittily clinical terms, and I can't improve on her diagnosis.

"Besides the neologisms that are splashed all over the body . . . like the daubings of a chimpanzee turned loose with finger paints," Jean wrote, "the poor thing has had its parts of speech broken to smithereens . . . and upon its stooped and aching back it carries an astounding burden of lumber piled on by the sociologists and the psychologists, the Pentagon, the admen, and lately, the alleged robbers and bug planters of Watergate.

"The prognosis for the ailing language is not good. I predict that it will not die in my lifetime, but I fear that it will be assailed by countless cerebral accidents and massive strokes and gross insults to the brain and finally will no longer be able to sit up in bed and take nourishment by mouth."

* * *

Take a stand on, say, the proper meaning of the word "transpire," and who your real friends and enemies are will soon—well, transpire. And my guess is they won't always be whom you'd expect. In the skirmishes, ambushes and pitched battles that are constantly being fought over language, the identities of the good guys and the bad guys are often surprising.

The very authorities whom you might expect to be manning the defenses and shoring up collapsing standards—the experts in linguistics, the dictionary makers, the teachers of English—are in many cases leading the onslaught. It's as if, in the middle of a coup, you turned to the palace guard for help and saw them coming at you with bayonets.

I once had several linguistics professors on my PBS talk show. They assured me that things like grammar, syntax and spelling were mere superficial details that shouldn't be allowed to get in the way of the deeper importance of self-expression. In fact they suggested that, in matters of language, rules and standards of any kind were snobbish, authoritarian and downright undemocratic.

When such people edit dictionaries, they completely cop out (*v. slang*. To fail or refuse to commit oneself, esp. out of timidity). They shrink from doing anything as undemocratic as suggesting that one meaning is more correct than another. They try not to deal in right and wrong at all, but merely in what *is*. They record, no doubt with impeccable scholarship, the language as it is spoke. The result is such ludicrous entries as the one in the Webster's Third informing us that "ain't" is "used orally in most parts of the U.S. by many cultivated speakers."

Most of my linguistics professors were apostles of a group called the Council on College Composition and Communication, which a few years ago put out a policy statement advocating "the student's right to his own language," no matter what dialect, patois, slang or gibberish it might be.

This idea could revolutionize education. I keep waiting for other departments to pick it up: the student's right to his own math, the student's right to his own history, even the divinity student's right to his own rites.

What the council meant by the student's own language was whatever the child was speaking around the house before being sent off to school; in particular, whatever poor black children were speaking. One of the experts on my show was Geneva Smitherman of Wayne State University, who argued that black dialect ought to be considered a bona fide language, sufficient unto itself, and that children who speak it should be taught English in the public schools virtually as if it were a second language.

A group of black parents had recently sued the Ann Arbor, Michigan, public schools in an attempt to win just such treatment for their children, and the case had blacks and educators all over the country in an uproar.

I suppressed my poor taste instinct to tell Professor Smitherman that the argument "didn't show me shee-ut." Instead, in my own language, I maintained that the notion of a separate but equal Black English rejected the immigrant experience of melting pot America. After all, children of Italian, Jewish and Norwegian extraction had their dialects too, just as I grew up piping my own peculiar Nebraskanese. But they —I—accepted that to communicate with the society around us, to get on in the world, it was necessary to go through the sometimes tedious effort of learning standard English.

Professor Smitherman cheerfully agreed. In fact, she said that was the whole point. She, who was black, said she was speaking for those blacks who did not *want* to submit themselves to standard English, which was the dialect of the white upper-middle-class establishment. To accept that group's dialect, she argued, was to accept its values and thus lose one's cultural identity.

For blacks, she said, it was a question of "Who am I?" or, as she solemnly insisted it would be quite proper to say, "Who do I be?"

And lest it seem that this argument divided only along racial or ethnic lines, she was supported by another of my panelists, the white linguistics scholar J. L. Dillard, author of a widely regarded book called —what else?—*Black English.*

(For the record, the judge in the Ann Arbor case didn't go nearly as far as my guests. He merely ruled that the schools should learn a little more about Black English and be more sympathetic to the children who spoke it—while getting on with the business of teaching them standard English.)

In Browning's poem "The Grammarian's Funeral," the grammarian himself was dead, obviously. Today the grammarian is underground in a different sense, or at least *a* grammarian is.

I'm thinking of Richard Mitchell, a brilliantly cranky zealot who teaches English at Glassboro State College in New Jersey. Nine times a year, using a clattery printing press in his own basement, Mitchell publishes a broadside called "The Underground Grammarian," through which he wages a funny, deadly one-man war on jargon, clichés and all shades of fuzziness, from "purple fustian" on down.

Once again, what is striking about Mitchell's campaign is who the enemy turns out to be. His barrages aren't aimed at the Philistines outside the ivied walls of academe but at his colleagues inside, at deans and administrators and even at English teachers sitting in the library —or, as they unfortunately might describe themselves, "language skills instructors" sitting in the "learning resources center."

Mitchell casts himself as a prophet in the academic wilderness, denouncing the false gods who have seduced his brethren. The false gods usually turn out to be the education professionals, or "education-ists." These are the folks who in all seriousness can maintain that "to language" is a verb meaning to represent "conceptualizations by prop-erly ordered sequences of signs," and can define "to aud" as to "listen to speech in order to language"—understanding, of course, that listen-ing means "selecting and attending to expectation in the auditory modality."

As Mitchell commented in "The Underground Grammarian," "If a man came to your door trying to peddle that kind of stuff, just how long would you aud his languaging before sneaking off to the telephone to call the wagon?"

With schools and campuses and other major organs of education so often in the hands of such manglers of the mother tongue, it's no wonder that the true believers, the real friends and practitioners of good language, are frequently amateurs, mavericks, guerrillas or double agents boring from within.

I don't count the dashing mercenaries, the William Safires and John Simons; nor any writers, really. They are by definition defenders of the faith. You take for granted that a William F. Buckley, Jr., will take to the barricades in this struggle, or at least ask his chauffeur to drive close by.

Buckley, in fact, once demonstrated his tactical skills by turning a retreat on the political front into a successful attack on the language front. He had been asked to deliver a commencement address at Vassar College, but when his selection touched off a storm of controversy on campus, he withdrew. A typical complaint against him was voiced by a professor of English, who wrote to the student newspaper: "It was Buckley who offered pridefully in those days the caste of mind and insinuating attitudes toward academe which intellectually veneered the crudities of Joe McCarthy, and in so doing, fueled 'McCarthyism' at its most virulent pitch with respect to the academic community."

In Buckley's letter of withdrawal to the president of Vassar (reprinted in the New York *Times*) he singled out the professor's charge. "That the man who composed that sentence should be teaching English at Vassar rather than studying it," Buckley wrote, "suggests that Vassar has much, much deeper problems than coming up with a suitable commencement speaker."

What you don't at all take for granted is that a former businessman now running the mammoth bureaucracy at the Department of Commerce (a worthy successor to Dickens' Circumlocution Office) would be an outstanding exponent of plain speaking and concise, vigorous writing. But that is precisely what Commerce Secretary Malcolm Baldridge is.

I don't deny that I take a special interest in Baldridge because he is another in the line of distinguished Americans who were born in Nebraska and majored in English at Yale. But I think any objective observer would have to acknowledge the breathtaking heresy of a federal official who can say of multisyllabic words, vagueness and Washingtonian smokescreens, "That's not communicating, that's covering one's flanks."

As befits a sometime rodeo rider, Baldridge has instructed his staff to learn how to write like a cross between Ernest Hemingway and Zane Grey. I can't imagine what could be made of this order by people who have spent their entire professional lives concocting viscous prose about hopefully having a mutually beneficial input prior to finalizing future plans contingent upon the management regime in the present time frame, but good luck to them.

Baldridge has had the audacity to put out a sort of hit list of bad English that he wants to eliminate from Commerce Department memos and correspondence, and it goes well beyond the predictable jargon and clichés. He actually expects people to avoid redundancies like "end result" and "new initiatives," to say "different from" instead of "different than," and to mind their plurals—"data," for example, and "criteria." (The singular-plural distinction may be a lost cause: if we already have "the media is," can "the phenomenon are" be far behind?)

No one man, not even Baldridge, could enforce such a list unassisted. Reforming any federal department's language is the linguistic equivalent of Hercules' task in tidying up the Augean stables. So Baldridge has hit upon a clever gimmick. He has had his hit list programmed into the department's word processors.

After somebody writes a letter or memo on one of these machines, he or she presses a glossary button to trigger a search of the text by the computer. If an offending usage is found, the computer causes it to light up, then flashes a message on the top of the screen: "Do not use this word."

I'm working on a variation of this device for my Apple computer at home. Instead of the flashing light and message, it would have a brief videotape of my high school English teacher, Miss Martin, pursing her lips and waggling her finger at me chastisingly.

Almost as unlikely a champion of good language as Malcolm Baldridge is Agnes De Mille, whose field is choreography, the most nonverbal of the arts. This indomitable lady has a graceful, intelligent prose style and a quick, tartly amusing tongue; she is not the sort of person in whose presence I'd want to be caught committing a solecism.

"I heard good English at home," she told me once on my PBS show. "At school I learned to parse. I learned all the parts of the English sentence. I learned Latin, which was a real help. Now, that's gone."

The show she was on happened to be a panel on language, whose other members were Edwin Newman, John Simon and John Kenneth Galbraith. Not only did she hold her own in this company, but she kept us all in line, pulling us back from our flighty digressions time and again to consider the basics.

"I think it begins with the way ordinary people talk," she said. "They don't talk expressively or clearly. They let their children grow up without ever hearing English—I don't know what they speak. Then the children go to school and apparently learn nothing, as far as I can make out, except how to plague the teachers. Then they get into college, or higher learning, and by that time they haven't yet tackled a simple declarative sentence. Children—I mean children up to twenty-five— cannot use the great tool, which is language and writing. It's all "You know—like—I say—oh man!"

Before she was through, she had also leveled Washington, "where the subjunctive is unknown" (except, of course, at the Commerce Department); Madison Avenue, whose ads "are not only untrue, but ungrammatical"; and the edifice of democracy in language. "You can't talk better than the other fellow, or you're a pig," she explained. "In order to be fraternal, to be like him or just sympathetic, you have to speak dreadfully, or not at all. And I think this is a pity."

Having her as a guest was a bracing experience, but I couldn't help wondering to myself, "What must it be like for the poor dancers who have to rehearse under her unsparing eye?"

Tony Randall is another notable amateur of language (and like all good amateurs, I'm sure he knows that the word derives from the Latin for "lover"). He is meticulously well spoken and knowledgeable, and even when he finds himself in some of the tackier precincts of television —as all of us performers do from time to time—he unfailingly upholds a standard of linguistic taste.

Well, not unfailingly.

Perhaps because my show was on PBS, allegedly one of the dignified precincts of the medium, or perhaps because he was seized by a perverse whim, Tony "played against type" when he came on with me. He still displayed a formidable acquaintance with the language, but hardly in the same spirit as Agnes De Mille.

I knew he was in an antic mood when he, well known as a vehement

foe of smoking, insisted on strolling onstage before the taping with a
lighted cigarette between his fingers. After the studio audience
guffawed, Tony turned to me and said, "See? I told you it would get
a laugh."

Then, as our microphones were being attached and sound levels were
being tested (making everything we said audible to the studio audience), he suddenly asked me, "How many slang words can you name
for the male organ?"

This caused a titillated murmur, and I thought he would be satisfied
with that. "Tony, this doesn't seem like the—"

"Your own name, of course, is one—dick."

"Well, yes, but—"

"Then there's peter and John Thomas. And slightly ruder ones, like
pecker and joint . . ."

"Sure, and stick, and peg too, but don't you think—"

"And the ones that sound sort of Chinese, like wang, and wong, and
dong . . ."

My discomfiture was misplaced, I guess, because the audience was
laughing good-naturedly at all of this. I could even see blue-rinsed
schoolmarm types covering their giggles with their fingertips. Apparently to them Tony is such a dear that they don't mind if he gets a little
naughty.

". . . tool, and wick, and third leg, and diminutives like weenie and
dinky . . ."

On and on he went, in a truly virtuoso catalogue. There was nothing
to do but let him finish.

". . . rod, and pencil, and *schlange,* which comes from the German
for snake, and of course *schmuck,* which is a Yiddish variant of the
German word for jewel . . ."

When it came time to tape our interview, I hardly knew what to
expect. What other mischievous surprises might Tony try to spring?

As it turned out, he settled back in his chair and conducted a
thoroughly straightforward conversation with me—full of humor and

good stories, of course, but delivered with perfect decorum. Until the end.

As I thanked him and prepared to sign off, he leaned forward and said very distinctly, "Good night, *Dork.*"

I never had the heart to send Tony the bill for the extra editing we had to do to cleanse the tape of that final entry in his slang catalogue.

Should we have edited it out? Or did we commit the phallus fallacy?

* * *

"Usage, schmusage—who needs all this pedantry? It doesn't affect me one way or the other. I can always get my meaning across."

This is the kind of impatient response I get from rough-and-ready communicators who feel that, because they are not writers or professors, they are above the language fray. However, like almost everything else, language is too important to be left to the experts.

It is "the defining mystery of man," in George Steiner's phrase. It is the index to our civilization, the history of our race, the living web of our shared values and emotions. When it breaks down it undermines the way we order our public life and common welfare. This is what George Orwell was ultimately getting at in the essay I mentioned earlier, "Politics and the English Language."

I once gave a commencement address on the subject at Vassar (somewhat disappointingly, I aroused none of the controversy that Bill Buckley did), and I told the graduating seniors that no matter what else they had concentrated on in their studies, they were still English majors. We're all English majors, willy-nilly, until the day we join Browning's grammarian. The breakdown of language isn't just something that's happening to language. It's happening to us.

Look again, if you will, at Thurber and the actress at the party. They were, to use Thurber's metaphor, on the shadow line, close to losing rational touch with each other. Nothing weighty was at stake, of course. On many occasions it doesn't matter all that much if words and meaning part company—if an undertaker advertises coffins with a "lifetime guarantee," for example; or if the New York *Times* prints this sentence about Nelson Rockefeller: "He was chairman of the Museum of Modern Art, which he entered in a fireman's raincoat during a recent fire, and founded the Museum of Primitive Art."

But E. B. White, who found that sentence in the *Times,* reminds us in *The Elements of Style* that muddiness of meaning is not always such harmless fun. "Muddiness," White writes, "is not merely a disturber of prose, it is a destroyer of life, of hope: death on the highway caused by a badly worded roadsign, heartbreak among lovers caused by a misplaced phrase in a well-intentioned letter, anguish of a traveler not being met at a railroad station because of a slipshod telegram."

Not to mention the anguish of the prisoner in the (perhaps apocryphal) incident of the fatally unpunctuated telegram: PARDON FROM GOVERNOR IMPOSSIBLE PROCEED WITH EXECUTION.

When the gravedigger catches Hamlet out in a bit of muddiness, Hamlet says to his friend Horatio, "We must speak by the card, or equivocation will undo us." E. B. White believes it, and so do I.

In Willard Gaylin's gripping book *The Killing of Bonnie Garland,* about a Yale undergraduate who beat his girlfriend to death with a hammer, much of the language from the murder trial is quoted verbatim. So is the language of the murderer, taken from tape recordings of the interviews Gaylin had with him.

At one point prior to publication, it was suggested that the syntax of the verbatim dialogue ought to be edited and tidied up. But to do so would have robbed the book of much of its realism, and would have eradicated the telling fact that the least effective attorney had the least clear syntax. Would anyone insist that this had nothing to do with the jury's sense that the other man had his eye more sharply on the ball, was surer of what he was talking about? (The reader would also have missed the fact that the murderer had clearer syntax and used the language better than both of them.)

We live a lot of our lives on the practical, everyday level, exchanging gossip at a party, giving and taking directions, and making and breaking plans. If our language is faulty, then these transactions will be faulty.

Each of us literally is in danger of not knowing what the other is talking about.

This is what makes me want to say to all those impatient people who dismiss the issue of language, "Wait a minute. *Can* you always get your meaning across? Are you sure?"

God knows, many of the transactions of *my* daily life are faulty, from garbled phone messages to staff meetings where everyone seems to be (as Peter DeVries said of Jesus and the Jews) at cross purposes. These contretemps may not involve lovers' heartbreak or death on the highway, but they can be inefficient, time-consuming and maddeningly frustrating. Some of my conversations with car rental clerks, telephone operators and waiters make me wonder if we're even speaking the same language.

Thanks to a malfunctioning answering machine, the following mini-ordeal with the telephone company—which, for me, is the prime baffler, muddier and confuser—was preserved verbatim. I doubt that it would have impressed George Orwell overmuch; nonetheless, I offer it here as a social document of some interest.

First, a little background information. I have two telephone numbers at home. I have four telephones. Two numbers, four phones. On one of the phones you can talk on either number, depending on which button is down.

That is all you need in order to grasp the picture perfectly, although to the woman from the phone company it was apparently incomprehensible and open to an infinite variety of misunderstandings.

The conversation took place on an otherwise ordinary Tuesday morning, when I awoke to learn that one of the phones (not the one with buttons) was dead.

> ME: I'd like to report a phone out of order.
> MA BELL: Certainly. What number are you calling from?
> ME: Seven-seven-seven, two-five, two-five.
> MA BELL: Your name?
> ME: Cavett.

MA BELL: What seems to be the problem?

ME: One of my phones is completely dead.

MA BELL: Do you have more than one phone?

ME: Yes. And I have two numbers.

MA BELL: Which number are you calling from?

ME: The one I gave you.

MA BELL: Then the other number is dead.

ME: No, I'm calling from the number that is dead. On an extension, of course.

MA BELL: I see. What seems to be the trouble with the phone you are calling from?

ME: Nothing. It's one of the other phones.

MA BELL: Could you give me that number?

ME: I did.

MA BELL: I'm afraid I'm not clear. You say something is wrong with the phone?

ME *(loosening collar):* It's dead. Out. Kaput. A lifeless prop.

MA BELL: The phone you are speaking from?

ME: What?

MA BELL: The phone you are speaking from is giving you trouble?

ME: Yes, of course; I'm speaking from a dead phone. It's one of my best tricks. No one knows how I do it.

MA BELL: I'm sorry?

ME: Never mind. Start again. I have two lines, four phones.

MA BELL: You have four instruments at your dwelling?

ME: Forgive me. *Instruments,* yes. Four *instruments* at my *dwelling.* In which I *reside.*

MA BELL: What seems to be wrong with the troubled instrument?

ME *(Resisting saying, "It is I who am troubled. The instrument appears quite calm"):* It won't work. It's as dead as a doornail.

MA BELL: And that is not the instrument you are speaking from?

ME *(in disbelief):* Hardly.

MA BELL: I beg your pardon?

ME *(beginning to throb at the temples):* No. I decided to speak from one of the phones that works. Could you perhaps send a repairman? It might be easier when you see the—

MA BELL: Yes. We won't be able to do that until next Monday.

ME: But Monday is five days off. That's unacceptable. It's my most used phone and I need it fixed immediately.

MA BELL I'm afraid you can't expect repair until Monday.

ME: And when can I actually get repair, as opposed to expecting it?

MA BELL: I beg your pardon?

ME: Never mind. I assume I pay the same amount for a dead phone as for a live one. Do I get a reduction for having a dead phone for five days?

MA BELL: You'll have to speak to billing about that.

ME *(whining):* Why can't I get service before Monday?

MA BELL: I'm afraid we're very busy.

ME: So am I.

MA BELL: Unless all your phones are out, we cannot consider it an emergency.

ME: I see. So if I rip out all my phones, I can get service immediately.

MA BELL: Well, if that's the way you want to put it.

ME: Can I speak to one of your superiors? *(Hoping she will say, "Who would that be?" so I can say, "Anyone on the face of the earth" and hang up.)*

MA BELL: None is available at the moment. If you give me your name I will have my supervisor call you.

ME: On the phone that works, I assume.

MA BELL *(grimly):* Your name, please?

ME: Cavett.

MA BELL: Cabot?

ME: Cavvvett.

MA BELL: Can you spell that?

ME *(through gritted teeth):* Yes. I've been able to spell it for years. "C" as in clodpate, "A" as in awfully dumb, "V" as in very stupid, "E" as in egregiously thickheaded . . . *(She hangs up. Apparently, at last, I have been understood.)*

Their meaning, alas, is usually one of the last things to be gotten across by those people who believe it doesn't matter what words you use to say something. But there is something else they miss even more totally. Consider the following:

"That was no lady, that was the woman I'm married to."

I know someone who remains a friend although he insists he detects no difference between that and the classic punch line, "That was no lady, that was my wife"; and I'm afraid his is the voice of multitudes.

The get-your-meaning-across people take in only that both versions convey the same information. They simply don't see that one is (reasonably) funny and one is not. Such people are as incomprehensible to me as those who hear no difference between the third and fourth notes of Beethoven's da-da-da-DUM.

B. Iden Payne, the venerable English director who was presiding over the Oregon Shakespeare Festival when I was a summer intern there a quarter-century ago, used to tell about the time a famous tragedian took on a role in a Bernard Shaw play. The actor—Forbes-Robertson or Granville-Barker or one of those double-barreled eminences of the day—felt himself to be slumming by appearing in a comedy, and as a result he condescendingly mugged and camped his way through rehearsals until Shaw himself brought him up short. "What you're doing," Shaw castigated him, "is all very well for tragedy, but comedy is serious business."

Beneath the playful paradox, Shaw had a real point—about plays, about acting, and perhaps above all about language. Comedy is in many ways the most exacting of verbal forms. It puts a mercilessly high premium on the clarity, precision and grace that I've been talking about. The kind of loose, casual language that may be all very well for other purposes simply won't do for being funny.

That is one reason why comic writers and performers tend to be our sharpest and most crystalline stylists. Any examples I give are bound to start arguments, but think of Lewis Carroll, Mark Twain, P. G. Wodehouse, James Thurber, Groucho Marx, Evelyn Waugh and Woody Allen, just for starters.

And talk about your word prigs! Noel Coward was once rehearsing Edith Evans in his *Blithe Spirit.* There was a moment where Dame

Edith was supposed to gaze out a bay window in the direction of a nearby town and comment, "On a clear day you can see Marlow." For some reason she delivered the line as, "On a very clear day you can see Marlow."

The insertion of the extra word nettled the fastidious playwright. He stopped Dame Edith and corrected her. Again she said it wrong. To Coward's mounting exasperation, no matter how many times he had her do it over, she continued to misread the line.

Finally, he exploded. "No, no, no, Edith! On a clear day you can see Marlow! On a *very* clear day you can see Marlowe, Kyd and Shakespeare!"

A joke, an aphorism, a witty saying can be worded only one way. The slightest change—one too many syllables, a substituted word—and its force and beauty are ruined. To those of us who deal in this sort of thing, a misquoted joke or funny line is as painful as it is for a musician to hear Chopin sharped and flatted in the wrong places.

I once read a biography in which Oscar Wilde's transcendent wit was purportedly being appreciated. The author referred to the time after the homosexuality scandal when Wilde, his career and life in ruins, was required to stand on a public railway platform in chains. Wilde remarked to a friend, "If this is the way Her Majesty treats her prisoners, she doesn't deserve any."

It is a wonderful remark, but it is more wonderful when quoted correctly. As Wilde instinctively knew, even under the duress he was under, the sentence needs two more words to make it clearer and funnier, and paradoxically, to make it seem shorter. What he actually said was, "If this is the way Her Majesty treats her prisoners, she doesn't deserve to have any."

The omission of those two little words dulls the edge, and if it doesn't entirely kill the joke it lops off a couple of its limbs. One imagines Wilde saying, "Now I have been worse than imprisoned, I have been misquoted."

Closer to our own time, there is a gleaming example of perfect wording by Fred Allen that is almost always misquoted and ends up badly crippled. Allen once said, "You could take all the sincerity in Hollywood, place it in a flea's navel, and still have room for four caraway seeds and the heart of an agent."

You can readily see how the first half could be turned around and unnecessary words added ("... still have enough room left over for ..."), but the more subtle distortion comes at the end. "The heart of an agent" almost invariably comes out "an agent's heart."

People still laugh, but they miss the rich deftness of the original. True, the heart of an agent and an agent's heart are the same thing (and equally minuscule). But the lofty, poetic construction of "the heart of" followed by the mundane word "agent" provides at least two levels of humor, whereas the misquote has less than one.

Would the people who settle for the misquote say there is no difference between "She has the grace of a swan" and "she has a swan's grace"? Or even "she has swan grace"?

A journalist writing a tribute to Fred Allen once brought off the amazing feat of misquoting five out of five of the comedian's funniest lines. I can't put myself through the agony of itemizing them, so one will have to do. Allen made a famous crack about a town in Maine that was so dull that "one day the tide went out and never came back." The offender rendered the line as, "... and never came back again."

I realize that in both cases you have a non-returning tide, but the extra word betrays an ear of tin, if not tinfoil.

To writers or performers with a finely tuned sense of comedy (and hence of language), no detail is too small, no shading too fine to be worth polishing, precisely because the tiniest blurring can be fatal to the effect. I never met anybody who exemplified this punctilio, in his person as well as his work, better than S. J. Perelman.

If you've read even one of his *feuilletons,* as he liked to call them, you know how immaculate his published prose was, despite incorporating and sending up great gobbets of slang, jargon and verbal sludge (another of his favorite terms).

With Perelman, anything that he committed to paper—including, for all I know, his grocery list—had to be brought to a diamondlike hardness and gloss. Years ago, I lived in a Manhattan apartment that previously had been occupied by the actress Patricia Neal, and that still contained some of her furniture and effects. One day I came across a book Perelman had inscribed to her. Where many authors would have scrawled a "fondest regards" or a facile joke, Perelman had wrought a tiny marvel: "For Pat, this extravagant gallavantry—conceived in anguish, executed in want, and remaindered in toto. Sid."

But he was equally stylish in his dapper bearing, his steel-rimmed spectacles and neat mustache, and most of all in his conversation. He had the ability—rare enough in writers, nearly unheard of in the rest of us—to speak in shapely, complete sentences. I think nearly every one he ever uttered could have been diagrammed to the last prepositional phrase on the blackboard of Miss Martin's English class in Lincoln, Nebraska.

Of all the Paris Review's many interviews with writers over the years, the one with Perelman is my favorite. Since many readers are aware that the Paris Review interviewees often touch up the edited transcript before publication, they probably think that Perelman's felicitous lines are more the product of his writing table than the tape recorder; but the fact is he actually talked that way.

When asked by the Paris Review whether distrusting the first inspiration that leaps to mind was a sound practice in writing comedy, he replied, "In writing anything, sweetie. The old apothegm that easy writing makes hard reading is as succinct as ever. I used to know several eminent writers who were given to boasting of the speed with which they created. It's not a lovable attribute, to put it mildly, and I'm afraid our acquaintanceship has languished."

A few days after Perelman's appearance on my PBS show, a woman was exclaiming to me about it at a party. "I loved his line about the men running Hollywood having low hairlines like apes," misquoth she. I'm not saying that the woman is despicable for miswording the gem that Perelman dropped in passing (". . . the studio executives, who have foreheads by dint of electrolysis . . ."), any more than someone should be thumbscrewed for loving the theme from "Casablanca" and referring to it as "As Time Moves Along." It's just that if she thinks that's what Perelman said, she probably wouldn't see the difference between the Mona Lisa and a passport photo of a smiling woman.

In Perelman's remark, by the way, the selection of the slightly archaic "dint" was perfection itself. You know what it means even if you don't. The line wouldn't be memorable without it; "by means of" and "thanks to" don't make it. Mark Twain said it for all time: "The difference between the *almost* right word and the right word is the difference between the lightning bug and the lightning."

Allen Funt, that wicked sociologist, once conducted a fascinating experiment in the relation between language and humor. On his show "Candid Camera," he told various people a joke and then filmed their attempts to retell it. As with all his best stunts, the results were not only hilarious but somewhat poignant in their innocent wrongness.

One of the jokes Funt used went like this: In olden times a man in armor dashes in out of a storm and tells the innkeeper that his steed has perished. He is on the king's urgent business and needs a fresh mount immediately. None is available, but he points to a large canine in the corner and offers to ride it. To which the innkeeper says, "Are you crazy? I wouldn't send a knight out on a dog like this."

The retellings defied belief.

Here is one, based only on my recollection of the show but I assure you not exaggerated: "It seems two men take a horse into an old castle type place where there's a bar, see . . . and . . . let's see . . . oh, and somebody shoots the horse. Now the king is waiting for the guy to bring home some gold or something, so he says, 'I have to have a horse.' Just then this giant dog walks in and somebody says . . . let's see . . . something about . . . oh, yeah, he says, 'I'm a knight. I couldn't get up on a dog like that.' See?"

The tendency to add irrelevancies was striking. One man laid on endless details of what the knight was wearing and what he had to drink, and finally worked his way to the end with the innkeeper saying, "Hey, I can't send a knight out on a chihuahua!"

Another mangler got the story almost right until near the end, when he finished off with, "Are you kidding? I wouldn't send my dog out on a night like this." Apparently he felt the humor lay in the barkeep's willingness to have the dog ridden but not in inclement weather. Or something.

Woody Allen, who has written more than his share of memorable (and presumably retellable) jokes, has had real life experiences of the same kind.

He told me once of a man trying to quote one of his jokes to him at a party. "I'm a great admirer of your humor," the man began. "I was particularly amused by a joke of yours in which you, uh . . . it seems that you were discussing some topic or other with your psychiatrist and, uh . . . you, in some fashion . . . misunderstood or misinterpreted a remark in a manner that led to a highly amusing . . . uh . . . set of circumstances. Do you know the one I have reference to?"

I like to think of Woody telling the man he wasn't precisely sure which joke he had reference to but was glad he liked it, then moving away with an aside to a friend, ". . . guy should put together a few more like that and have himself an act."

Nor is it only amateurs, outside of show business, who are tone deaf to how humor must be worded. Years ago the brilliant comedy writer David Lloyd and I spent a week working as writers for Art Linkletter. David's and my experience was that Linkletter was amazingly adept at those things that he did well, but he was to comedy what Jack the Ripper was to etiquette.

There is such a thing in humor as spelling it out, i.e., making a joke *too* clear. It tends, unhappily, to make the joke less funny as well. What happened one day when David and I were assigned to come up with some jokes on the subject of comedy teams is etched indelibly in our memories.

David submitted the line, "There have been many great comedy teams: Laurel and Hardy, Abbott and Costello, Jack E. Leonard . . ."

Apparently fearing that listing the rotund comedian among comedy teams might be too subtle for the audience, Linkletter (or a colleague) reworded the line so that a head of cabbage would get the point. It came out thus: "There have been many great comedy teams: Laurel and Hardy, Abbott and Costello, and big, fat Jack E. Leonard, who is so fat he's a one-man comedy team all by himself!"

The fact that the emended version was greeted with less mirth than an unfavorably jury verdict restored one's faith in the public.

The last word on this matter, as on so many matters, was said by Groucho. His witticisms used to be quoted frequently by one of our leading columnists, but always, *always,* inaccurately. Groucho grew more and more frustrated and perplexed.

"What can you do?" I asked him.

"Nothing," he said. "It's hopeless. The only way to get him to print a joke right is to *tell* it to him wrong."

THE CAVETT
ALBUM—II

WHEN YOU HAVE DONE as many TV talk shows as I have you will find that one of the banes of your existence is the question, "Who was your most interesting guest?" As should be obvious (but apparently isn't), to be able to choose among thousands of guests and dozens of categories, singling out one person and crowning him or her with that pallid label "interesting," is an impossibility.

The most interesting person I didn't have on my show, however, is easy: the writer Jean Stafford.

What distinguished her was elusive and uncapturable, and I'm uncomfortably aware that it is foolish to try to convey a true impression of her in print. After she died, a college quarterly put out a special issue on her that included many portraits and reminiscences by friends and colleagues. No two of them seemed to be about the same person, and none of them was the Jean I knew.

The Jean of the love letters to Robert Lowell, her first husband (quoted in Ian Hamilton's biography of Lowell), was still a further revelation to me. I was accustomed to hearing Jean speak of Lowell in long-suffering terms, and to hearing her refer to husband number two, Oliver Jensen, as "that other man I was married to whose name escapes me at the moment."

I blush to confess that I didn't know who she was when we met. My wife and I were attending a Christmas cocktail party given by Leueen MacGrath, the actress and former wife of George S. Kaufman. Leueen's wide acquaintance in the theater and literary world always produced an impressive collection of party guests. "My God," said my wife. "That's Jean Stafford."

My single monosyllable "Who?" loosed a torrent of my wife's abuse upon me for being ignorant of one of America's best writers of fiction, a Pulitzer Prize winner, of whose work my wife had read virtually all.

Jean's husband, A. J. Liebling, another fine writer, was at that moment on the verge of death in a New York hospital (as I later learned), and Jean's eyebrow-raising presence at the party indicated not so much a lack of concern and devotion as a highly developed penchant for seeking escape.

From the first words I heard her utter it was clear that here was one of the funniest and most brilliant women I would ever meet. Also one of the drunkest.

Jean's distinctive timbre, low register and variety of inflections combined to produce the wittiest *voice* I have ever heard. Anything she said seemed richly shaded with meanings. Her dark hair and large, luminous eyes highlighted a shrewd yet slightly girlish face that had been extensively reconstructed following a near-fatal car crash. The mishap gave us her marvelous story "The Interior Castle," which seems to be anthologized in virtually every collection of prize-winning American short stories.

Jean and my wife, especially, formed an instant bond of friendship that lasted until Jean's death. That first night we signified it by accepting the duty of getting Jean home. Leueen and others to whom the task had fallen in the past seemed greatly relieved that someone new was taking on the job.

After a cab ride filled with laughter, I recall Jean finally managing to align her key with the keyhole and letting us into an old and comfortable apartment that was then the Liebling-Stafford residence.

While Jean, at her insistence, fixed a drink for everyone, I asked for directions to the bathroom. She said, "Straight ahead. Through Joe's room." I *had* read Liebling: his war correspondence; his masterpiece on boxing, *The Sweet Science;* a selection from his hilarious book on the Longs and Southern politics, *The Earl of Louisiana.* I had also seen him on David Susskind's early "Open End" shows. He looked like a Jewish buddha, his eyes and face sparkling with enthusiasm and wit.

I paused to gaze with a fan's avidity at his typewriter, his bathrobe and well-worn carpet slippers, all of which, as it turned out, he had used for the last time.

A few minutes later, Jean insisted on hauling out a ouija board and seating us across from her for a session. I had heard of respectable people taking ouija boards seriously—S. J. Perelman, for example—but I had never seen it happen. Jean, who could *just* navigate, lowered the lights and began the solemn business with the hands and the pointer.

She seemed suddenly sober and deadly serious. As the pointer began to move I was too taken with Jean's clear-eyed concentration to notice what, if anything, was being spelled out. Apparently it was a man's first name. Jean shot from her chair, knocking it over, and lurched sideways against the wall. She let out a Medea-like wail, followed by a heart-breaking, "My . . . brother Dick . . . *hates* being dead!"

I don't remember much of anything after that. It was such a shocking and vivid moment that it has erased everything around it. Somehow Jean was gotten into bed. Joe Liebling died hours later. It was spooky seeing his obit in the later editions of the next morning's New York *Times* and recalling my moment in his room and the night's strange events.

Over the remaining decade or so of Jean's life she became a neighbor as well as a friend, since she settled near us on Long Island, in the antique-filled, shingle-style house that she and Liebling had bought in the town of The Springs. (The names "Jean Stafford and A. J. Liebling" on the country mailbox were never altered.)

Knowing her during those years was one of the joys and burdens of
being alive, as we enjoyed her wicked charm and colorful rages and silly
presents and gloriously funny phone calls and letters, balanced against
her appalling self-destruction with cigarettes and booze.

She had, as she described it, an "adder's tongue." She once described
a bulky feminist leader as "looking like she was pregnant with farm
machinery." Her nickname for a famous female writer whom she
despised was "Miss Scaly Bird."

One day she called up because another less-than-admired colleague
had written an article for the paper that had her snapping. "Have you
seen today's New York *Times?*" she asked in a voice curdling with
disgust. "Willie Jones [we'll call him] just went to the *bathroom* all over
the Op-Ed page!"

Her vocal diction, like her writing, typically rolled out in elegant and
shapely fashion, then climaxed hilariously in some earthy colloquialism:
"Did you see the Chief Executive of these United States declare
emphatically last night on television that he is not a crook? In a pig's
valise!"

I think this alternation of "true American" with a more ornate style
reflected the influences of her two favorite authors, Mark Twain and
Henry James. I once heard her spin out a long description of the
achievements and admirable qualities of Harold Ross, the founding
editor of The New Yorker, all in an elaborately wrought verbal prose
that ended with the words, *"He* was a *cash customer!"*

Jean had a rubber stamp that convincingly simulated the curlicued
signature and title, "Miss Henrietta Stackpole, secretary to Miss Stafford." Over this pseudonym she answered much of her mail, confident
that, as she might say, "nary a one" of her correspondents would
recognize the name as that of a character in Henry James's *Portrait of
a Lady.* When a literate sailor did, she sent him a splendid congratula-
tory note over her own signature.

Her personal letters were delightful mixtures of the informal, gossipy
Jean and the poised professional who could never write anything badly,
as in this account of some literary awards committee she had been on:

". . . To my unbounded delight, I have just discovered that next Thursday I shall for the last time meet with a committee on which I have served (without emolument and, for the most part, without effect) for three full calendar years and for which I have been obliged to read upward of 6742 long hard books of fiction and (mercy on us) criticism and (more mercy) poetry and (HELP) plays. The meetings themselves are rather good fun because there's scarcely anything meaner in this world than a batch of writers getting together to cut up other writers. Last year, to our considerable relief, we lost Loren Eisley (I asked Joe Mitchell who he was and Joe said, "Oh, he writes about science kind of the way Anne Lindbergh does."), but he was replaced by Kurt Vonnegut who keeps saying "Gee!" and recommending the funky serious one-act plays wrought by Black albino paraplegics. I dearly love Henry Steele Commager (he and I agree on just about everything) but I do not like a pig-eyed woman poet who sniffles into Kleenex and whose large woman housemate comes to pick her up in a peanut-butter colored Volkswagen truck: they always try to get me into it, so I hang onto Mr. Commager as tight as I can, feeling as I do, that it would be discomforting for a woman at my time of life to be gang-banged by two strapping tomboys, one of them afflicted with chronic catarrh . . ."

When Jean came to our house for a visit, she usually brought a rare bottle of wine from the rapidly diminishing wine cellar of Joe Liebling, a zealous oenophile, or a comic gift of some piece of tasteless kitsch (one is on my desk to this day—a plastic statuette of a hula dancer with an opening in her pelvic region for sharpening pencils), or a piece of writing from some unheard-of magazine or newspaper, annotated by Jean in a lethal parody of what she called, her voice dripping with malice, "the learned journals of the Modern Language Association."

Her eye for priceless tripe was keen. She and her friend Randall Jarrell had discovered the incomparable works of a lady poet from Ohio

named something like Maude Dooley. She often regaled us with sample
verses by this sweet singer of Sandusky, or wherever, declaiming them
with lyric seriousness, like a young Ethel Barrymore, then whooping
with laughter.

Unhappily, I can bring to mind only one fragment from a romantic
ballad about a moonlit boat ride on the Winsocket River, or some such
name:

> (Da *dum* da da *dum*
> Da *dum* da da *dum*)
> And the night it was tender and real.
> The hours they flew by,
> The stars they knew why,
> As my friend and I sat on the keel.

On these occasions I was continually struck by the mixtures in Jean
—her still elegant yet eroded beauty, her engagingness when sober and
her mordant humor when drunk, her sudden and baffling shifts of
manner.

One night when she stayed over as a house guest, I looked in to be
sure she had reached her bed successfully, since moments earlier she
had been quite drunk. A miraculous transformation had taken place.
She was upright in bed in her smartly tailored bathrobe, had clapped
on her reading spectacles and was sternly and precisely editing the
manuscript of an article she had written.

Driving her home the next day, I asked if she thought she *could* stop
drinking. She stared out the side window for a long moment without
speaking, and I wondered if I had put my foot in it. Then she said in
a tone that was neither offended nor melodramatic, but chillingly
matter-of-fact, "I loathe alcohol. It is my enemy. And my seducer."

We rode in silence for a while and then changed the subject.

Later our conversation touched on the poet Delmore Schwartz,
whose severe mental problems Jean jokingly attributed to his mother's
decision to name him for the apartment house where the family lived

when he was born, the Delmore Arms in Brooklyn.

I said, "Would this, then, be the ultimate example of the edifice complex?"

She replied, "You would have the crown jewels for that, were they mine to bestow."

Whenever I was at Jean's house, I loved peeking into her workroom. It was crisply organized, with filing cabinets that contained letters from a Who's Who of American literature, many of them doubtless scandalous. There were also intriguing folders of raw material, some belonging to Jean, some left by Liebling. I caught a glimpse of a bulging manila file of notes that Liebling had intended to use for a devastating dissection of the most famous of Luce publications. He had labeled the folder *"Time* Bomb."

My other favorite room was Jean's upstairs library, with comfortable overstuffed chairs and walls lined with books. There is an unmistakable look to the bookshelves of people who actually read and write books instead of merely buying them; the volumes have a well-worn and handled appearance. Jean's were a treat to look through because many of them were amusingly inscribed to her by the (often famous) authors.

Often after one of Jean's dinners, we sat up in that library as Jean discoursed into the wee hours on the sex lives of American short story writers, the Watergate follies or—one of her favorite topics—the lore and literature of the West.

She was Colorado born, and her father—who looked like a grizzled gold prospector and mountain man, judging from a snapshot she showed us—had been a writer of western novels. One of her favorite old books was *A Lady's Life in the Rocky Mountains,* a well-born Englishwoman's memoir of her solitary travels on horseback in the rugged Colorado terrain in the 19th century. The woman befriended a mountain man (and undoubted psychopathic killer) named Mountain Jim, with whom she may well have had a romance.

Jean, legs tucked under her in the chair, recounted with goosepimply drama how she and a friend on the faculty of the University of Colorado set out on a half-serious quest to find Mountain Jim's cabin, using descriptions of the surroundings in *A Lady's Life*, old issues of the *Rocky Mountain News* and other archival sources. A scornful laugh from a colleague set them to the task in deeper earnest, and through digging, calculating and triangulating clues they found it.

They decided, however, that they didn't want historians and tourists trampling their private find, so they kept it a secret. Years later Jean tried to retrace their path to it, but a road had gone through and nothing of the cabin remained.

Remembering such tales, I regret never having Jean on my show, but at the time the subject never came up. I wonder if she wanted to do it. I had some vague fear that I knew her too well. It also occurred to me that she might show up the worse for drink, and then there would be the problem of whether to air the show or edit it or face up to a situation that could embarrass us both and even damage our friendship.

As it was, her name came up fairly often on the show when writers like John Cheever or John Updike appeared, and in particular when Saul Bellow mentioned a brilliantly descriptive paragraph of Jean's that made him sit back in awe.

One day, while deploring her persistent "filthy habit," Jean said that she finally had the clinching reason to quit smoking forever: "My doctor used a word today that he has never used before—stroke!" It was the affliction she dreaded most.

Yet then as on other occasions, she desisted only for a day or two, then switched to little cigars and after awhile began inhaling them. Then it was back to cigarettes.

I don't remember whether it was before or after she fell against one of those well-organized filing cabinets and cut her head open that she had her "cerebral accident" (a euphemism she deplored), but when it came it was the final indignity. It left her alive but unable to write; reading was difficult at some times, impossible at others. Since both activities were her life's blood, her existence from then on was an ordeal.

She continued her late-night calls to friends, but since the stroke had affected her speech the conversations could be excruciating, especially when she was drunk. There was nothing to do but wait them out. Often they ended with Jean, unable to make her brain come up with a word she wanted, snarling with disgust and slamming the phone down. At times she couldn't get even the first word out; there would be no sound at the other end except a kind of strangled croak and an immediate hanging up.

Her eagerly awaited novel, which by then had been about ten years in the making, never saw light. She hadn't published one since *The Catherine Wheel* in 1952. She had whetted the appetite of friends and colleagues—and perhaps made them nervous—by saying that this one would be the first clearly autobiographical work of fiction in her career.

After her stroke, one superb chapter appeared in The New Yorker under the title "An Influx of Poets," as if to give us all an idea of what we were going to miss. I called to tell her how many people I had heard rave about it and how, in the middle of reading it, I put the magazine down for a moment and said to myself with admiration, "My God, I *know* her."

She managed to stammer out, "That's . . . awfully nice . . . to hear."

In her later years none of Jean's friends was sure what her financial status might be. She told me one day that she had decided to sell some of her and Liebling's first editions. I wanted to buy them myself but held back for fear the offer would embarrass her, or that she might sell them to me for less money than she needed.

Months later, after a dealer had bought some of them and taken them away, she made a poignant comment. "I always thought I didn't give a damn about old books. Seeing them go, I realized that there's nothing I love more."

She was always changing her will, and her final mordant joke— perpetrated, no doubt, while she was in her cups—was to designate her partially lettered housekeeper not only as her sole beneficiary but also as her literary executor. It was an unfortunate move, but I can imagine her anticipatory glee at the widespread distress it would cause.

After she died I wished I had salvaged at least the carefully hand-lettered sign she posted on her back porch door, which she used as the main entrance to her house. Give or take a word, it read:

> NOTICE: We are at work and must not be disturbed. This applies to all solicitors, encyclopedia salesmen, collectors of petition signatures, distributors of tracts, donation seekers and other time wasters.
>
> P.S. *Anyone* misusing the word "hopefully" on these premises will be persecuted.
>
> Mrs. A. J. Liebling

For years afterward I kept having the experience (other friends have reported it too) of seeing something odd or amusing in print, of hearing some howling solecism or of encountering some horrid artifact of manufactured humor, then imagining that incomparable cackling laugh and thinking, "Won't Jean get a kick out of this?" And amending the verbs, of course, to the past tense.

ON THE DROPPING OF BRICKS

I WOULD LIKE TO meet the genius who said, upon being told of a remarkable coincidence, "But it doesn't mean anything. Think of the billions of coincidences that *don't* happen." I would like to tell him about one that did. I think it proves that whoever or whatever is in charge of arranging them has a malicious sense of humor.

It happened one summer on Long Island, where I was sharing a weekend place with several other people. On this particular foggy weekend, I had the cottage all to myself. I arose early on Sunday. The weather was out of Ibsen, and I decided that a walk on the undoubtedly deserted beach would be a moody pleasure.

Driving over to the beach, I stopped to pick up a Sunday New York *Times* and as I tossed it onto the car seat it fell open to the Arts & Leisure section. I noticed an item about a currently popular volume of humor that was being made into a Broadway musical. Let's say it was called *Lox and Bonds*. The item sort of half-registered on my brain and I thought I had no opinion about it one way or the other.

Twenty minutes or so later, my mind a blank, I was ambling on the deserted strand, crunching clam shells underfoot. A dim figure appeared in the distance, trudging toward me. The landscape was so bleak and empty that I felt like Robinson Crusoe upon finding the footprint.

The figure drew nearer and finally came into clear focus through the fog. It was a man who seemed to recognize me. I vaguely felt that I knew him too. We stopped and greeted each other.

After the obligatory comment on the weather we both fell silent. There was an awkward pause, which I finally ended with the only thought in the world that I could come up with. "Did you see where they're making a musical of *Lox and Bonds?* I guess the Broadway theater has finally admitted defeat."

He gave me a look that seemed to say why in hell had I brought that up? As it happened, I hadn't read *Lox and Bonds,* had no feelings against it and was merely casting about desperately for conversation fodder that sounded informed and even opinionated.

I pressed on. "I suppose next they'll have scraped *through* the bottom of the barrel and start making musicals of funny greeting cards."

A blind man would have been able to feel the look I was getting now, but I dug deeper, even while wishing that I had something else to talk about. "They used to make musicals out of Shaw plays, and now this." I put on a mocking intonation, my voice dripping contempt. *"Lox and Bonds* . . . onstage . . . Winter Garden!"

He finally spoke. "You're kidding, aren't you?"

"No, it's in today's *Times.* "

"You know I wrote it."

The words came to me as though from a resonant metallic tunnel. Numb with shock, I could just make out over the throbbing of my pulses another voice, which proved to be mine, saying, "I've . . . got to . . . stop putting people on."

I am blank, probably from a form of concussion, as to what happened next. To this day I am not sure I got away with it. A cold perspiration bespangles my brow even now as I type this.

On the way home I thought of calling a mathematician friend and asking him to calculate the odds of encountering on a remote beach the one person out of the billions on the face of the earth who happened to write the one book out of the forty thousand that are published each year that happened to be mentioned in the one article that caught my eye on the one page the paper happened to fall open to . . .

I need to lie down.

That awful experience turned me into a sort of collector of occasions when people have committed *faux pas* or, as the English say, dropped a brick. I keep a mental black museum of foot-in-mouthery, probably in a frantic quest for reassurance to assuage my still-squirming discomfiture. I offer here two of the choicer items from my permanent exhibit.

One concerns an actor friend who arrived slightly late at a dinner party for eight. He was introduced all around and was promptly seated with the other guests. A silence occurred during the soup course, during which he said, for no particular reason, "Whatever became of that nauseating child actor, Timmy Simpson?"

Suddenly the silence was deeper. He looked up to find the other guests, some with spoons halfway to their mouths, looking like a still photograph.

Panicked, he ransacked his memory for the names he had just half heard in the way we all do when being introduced to strangers. Of course, one boomed loudly in his mind's ear above all the rest.

To this day he can't hear the name Timmy Simpson without a wave of nausea. He remembers nothing else of the evening.

Another ill-fated acquaintance was at a large embassy party in London. He was trapped with a pin-striped dullard from the foreign office. In an attempt to liven up the conversation, he pointed to an overdressed matron, one of dozens of women in the room, and said, "Look at that. Which is it, a hooker or a transvestite?"

"It's my wife," was the angina-inducing reply.

The next day, the hapless insultee called my friend to assure him that there were no hard feelings. In fact, he went so far as to invite my friend to their country house for the weekend. Out of guilt, my friend accepted.

He reports that the ennui of the weekend was of an intensity sufficient to make one homesick for Devil's Island.

Why can't we handle these situations? Everybody present is aware of what has happened, and may even feel sympathetic toward the poor brickdropper, who after all has thoughtlessly done no more than anybody else might have in the same circumstances.

There are people with the courage to face hideous calamities, to lead men into battle against overwhelming odds, to leap into whirlpools to rescue drowning strangers, but I doubt that there have been three people in the history of mankind capable of saying in incidents like the above, "Terribly sorry, old chap. Really put my foot in it, didn't I? Well, better be moving on."

HOW I ALMOST BECAME A HOUSEHOLD WORD

ONE SUMMER MORNING A few years ago, I awoke feeling as if I had been keelhauled through Death Valley beneath a square-wheeled dune buggy. In fact, had I been offered a choice between that and what actually did happen, I would, in retrospect, have opted for the keelhaul.

I won't say you should have been there. I'm not sure even the Nuremberg defendants would've deserved to be there. What I had, in fact, been through was the taping of a new TV show, starring me and, according to the advance hoopla, revealing me to an unsuspecting world as a singing, tap dancing, skit performing variety whiz.

To say that the entire enterprise was misconceived and mishandled to the point of lunacy would be to understate the case. What should have taken perhaps two hours of taping, in order to yield a one-hour program, took eleven. Communications, as they are laughingly called, broke down, chaos reigned unchallenged, the temperature rose to boiler room levels and technicians and performers wandered stunned in a maze of equipment and scenery while a benumbed studio audience, arrayed in bleachers, beheld the spectacle and were sore amazed.

The planned order of events was constantly reshuffled, cues of all sorts went unrecognized, unexplained retakes were ordered repeatedly, all amidst frantic script changes that were scribbled illegibly on cue cards. As it happened, I nominally had the authority to do something about all this, since I owned the production company and was the producers' boss; but, as a distracted performer, I had followed my usual tendency to put creative decisions largely in the producers' hands.

One expected to awaken at any moment in one's own little bed, realizing that that pesky area of the subconscious illuminated so brilliantly by Dr. Freud had been doing its nocturnal dirty work. But no such luck. The bad dream was all too real.

And the dreamer was not alone. Guest stars like Liza Minnelli and the magician Doug Henning sat for hours unsummoned in their dressing rooms, wondering who had gotten them into what. So did I.

Talent (the cast's), money (mine) and energy (everybody's) were squandered by the truckload. All of which might have been bearable had the result been splendid. But, as a check of the microfilm records of the New York *Times* will confirm, in its four-week trial run the show fell considerably short of "Your Show of Shows" in both quality and ratings. To be fair, a critic somewhere in Michigan liked it.

How your humble correspondent got caught up in such an experience is a story that illustrates several morals. Stay home and stick with the family hardware business is one. Or, if it's too late for that and you're already in show business, try to capitalize on the things you do well and minimize the things you don't, which is a lot harder than it sounds, especially when everybody around you is urging the opposite. Or, beware of network vice-presidents who have a vision of a new and different you.

But I'm getting ahead of myself.

The sequence of events that led me to the battered, numb and exhausted state in which I found myself on this particular summer morning began many months earlier in Fred Silverman's office. Fred was still at CBS in those days, and was celebrated as the man with the golden gut—a programmer with a supposedly infallible instinct for popular tastes. Later, of course, after he moved to ABC and then NBC and ratings began collapsing around him, his gut was found to be composed at least partly of pyrite.

What took place in Fred's office was—I can hardly bring myself to use the word—a meeting. Programmers, lawyers and money people in TV thrive on meetings, which they regard as a form of activity. To them, a day-long meeting is a day well spent.

To me, a meeting is a nullity, a negation, something you do *instead* of doing something. When I'm unavoidably trapped in one my gaze, quickly followed by my train of thought, usually goes out the nearest window. The other people in the room then proceed to conduct the meeting around me, which is reasonable, and begin referring to me in the third person, which annoys me.

Once, after an associate of mine repeatedly prefaced remarks to a network executive with phrases like, "What I think Dick wants" and "As I read Dick," I cut in with: "Why don't we ask Dick? I believe he's here."

But sometimes I'm smart enough to stay away, which is what I did for the Silverman meeting. My representatives, a phalanx of four, pitched several program ideas on my behalf. My late-night show on ABC had gradually faded from the airwaves; I was more or less at liberty; Fred had indicated some interest in bringing me to CBS.

In fact, it quickly became clear that Fred had more than "some" interest. The usual scenario for such meetings, in which, for example, producers propose a twelve-part series and Fred says he'll buy one episode with an option, was reversed. My representatives offered up some celebrity interview specials, a string of documentaries on American Indian history, a TV film. A mere bagatelle, Fred said in effect;

he was going to show them how to really think big.

He had a notion that, potentially, I was a latter-day, more sophisticated Arthur Godfrey—an ad lib personality with an off-the-cuff,
believable appeal who, while not doing any high-powered performing
himself, could serve as the catalyst for a gang of regulars gathered
around himself and thus deliver a show with an impact far beyond the
sum of its parts.

To develop the latent Godfrey in me, Fred wanted to put me under
exclusive contract to CBS. He would use me throughout the schedule
in guest appearances and specials until just the right chemistry and
format evolved, and then he would launch me as a prime time fixture.
He would, as he put it, make me a household word.

My representatives left Fred's office roughly in the position of sales-
men who had hoped to close a tidy deal and had ended up tripling their
quota. My lawyer reported that it had been "a thrilling meeting." It
was the first time I'd heard anybody use that kind of language about
a meeting since I'd read Merle Miller's and Evan Rhodes' wonderfully
scathing memoir of network TV, *Only You, Dick Daring!* Maybe
everybody was just lightheaded from having gotten up so early in the
morning and assembled at breakfast for a meeting *about* the impending
meeting.

Not that I wasn't pleased about it all. I was. I had checked CBS's
references and they came highly recommended. Only the household
word part left me a little dubious. "Dustmop," after all, was a household word. More to the point, so was "toilet."

One of the most curious things about Fred's visionary gaze into my
glorious future was that it depended on his ability to define me as
nobody had defined me before. It started from his perception of the
Godfreyness that my personality could be molded into. Yet I felt that
I was already defined, thank you very much; my personality already had
a mold of its own, lumpy as it might be. It's disconcerting to be told
that you could really amount to something once people figure out who
you are.

I must admit, though, that who and what I am, as a TV performer, are questions that have long perplexed some of the keener minds in the medium. (At last count, there were six.)

Why should this be? In many ways I would seem to be a creature absolutely made for TV. I have a faculty for being what is called "natural" in front of the camera, and for connecting with an individual viewer at home. I can almost always think of something, if not witty or profound, at least pointed, to say. I thrive on spontaneity and a loose (or nonexistent) structure. I actively enjoy the unexpected.

The very things, in other words, that reduce some talented actors and comedians to mute, terrified stupefaction—appearing as themselves "in front of the curtain" and trying to entertain an audience without benefit of a script or maybe even a plan—are the things that bring out the best in me, such as it is.

Yet over the years TV programmers have scarcely known what to make of me and my "pure" TV instincts. Labeling me a "talk show host" and using me as such has been a kind of provisional solution—often a very happy one, let me hasten to admit, and one that has suited me well. But even talk shows can begin to seem formula-ridden and confining, and can start me wondering whether beyond them there isn't some freer, bolder kind of programming I could try.

When programmers, however, think of taking me out of the talk show ghetto and using me in some more intensive way—on prime time, for instance—their minds tend to wheel like homing pigeons to all the old familiar devices, premises and formats. Their message, in other words, is "Let's be different in the same old ways."

These ways, I know, have generated many excellent programs and served as highly appropriate vehicles for many brilliant performers. But because my most distinctive gifts not only have no particular need of the tried-and-true devices but sometimes can actually be tripped up by them, the programmers and I usually end in a standoff. It is as if somebody came along with the first highwire act without a net, and the circus owners said, "Sorry, we've already installed a net, so we can't use you."

At least Fred aimed to break this impasse. It was his means, not his ends, that bothered me. For example, I can't say I was encouraged by the "notion" that he and another CBS executive, Oscar Katz, had for a comedy sidekick to be paired with me. Over his usual lunch of steak and iced tea at the "21" Club, Fred proclaimed to me one day, "Rocky Graziano and Dick Cavett—now that's funny!"

Cavett and Graziano, I repeated to myself (discreetly rearranging the billing). Somehow it didn't have quite the ring of Laurel and Hardy or Hope and Crosby. As things turned out, that didn't matter, since Fred never mentioned the subject again, perhaps realizing he had extracted most of the funniness from it by merely stating it.

Fred settled on a method for my remolding that consisted of pushing me first into one programming pigeonhole, then another, to see which shape fitted. During the eighteen months of my CBS contract, I did guest spots as a comedian, I emceed awards ceremonies, I delivered public service announcements, I conducted interviews, I starred in a special about Hollywood back lots and I developed, through my own company, one of the most promising never-to-be produced TV movies ever never produced. I did everything but the weather report. (In fact, during a publicity tour, I actually did read the weather as a lark on some local radio station, but I don't think it was a CBS affiliate.)

The most unsettling thing about the Silverman experiment, however, was that most of it had to be carried out without Silverman. The ink was still tacky on my contract when Fred jolted the industry by announcing that he was leaving CBS to become programming chief at ABC.

I called him as soon as I heard the news. "I assume you're not taking me with you," I said. "Under the circumstances, do I do the honorable thing by stepping down?"

He insisted that his departure would change nothing. All would be well, he said, and he gave me a pep talk about carrying on the noble work he had begun. "I'll call you right after your first show airs," he promised.

Contrary to his assurances, Fred's departure changed everything. I was left to the tender mercies of other CBS executives whose sense of what Fred was trying to do with me appeared to be just below nil. The ambitious among them had every reason to dissociate themselves from Fred and all his works, and hence regarded me with wary suspicion as an expensive legacy from the old regime. I was tainted. Overnight I had been transformed from Fred's Favorite into Fred's Folly.

Most of my appearances during those eighteen months were thus P.S. (post Silverman) and consequently were arranged in a spirit of "Let's give this a try" at best, and "Let's get this over with" at worst. Instead of exploring the possibilities to see where they might lead, CBS and I fell into that unmistakable mode known as "fulfilling the contract," which precedes "going separate ways," which in turn is followed by "pursuing other projects" because one has "several irons in [or near] the fire."

All the more so after the disastrous summer variety show. That was the watershed. Or do I mean bloodshed?

*   *   *

Despite my best efforts at amnesia, despite everything from hypnosis therapy to a transcendental meditative discipline passed on to me by a Hindu swami in Port Arthur, Ontario, I can still remember it all with breathtaking clarity. Like so many other things in the CBS venture it began while Fred was still at the helm, steaming proudly toward a brave new format, and ended up foundering in his turbulent wake, among the oil slicks, orange peels and used contraceptives.

"How about doing a summer variety show?" he suggested to me over another lunch at "21." His tone was blandly casual, as if he were suggesting that I try the fresh strawberries. "We don't have anything for the Carol Burnett time slot during the month of August. There wouldn't be any pressure. We wouldn't even *look* at the ratings. You could try out some ideas, do anything you want. If it catches on, fine; we'll find a place for it in the regular schedule. If not, no harm done."

When I replay the story of the summer show in my mind, I always stop the action on a freeze frame, as it were, at those points where, with a simple word, I could've headed it all off and turned back before it was too late. That moment at a table in "21" was the first.

Instead, I soon found myself sitting in a solemn you-know-what with my agent, manager, lawyer and other advisors, weighing how much I had to gain and how much to lose by acting on Fred's proposal. As I recall, every one of us grown men accepted his minimal description of the risks at face value.

By the time Fred was hanging up the pictures in his new office at ABC, I was committed. The project was to be packaged by my company, which meant that CBS paid me a lump sum per show, out of which I hired the staff and covered the production expenses. If anything was left over I could keep it as profit. More important, if costs exceeded the lump sum then I, not CBS, took the loss. One must, after all, be fair to a giant network.

Incidentally, as a quaintly amusing historical detail, the lump sum was $110,000 per show. Nowadays such a risible amount would scarcely keep a prime time variety show in coffee and doughnuts (or a movie company in cocaine nostril spoons).

At this point a new CBS vice-president, a sort of surrogate Fred, entered my life. He was Alan Wagner, the executive who was designated to shepherd my show onto the air and, if possible, into the bonanzaland of the regular season schedule.

Soft-spoken, slightly owlish, Alan seemed quite a decent and intelligent man, almost as if he were miscast in his assignment. When he used the obligatory word "excited" during his obligatory complimentary remarks about me and the forthcoming show (". . . very excited about this . . .") it lacked the glib, hollow sound that the really convincingly crass programmers give it. True, the Gelusil on Alan's desk seemed a plausible touch, for a pained edginess did filter through his affability. But such was his evident sincerity that I could hardly believe my ears when I heard the following exchange in his office.

Alan and another executive were discussing the previous night's CBS shows and the numbers, or ratings, that had come in on them overnight. When the other man mentioned watching a particular program, Alan said, "Oh, I missed that. How was it?"

"I don't know," came the reply. "I haven't seen the numbers yet."

These, you'll recall, were the people who weren't even going to *look* at my ratings.

My first task, in consultation with Alan, was to select a producer. Dorothy Parker once said that the two things she had never understood were the working principle of the zipper and the precise function of Bernard Baruch. If you substitute a TV producer for Bernard Baruch in that sentence, you get my outlook as well. Nevertheless, even though the ways of a producer are as mysterious to me as the mating habits of the Australian bowerbird, I wouldn't want to do a show without one, all things considered.

The problem was to find the right species of bowerbird, so to speak. Most of the producers I knew—leaving aside a generous pool of incompetents and madmen—were talk show producers, with little experience in staging comedy routines, musical numbers and the like. On the other hand, the few variety producers I knew anything about and could imagine entrusting myself to, like Carol Burnett's husband Joe Hamilton, were 1) not available, or 2) not available at the price I could pay.

If this little narrative were a 1930s movie, we would now segue into a montage sequence, with leaves of the calendar falling away intermittently while, over perky, up-tempo music, I meet in my office with one producer after another, perhaps with some running gag strung throughout, like a secretary arriving brightly with coffee just as each session is breaking up (capper: after the final scene she sits down in my office and drinks the coffee herself, as audience knees remain largely unslapped).

The producers breezed in, flaunting Palm Springs or sunlamp tans or London pallors, on their way to or from the Coast. (In showbiz geography there is only one coast, in California; the line of conjunction between the Atlantic Ocean and the North American continent is never referred to.)

Some struck me as thoughtful and interesting, others as bores or yahoos (one called me "Jocko"); some were guys who had once happened to be on the premises when a show became a hit and had been living on their reputations ever since, others were hypermanics whose imaginations ricocheted alarmingly off my office walls.

Danny Simon, the older brother of the playwright Neil Simon and himself an accomplished comedy writer, is legendary in the trade for being able to improvise script ideas for programmers or producers, ingeniously adjusting as he goes along to minuscule reactions that he senses in his auditor's facial expression or body language. Based on the shift of a gaze or the tapping of a pencil, he will skillfully backtrack along a plot line, switch a locale from the Klondike to Bora Bora, sex change the hero's macho sidekick into his invalid mother-in-law. Several of my conversations with prospective producers went the same way, with them in the Danny Simon role and me as the barely scrutable auditor.

"Well, Dick," they would say, "I'm just bullshitting off the top of my head, but the whole show could take place, like, *behind* the curtain, or in your dressing room . . . the guest stars do their numbers as if they're auditioning or rehearsing . . .

"No, no, I see where you're coming from now . . . it's in front of the curtain, and you're the host, casual—no, in black tie . . . class all the way . . . in fact there's no curtain at all—the show is a party in your apartment . . . it's on a roof garden . . .

"Doesn't do anything for you, right? How about a cellar made to *look* like a roof garden? Forget it . . . okay, maybe you go out on the street with a hand held camera, just stop people at random and talk to them, see what develops . . . suddenly you stop someone and it's, like, Sammy Davis, Jr., and . . ."

In the end I realized that the right man for the job had been in New York all the time, practically down the street from me. He was Bob Precht, who had produced the Ed Sullivan Show and now presided over one of Ed's legacies, a company called Sullivan Productions. His experience seemed perfect. In fact, now that I thought of it, the idea of making the summer show an open-ended, low-key variation on the old Sullivan format might not be bad at all.

Besides, I had liked Bob ever since meeting him in the early 1960s, when I made my first appearance as a nervous young comedian on the

Sullivan Show. He was a lanky, sandy-haired, rather boyish fellow who dressed with casual elegance and had a quality that I can only call serenity. Both his brow and his trousers were miraculously wrinkle-free. The sight of him strolling into an office or onto a studio floor was reassurance itself. In the face of his ease and geniality, you felt that *nothing* would have the ill grace to go wrong.

Bob was not available at the price I could pay either, but I had a solution for that. I paid him more.

We now segue into another montage sequence—same perky music, later dates on the calendar leaves—in which Bob is seen interviewing one comedy writer after another as he sets to work assembling a staff (this time the last departing writer takes the coffee from the surprised secretary and pours it into a flowerpot on the receptionist's desk on his way out).

There is one universal piece of received wisdom about comedy writers in New York: they've all gone to California. Bob's efforts showed how wrong that could be. Among the talented people he hired were Tom Meehan, a former New Yorker humorist who, a couple of years after my show, would go on to write the book for the musical "Annie"; Tony Geiss, an old pro of a press agent, producer and writer who would later become head writer for "Sesame Street"; Marshall Efron, a short, rotund writer-actor who had created many imaginative sequences on "The Great American Dream Machine"; and Alfa-Betty Olsen, a petite blonde whose devoted collaboration with Marshall seemed as unlikely as her name.

What would prove to be the most significant bit of staffing, though nobody knew it at the time, had already been set. As head writers, CBS had urged me to take on a young husband-wife team whom I shall call Bill and Mary Lane, at least partly on the grounds that they would bring a hip, contemporary touch to the proceedings. All I knew about them was that their chief credit was writing and producing an award-winning special and LP record for one of TV's brighter comediennes.

Was it Bob who made the lukewarm response, "I guess I can work with them"? Or was it the Lanes who said of Bob, "We guess we can work with him"? I can't remember. Either way, I ratified their selection with about the same amount of enthusiasm.

Alan Wagner at CBS said, "Oh, we're crazy about the Lanes, crazy about them. They've got several things under development for us." In TV, the term "under development" can cover a multitude of sins, and usually does. And speaking of cant terms, my interior alarm bells should've gone off when, during my first conversation with the Lanes, they used the word "concept" to refer to the shape or format of my show.

But there was no time to brood about that, for events now began to move quickly. Without warning Bob did something that seriously undermined his usefulness to me. He resigned. His reasons were personal and compelling, having to do with his wife's health, so I had no choice but to acquiesce regretfully.

Then, as if the fates were determined to cut me off from anything even remotely connected with Ed Sullivan, I was informed that the Ed Sullivan Theater, the CBS-owned TV studio on Broadway, was booked during the period when I needed it. I had long since canvassed the studios in the city and decided that the Sullivan Theater was not only the ideal facility for my show but, in a word, indispensable. Accordingly, I'd been promised full and unlimited access.

Now it transpired that CBS would be using the place for some cockamamie game show and, to add insult to injury, would be renting it to ABC for a live variety show hosted by Howard Cosell.

When I appealed to Alan Wagner, he vowed to move heaven and earth for me. He may well have moved both entities, but he failed to budge the game show or Howard. No Sullivan Theater.

I sat down and wrote Alan the kind of letter that ought to be put into a desk drawer overnight and reconsidered in the cool light of morning. But, characteristically, I pressed it into the hands of the nearest messenger.

"I am being asked," I wrote, "to make do with hind tit. I won't." (I did, of course.) I went on to summarize the situation as I saw it. Not only did I have no place to do a show, but I had no show—and I was scheduled to be on the air in a month. I was without the services of a producer, let alone a director, set designer and musical director. Not a single cast member or guest star had been lined up. I had spoken to big-name performers like Cher and Lucille Ball about making guest appearances, but I was becoming deeply embarrassed because, despite my repeated promises to call back soon, I was unable to confirm anything or be specific about dates.

"I am getting the distinct sensation," I wrote, "of one being urged to fly by the seat of his pants in what looks more and more like an un-airworthy craft."

The only upshot of my letter, except for a succession of would-be reassuring noises emitted by Alan, was a decision to let the Lanes take over as producers of the show, presumably on the theory that it was desirable to have somebody at the controls whether they were flying by your compass or not.

The Lanes, after all, were the head writers. They were the ones with the concept. Last but far from least, they were the only candidates in sight, which gave them a definite edge. Starting that montage sequence over again in search of another producer was out of the question.

Here we have the second freeze frame in my mental replay, another point at which I still could have bailed out.

I didn't, of course.

* * *

"I divide people into two groups: those who divide people into two groups and those who don't."

Robert Benchley said that, but I'm not going to let it keep me from dividing TV people, and maybe all creative and artistic people, into two groups: those who believe in leaving nothing to chance and those who put more trust in, as the song says, doing what comes naturally.

The former impose a carefully controlled structure on their work ahead of time. They detest loose ends. They believe everything should fit into their plan or it goes out the window, no matter how good it might be in other respects. At home they probably have their socks neatly lined up in their dressers.

The doing-what-comes-naturally people believe in gathering the best elements, however motley, giving them plenty of room and letting a rough and ready structure emerge organically. They believe loose ends are a small price to pay if the basics are sound.

I am of the latter persuasion. And, incidentally, my dresser drawers are a mess.

Bill and Mary Lane, as I'm calling them, were planners with a vengeance. The special and LP they had done with the comedienne were nothing if not meticulously structured. They had assembled it by shooting the bits and pieces separately and then weaving—you might say tightly braiding—them together in the editing room. The result was highly skillful, but to my taste tight and airless, with every line, every song, burdened by a self-conscious Point.

In retrospect, I should have seen on day one that the Lanes and I were on a collision course. They readily agreed when I reminded them that my style was different, that with me they'd have to adopt a more relaxed approach. They nodded earnestly when I said I wanted to do the show in something close to a single, continuous stretch of "real" time, almost as if it were live, and not tape it in dozens of mosaic fragments to be pasted together later.

But my breath went for nought. We simply inhabited opposite sides of the loose ends question. For all their gifts and energy, two producers less likely to create a setting in which I could be comfortable and perhaps show up to advantage would be hard to imagine.

They infused my erstwhile raffish offices with a sort of febrile tone —Mary slightly taut of feature, bereft of makeup, smoking nervously; Bill more cheerful but equally intense, with a *bandido* mustache that drooped at the ends. You might cast them as a zealous Peace Corps couple who had stayed too long in the jungle. With their jeans (his) and fatigues (hers) they had a quasi-military look, like guerrillas. You could easily imagine them with bandoliers and a grenade or two dangling at the belt.

Our first open clash was over—can you guess?—their "show concept." They proudly plunked on my desk a thick, scriptlike document summing up their conviction that the show needed a binding, overall *theme.* Everything I did or said within its framework would then express a consistent "attitude" or "point of view."

The tome further informed me that I was not a totally glitzy showbiz type but still retained a shred or two of midwestern authenticity, and hence should be seen on the show, casually but not too casually dressed, in a setting that was theatrical but not too theatrical. Phrased more succinctly, this mainly translated into: no tie and a simple set. The studio's brick walls were to be exposed in a manner carefully calculated to strike the viewer as offhand. And honest.

My attitude, I gleaned, was to be that of the Wryly Bemused and Skeptical Observer of the Fads and Pretensions in Modern Society. The show's comedy was to be based on my skewering of such phenomena as pop therapies, plastic pre-packaging and the then current vogue of talking to houseplants and otherwise treating them as sentient beings.

All this was very well (as people say when they mean the opposite), but my somewhat impatient response was to ask, "Where are the jokes? Who are the guests?" My gut told me we should book some people for me to be wryly bemused *with* in front of those honest brick walls, and do it fast. Time was short. We were moving nearer the buzzsaw by the minute, and its increasing proximity was already causing me to lurch in my sleep.

Not that I had anything against themes or attitudes, you understand. In fact, I was fairly sure that I had an ample supply of each tucked away somewhere in my performing luggage. It's just that as a devout loose-ender I had always believed such things could be trusted to take care of themselves, to arise as byproducts of a whole series of ad hoc choices I might make along the way about what is funny or entertaining. In my authentic midwestern way I felt strongly about putting first things first, and I knew that the first thing was *not* a set of abstract criteria that would shape our production decisions.

I pointed out that in all my experience of television no one had yet risen up out of the crowd to say, "That was a good show, the guests were terrific and so were you, and I laughed a lot, but where was your concept?"

Bill was soothing and patient with me, a little bit as if I were a houseplant. "You see, Dick," he said, "we want the show to have its own integrity and momentum, so it can go on with or without guest stars. That way it's not at the mercy of the bookings."

This had the fine ring of sense to it, but in my view it could also be paraphrased, "It's at the mercy of the producers."

When we eventually signed Liza Minnelli and Doug Henning, among others, for the first taping, the Lanes thought it would lend "valuable cohesiveness" if Doug's segment of conjuring with handkerchiefs, coins and cards were followed by Liza singing "Magic to Do." (Magician, "Magic"—get it?) That the song was hardly Liza's first choice got shunted aside by the "need" for "logical flow." One too many hearings of this phrase in the weeks ahead was to cause a barroom song to form in my head: *"They called her Logical Flo . . ."*

"What if we let Liza sing whatever she wants?" I asked. "We might get a better performance that way. Let's let Doug do his act and Liza do hers."

The drooping ends of Bill's mustache twitched as he gave a tight smile. "That's just not our esthetic," he replied.

Beware of those who use the word "esthetic" as a noun—Dick's Almanac.

Later still, when we got into the studio, the much cherished bare brick walls turned out to be all but imperceptible on the screen. To preserve the sense of taking-the-viewer-behind-the-make-believe, several giant wooden crates were hastily ordered up for the set, inspired by the "road boxes" in which touring troupes transport their costumes and props. For a feverish day or two, if I recall correctly, there was even a plan for me to discover my guest stars in these crates, or (surely I imagined this one) for me to have a regular routine with a bag lady who had taken up residence in one of them.

The real problem with the crates, however, was that most laymen and quite a few theater folk who saw the show hadn't the vaguest idea what they were supposed to be. They looked like wooden dumpsters accidentally left on the set by the custodial crew.

This literal-minded objection was brushed aside. We were far too close to taping to consider changing them. And, of course, they did conform to the concept.

In between arguments over such matters the work of pulling, or slapping, together the elements of the show went hastily on.

The Lanes took over an office across the hall from me, pushing their desks together the way some devoted couples push single beds together in hotel rooms. Facing each other across the double desktops, they typed and conferred while cradling phones on their shoulders, and the air grew thick with esthetic and Mary's cigarette smoke.

In the other offices new phone lines were installed, with new staff members at the ends of them. Activity abounded. In the background could be heard, above the phones and typewriters, the constant sound of the Xerox machine, a happy hum or a whine of desperation depending on how your ear was attuned. It earnestly multiplied memos, letters and script segments, the latter appearing in various drafts on white, green, pink or yellow paper according to a color code that I failed repeatedly to crack.

From time to time Alan Wagner, attended by a retinue of numbers watchers, would come over from the CBS building for a briefing with the Lanes and me, then walk down the office corridor, poking his head in a door here and there to offer encouraging comments—a brigadier from HQ touring the trenches. He was affable as always, but kept glancing around dubiously. His voice said, "Well, things seem to be coming along fine, just fine," but his eyes seemed to say, "Are you guys *serious?*"

The Lanes announced with considerable fanfare that they had lined up Clark Jones to direct the show. Clark had a list of credits a yard long, single spaced. Some were for shows I had watched as a high school student in the early 1950s. My pessimist side couldn't help wondering

whether after all those shows and all those years Clark might not be
. . . well, *tired.*

Still, I was grateful for all the experience and professionalism I could
get; and besides, my own first choice, Art Forrest, who had directed
my ABC talk show, had long since proved to have that status-enhanc-
ing quality, unavailability.

Clark had directed most of his hundreds of shows on his own, but
the Lanes felt that, with him tied up in the control booth, Alan
Myerson, a director seasoned in comedy and improvisational theater,
should be flown in from Los Angeles to work with the performers—
in case, I suppose, the performers felt lonely and neglected out in the
studio.

As yet, of course, there still weren't any potential neglectees out in
the studio, but I'm coming to that.

After finding a set designer, the Lanes added an overall design
consultant whose fee, as near as I could make out, was earned by
insuring that the set designer didn't violate the sacred canons of the
visual concept, whatever they and it were.

I now had two directors and two designers: matched sets, so to speak.
I didn't ask where the money was coming from for these extra people.
That would have been the responsible thing to do. But by this time the
meter was running so fast that the digits were blurs.

I sometimes felt that the Lanes' predilection for pairs (reflecting
their own doubleness?) might, if unchecked, have extended indefinitely
into the production ranks. One day they brought in a black duo called
Ashford & Simpson, recording stars in a sort of disco rhythm-and-blues
genre, as candidates for the job of musical director(s).

Ah, I thought when I saw them come through my door: the hip,
contemporary touch I was told that Bill and Mary might provide.

For reasons that escape me to this day, the Lanes thought that the
"chemistry" between me and Ashford & Simpson would be "interesting." Since my tympanic membrane had never been tickled by so much
as a note by either chorister, I had almost nothing to say to them. After
we all sat around for a few minutes looking bewildered—except for

Ashford (or was it Simpson?), who glared out fiercely from a tangle of dreadlocks—even the Lanes admitted that the chemistry was as flat as last month's seltzer.

Intermittently I got back on the long distance phone, returning to the increasingly pressing and always a little soul-sickening task of trying to persuade "names" to make guest appearances. In this case the task was exacerbated by the fact that I wanted them at ridiculously short notice and ridiculously low fees, for a show that I still could describe only in the most amorphous terms.

An abridged *Who's Who of Show Business* said no. Lucille Ball said she could only pretape a short segment from California—mail it in, in effect. Others gave the classic answer: a firm maybe.

What did I want them to do, many asked—sing? Dance? Act? Be interviewed?

Well sure, all of the above. Or none of it. How in the name of the William Morris Agency did I know?

At times I had to close my door and vent my anxieties by writing secret notes to a friend who was serving as "creative consultant" to the show—gratifying temporarily, but not the most effective method of correcting the situation. Better I had simply opened that door and confronted the problems directly and decisively.

"Destroy this upon finishing," went one of my memos to him, recently unearthed. (I think it fluttered from the pages of a well-thumbed copy of *The Power of Positive Thinking.*) "The fact that we cannot get anything but everybody's second through fourth choices to direct, produce, perform, etc., is enough to make the captain of the *Titanic* feel right at home. Perhaps it is too early to be thinking this way, although it also occurs to me that it is too late . . . and perhaps time to be thinking of some fallback position, like 'Dick Cavett Presents Carol Burnett's Favorite Re-Runs.' "

* * *

The only people who appeared to be having any fun getting ready for the show were the writers. But since writers are by definition crazy, what did that prove? They gathered periodically in Bill and Mary's office for writers' conferences, and from across the hall I would listen wistfully as their low murmurs suddenly crested into waves of giddy laughter.

Comedy writers' conferences are among the livelier, more bizarre rituals in TV land. They are seminars that are licensed to be silly, instant think tanks in which the thinking is done out loud. They are arenas, forums, round tables, encounter groups, bull sessions, psycho wards.

But they are intensely verbal, not written. Much of the hilarity that is uncorked in them evaporates *instanter*. What may seem at the time a robust comic notion looks the next morning like something that tried to leave Shangri-La.

Since many comedy writers are also performing comics—former, part-time or would-be—they sometimes do fullblown routines in conferences and then, their creative urges gratified, somehow don't get around to filling paper with them.

The talented Marshall Efron was one of these. He fractured conference after conference with his improvisations but, even with Alfa-Betty Olsen as his amanuensis, never seemed able to duplicate them at the typewriter. Eventually, after the tapings began, we solved this difficulty by short-circuiting it. We put Marshall right on camera with me to repeat one of his best conceits, in which he—bespectacled, woolly browed and mustached, with a belt circumference within which four of me could rhumba—came on as the winner of the Dick Cavett Lookalike Contest.

Although I too was functioning as a writer, I absented myself from the conferences in order not to dampen or inhibit them; but I soon sensed a more serious separation between me and the writers.

I became aware that none of their copy was passing across my desk. The whole muddy current of rough drafts was dammed up in the Lanes' office, and the trickle that was reaching me had already gone through their zealous filtration.

I took a keen, sudden interest in what was being rejected. The writers

Exchanging repartee with Bob Hope on the set of a PBS show.   WNET/THIRTEEN

Lauren Bacall provokes an open-mouthed reaction.   WNET/THIRTEEN

Jazz pianist Oscar Peterson: much music, few words.   WNET/THIRTEEN

Sharing a laugh with the late Tennessee Williams in a New Orleans courtyard.   ABC

Cutting up with Steve Allen and Marshall Efron on CBS variety show.

Tony Randall learns the art of the trick pencil-grip.

Photo by Emil Romano, CBS

WNET/THIRTEEN

Tennis great Arthur Ashe gets a shoulder massage.

Gene Kelly in a nostalgic mood during a stroll on a Hollywood back lot.   Photo by Lee Green, CBS

Eyeball to eyeball with Peter Ustinov.   Photo by Irv Haberman, CBS

Muhammad Ali pulls no punches in a bout of verbal sparring.   WNET/THIRTEEN

Richard Burton reminisces about his life on PBS show.   WNET/THIRTEEN

A dance routine with Bob Hope and Charles "Honi" Coles.

Displaying his irrepressible magician's style.

With Nicholas Koster in *Otherwise Engaged* on Broadway.

With John Horton and Carolyn Lagerfelt in Broadway's *Otherwise Engaged*.

Photo © 1983 by Martha Swope

In the title role of *Charley's Aunt*, Williamstown Theatre Festival.   Photo by Marcia Johnston

With Tim Matheson in Noel Coward's *Nude with Violin*, Williamstown Theatre Festival.
Photo by Jessica Katz

A Manhattan stroll with his wife, the actress Carrie Nye, and pet poodle.

Photo by Judy Gurovitz, People magazine

Taking a reading break on horseback at Montauk, Long Island.   Photo by Barbara Walz

Gazing out over the Sands Hills in his native Nebraska.

apparently had been discouraged from speaking to me about their work, let alone showing me fragments, on the grounds that this would lead to "confusion" and make the show "schizoid in its point(s) of view," not to mention being a breach of the chain of command.

When I sought suggestions from sources outside the chain, like the writer and director Marshall Brickman, an old friend, the Lanes went into a partial snit. I surmised that they not only felt left out by my meeting privately with Marshall, but scented a danger that he would be full of appealing ideas that wouldn't "fit in." He was, and they didn't.

One day Bill announced that my opening monologue in the first show should revolve around the frustrations of mass-production packaging. "This pen," he said, brandishing an inexpensive ballpoint sealed in clear plastic, "is so well wrapped that you can't open the goddamn thing. This is what industrial efficiency has brought us to. It's given us a pen that you can't even use."

Bill was entranced with the notion of my inviting a member of the studio audience to try to open one of the pens on the air. After the volunteer struggled helplessly with it for a few seconds, I would get off a volley of devastating jokes on the subject.

I shared only a fraction of Bill's indignation about plastic-wrapped pens and none of his estimate of their comic potential. He and Mary, however, considered the pen gambit the perfect embodiment of the stance I was to adopt on the show. So although it wasn't my real attitude, it served as my "attitude."

What all this came down to was that I, no less than that defenseless ballpoint, was being made a product of mass-production packaging. (I wish I'd thought of that argument at the time.)

I didn't even find the plastic wrapping particularly impenetrable, but I *assumed* that its resistance had been carefully tested. Listen closely, now, and you will hear one of the profoundest truths gleaned from Uncle Dick's lifetime of frustrating experience. The word "assume" should be banned from the language. I shall pause while you jot that down.

In fact, I plan to stamp out the word myself, unassisted, just as soon as I finish using it to teach one cardinal rule to myself and all those around me: never assume anything.

I don't mean "assume" as in "assume a pose." I mean "assume" as in, "I assumed someone mailed it." Or, "I assumed he was a union member." Or, "I assumed it had been cleared with the legal department." Or, "I assumed he knew we were taping *today.*"

When I eventually tried the packaging bit on camera, the first member of the audience to whom I handed the sealed pen extracted it in half the time it takes a short order cook to crack an egg, then handed it back to me with an expectant expression, innocently wondering what merriment was to follow.

As I recall, after several retakes (and pens) we finally located an audience member with a suitable lack of digital dexterity.

Another ideological tug-of-war that affected the show's comedy was over feminism. When another writer and I concocted a little sketch for Lucille Ball to use in her pre-taped segment, Mary chose to veto it on the grounds that it was "demeaning to women."

So, now (I said mentally), we rewrite the theory of comedy. Never mind what comedians have practiced since the days of Aristophanes or, probably, Cro-Magnon campfires; never mind what sages like Aristotle, Bergson and Mae West have concluded. Henceforth anything that touches on procreation or the war between the sexes in a manner that could be viewed as "demeaning to women" is no longer funny.

I felt a hot rush of anger as I said (out loud), biting off each syllable as if it were one of Mary's fingers, "Let me just state categorically, and for all time, that one reason that will never, ever be used on any show of mine for rejecting a good piece of comedy material is that it is *demeaning to women.*"

The perhaps excessive sarcasm with which I pronounced the last three words cast a tense silence over the room (which happened to be my office), though one or two of the writers present appeared to be cheering behind poker faces.

Another argument I could have cited for keeping the sketch was that we needed every scrap we could come up with. For weeks a remark of Alan Wagner's had been causing me to break out in something moist and prickly whenever I remembered it. He had said, innocuously enough, "I see this show as an hour of comedy." Here we were, a matter of days from the first taping, and we had maybe three minutes and forty seconds of comedy in hand.

I decided it was time for a stiff memo to the producers and the writing staff, to wit (and, I hoped, to wits):

Here is my main thought about the writing situation: I want to start seeing monologue fast.

If several jokes can be done on a subject, fine. But I do not feel that a monologue has to be *about* anything, and if anyone has an isolated joke that will work, or any number of them, fine. I don't care if no two jokes relate to each other.

The subject of the joke can be literally anything. (Incest involving public figures, perhaps, should be soft-pedaled.)

Here, for illustration, are a handful of jokes I wrote for myself years ago which are very good:

"I once went to a wedding where the bride was pregnant, and they threw puffed rice.'

"My dumb cousin Norman just got fired from his job as director of the St. Louis Zoo. He took down all the cages and tried to run it on the honor system."

"At the wedding they definitely served cheap caviar. I don't know much about caviar, but I do know you're not supposed to get pictures of ballplayers with it."

"The walls of my apartment are so thin that I can't sleep if the neighbors are watching television. I don't mind so much being able to hear it, but being able to *see* it . . ."

One of my best jokes was about a restaurant that served Chinese-German food: "The only problem is, an hour later you're hungry for power."

The bottom line is: I would like to see at least two pages

of monologue from everyone (at least ten jokes) by Thursday
noon.

Please see *me* if you have any questions.

To the Lanes separately I sent a briefer missive underlining my
point:

> I would like to know of everything that is being and has
> been written, see it in its earliest stages, answer writers'
> questions about it, and circulate it as widely as possible for
> criticism, suggestions and improvements.
>
> Writers may submit anything to me they want to—the
> more the better—as an idea, suggestion, premise to try,
> rough draft or finished piece without limitation of any kind.

Crisp executive stuff, eh? Unfortunately, even after the monologue
material began flowing, we still had the better part—or should I say the
larger part?—of an hour to fill. Which brings me to the burning issue
of sketches.

Sketches, of course, are the short comic vignettes, played in broad
revue style, that came down from burlesque and have been a staple of
TV variety shows since the heyday of Milton Berle.

I had insisted from the outset that they weren't going to be the staple
of *this* variety show, because I wasn't going to play them. I'm not
comfortable within their tightly scripted confines, I don't do them
terribly well, and I think they're a waste of what I *can* do well, which
is talk, improvise, indulge in unstructured give-and-take and byplay of
all sorts with the audience and guests.

This too can be comedy, judging from the laughs I've gotten over
the years, but you could never prove it by most producers, much less
the Lanes.

Also, in the history of television, there have been a *handful* of people
who could really write sketches, and they either worked for Carol
Burnett or went on to become Neil Simon and Woody Allen.

Nor did I want to stand up and be counted as a singer and dancer. At least not seriously, as if I really meant it. I do enjoy fooling around with real singers and dancers, joining in their acts and even occasionally surprising people when I bring off a neat twist, melodic or terpsichoreal. Still, Fred Astaire doesn't toss uneasily on his laurels while I'm at it.

The process of undermining my resolve had been started by Bob Precht. When I told him how I felt, he said sympathetically, "Sure, I understand perfectly." He flashed his most reassuring smile. "On the other hand," he went on, "there's a certain interest in your tackling unexpected roles. The audience enjoys seeing a star in situations of jeopardy."

Simply being on stage and trying to talk coherently under the gaze of, say, twenty million people was a situation of enough jeopardy to satisfy my standards.

When the Lanes took over they eagerly incorporated the jeopardy idea into their Concept. I, of course, was still struggling to put the Concept idea into jeopardy.

As for sketches, I began to think that the Lanes were committed to them by instinct, conditioning and necessity—necessity because what else but such neatly dovetailed, carefully worked out scenes could insure that not a single detail, not a single gesture or line of comedy, would stray into a schizoid point of view?

It was the old argument again. The lined up socks versus the jumbled ones, the latter now increasingly stretched and frayed.

The result this time was a compromise, if you define a compromise as an arrangement whereby people who can't get what they want make sure that nobody else does either.

It was decided that I would play sketches after all, but in a kind of loose, improvisatory style, working around the other performers. If the Lanes didn't actually add out loud, "Then we can tighten things up in editing," I'm sure I detected a mental note being made.

I prevailed in my desire to build into each show a lengthy, unstructured talk segment with at least one guest—Liza in the first, Peter

Ustinov in the second, and so on. But when I asked what was considered lengthy, Bill said, "Oh, five minutes."

To somebody whose script was stitched together in allotments of a minute and thirty seconds for this and forty seconds for that, with ten-second introductions in between, I suppose five minutes really did seem like a tundra of unfilled air time. To me, who had conducted one-on-one interviews for ninety minutes without even getting around to some of my main questions, it seemed scarcely sufficient for clearing my throat.

It was also decided, moving a little higher on the jeopardy scale, that I would sing after all, but in a casual, self-deprecating way, like a parlor baritone who allows himself to be maneuvered to the piano after dinner. Clark Gessner, composer of the rather cute off-Broadway musical *You're a Good Man, Charlie Brown*, was asked to write some special material for me in what was taken to be my distinctively wry, whimsical tone. He did.

When the Lanes learned that I had been taking tap dancing lessons, something I thought I'd been doing for my private enjoyment, their reaction gave me a rough idea of how Moses must have taken the news from the burning bush about God's real estate plans for Israel.

"That's it!" they exclaimed, more or less in concert. "Don't you see! There it is—the opening for the first show!"

The idea, I gathered after applying the psychological equivalent of cold compresses, was that while a rehearsal piano tinkled in the background, the camera would pan across a line of tap dancing feet, pause on one pair of size eights that was earnestly tapping in unison with all the rest, then sneak up the limbs and torso, ultimately revealing your humble servant. I would then welcome the viewers and introduce the show while continuing to tap up a storm, or at least a gale.

"The image itself makes a statement," Mary explained. "It shows the viewers right away that this is not Dick Cavett the interviewer, with a dark suit and a camera shot that rarely goes below his third shirt button, but a looser, surprising new figure in rehearsal togs, Dick Cavett the entertainer, on his feet and dancing, yet."

I suppressed the desire to say, "Gee, I always had the crazy notion that as an interviewer I *was* entertaining." It was not a remark likely to have much effect on someone seized by a blinding revelation.

What really concerned me was that I was having an attack of the literals again. Would it be possible to deliver an introduction while simultaneously performing the Lancashire time step? Wouldn't the tapping distract from the introduction, or vice versa? Most important, was I certain that I wanted to make this initial "statement," presenting myself as a sort of capering jackanapes instead of starting with something simpler and more natural and letting the surprises, such as they were, crop up along the way?

I decided to avoid answering these questions. Had I stopped to do so I might have saved us all a lot of trouble. But we were now heading into the final days before taping and there wasn't the luxury of time to think.

Members of the production staff shuttled frantically between the office and various rehearsal halls, where sketches, songs and—well, yes —tap dances were being worked out. (Naturally a choreographer was now necessary, and this added to the swelling budget.)

New script inserts seemed to arrive hourly. We had all but exhausted the spectrum for these successive drafts. Some people had simply lost track of the color code, so that now each script, looked at edgewise, had a slightly different rainbow pattern.

After losing the Sullivan Theater we had settled for a studio in the CBS Broadcast Center, on Manhattan's West Side near the waterfront, and there the set was being assembled.

The facilities provided in such a studio, by their nature, were the opposite of everything I had wanted. Instead of a theater with a stage, curtains and a bandstand, we would be performing in a vast, brightly lit, sterile rectangle resembling a gymnasium with bleachers.

The set was divided into a musical performance area, a comedy performance area and a talk area, each with its own cryptic arrangement of the bloody road boxes. The trouble was that these areas were dispersed like separate islands on the expanse of the studio floor. How in the world would we maintain the flow from one segment to the next that I considered so essential to the show?

Even assuming that a forward unit of cameras and technicians could be sent ahead to the next area while the preceding segment was being completed—not likely, given the sparse crew at our disposal—the performers would have to jog briskly to get into position, or ride golf carts, like relief pitchers coming in from the bullpen. And the audience in the bleachers would need field glasses to follow the action down on the field.

"Maybe we should just dump the set and stage a soccer game instead," I suggested, only partly in jest.

Confronted by the actuality of tangled cables, bewildering light grids, heavy, cumbersome flats and milling stagehands, my staff too seemed daunted, and began muttering phrases like ". . . probably a few tape stops . . . breaks to reset . . . if the last few segments run a bit late we may need to bring in a second studio audience . . ."

My question was, "How about bringing in a second cast?"

The cast, the cast.

Part and parcel of the Lanes' determination to build the script around comedy sketches was their determination to assemble a mini-repertory company to play them.

"I've seen and written on too many shows," I told them, "where in the first episode they introduce the 'family' you're going to get to know and love, and two weeks later they've been canned and paid off and they're never mentioned again."

The Lanes did their best to sway me by urging Imogene Coca as one of the regulars. Since her days with Sid Caesar on "Your Show of Shows" she had reigned in my personal pantheon as one of the few *artists* of television comedy.

"I love Imogene Coca," I said, "but she's a huge star. Why not wait until we have the right piece of material for her instead of having to shove her into something because she's *there* and on the payroll?"

Again we "compromised." We proceeded without a mini-rep company, but we did acquire a gang of two regulars.

The first was Leigh French, a sexy, funny young actress who had done some sparkling bits on the Smothers Brothers show. The second *was* Imogene Coca.

Both were performers with whom anybody would be happy to appear. But gifted and likable as they were, in our production they turned out to be two characters in search of an author, a premise—indeed, they were two characters in search of a character.

Leigh French somehow withstood the frustrations and stayed on through all four shows. Coca, as we shall see, did not.

Thus progress, or its reverse, accelerates rapidly as a production builds up momentum and show time approaches. Course corrections become harder and harder to make, because with each wrong turn more time is gone and fewer options remain open. You give in against your instincts to save priceless time.

For the performer—even one who is also the boss, as I was—it is a little like being trapped in an airliner that is losing altitude alarmingly. He may own the airline, but no matter how much he pulls upward on the arm rests, yells or lurches to the cabin and claws at the locked door, he cannot get his hands on the controls and pull the plane up.

And there was no doubt about it: as we reached the beginning of August we were no longer *edging* toward zero hour. We were plunging "ass over teacup," as my uncle Paul used to say, and the ground was coming up fast.

* * *

It was not the show's first broadcast that constituted the crash, you see; nor the reviews, nor the ratings, nor any verdict handed down by CBS.

It was that first taping.

Those of us who went into it with intimations of disaster had them fully and absolutely and irreversibly confirmed. Those blessed few on the production staff who had been unaware of the dire truth could no longer escape it. From the TV public's standpoint the show might still be a coming attraction, but we all knew, after the taping, that it was a closed case. Our little caper was *kaput.*

Which is why the next morning—the morning with which I began this saga—I awoke in the gray dawn and lay in bed trying to decide between making tea or stepping in front of a crosstown bus.

Disjointed images from the previous day flickered before me in the half-light. Were they real or imagined?

An audience streaming into the studio, gasping from an hour's wait on the baking sidewalk outside; then, a few hours later—long before we were finished—streaming back out again, gasping from what they'd just witnessed.

A cue card being waved in front of me, right in the midst of taping a sketch, with lines scrawled on it that I'd never laid eyes on before.

A technician slumped over his console, whether conscious or not I couldn't tell as I glanced hastily into the control room, but looking like a survivor of the Bataan death march—or possibly a non-survivor.

A disconcerted Imogene Coca wandering the studio corridors at nearly one A.M., looking for the door and a taxi home, unassisted by anyone from my staff.

Images of struggle, confusion and rout, not to mention poor ventilation.

Viewed from my sweaty pillow they oppressed me to the point where I considered, as an alternative to killing myself, simply never stirring from beneath the counterpane again. I would fade mercifully from the public's memory, then, much later, recapture a modicum of fame as a legendary recluse.

Finally I hauled myself up and tottered to the typewriter, something I occasionally do in the early mornings to try to get a grip on things.

"Dear Diary," I wrote. "What do the Lanes think went wrong? How do they see the project now? How soon can I get them into the world's largest catapult?"

No, no, that would never do. They had, after all, been tireless and conscientious and certainly weren't to blame for the seemingly unprecedented series of mechanical breakdowns and technical delays.

I started typing again and filled three single-spaced pages with questions beginning with the word "why."

Why, for instance, didn't we get the rehearsal and run-through we'd been promised? Perhaps partly because of the technical delays, we seemed to be still preparing for it when tape began to roll, like feckless aborigines who fail to finish building their huts before being overtaken by a monsoon.

In one case I found myself trapped in a classic variation on the actor's nightmare. This was the Lucille Ball sketch; she had pretaped a scene in California in which she answered the phone and carried on half of a conversation (her half, of course). The idea was that on a split screen I would purport to place a call to Lucy from our set, while the control room intercut my lines with her tape; I would make it look natural and shade the comic timing to a nicety by following her tape on a TV monitor on the studio floor.

It was an amusing enough conceit that might have yielded some fun, except for one thing. I had failed to look at Lucy's tape prior to going in front of the cameras. (Had I seen it, I might have picked up from her the old pro's technique of holding a prop phone so it doesn't obscure your face.)

Why did everything, but everything, take so long? Before the day was half over I was exhausted from standing around and waiting between setups, and even between shots, while stage managers extracted either no message or contradictory ones from the crackling garble on their headphones, only to have to wait longer while one of the Lanes picked his or her way laboriously from the control booth to the set to try to get the message through.

Then I would inexplicably be sent back to my dressing room, at times with instructions to change into a new set of clothes that would later prove to be the wrong ones, or to pick up revisions in the script (still, at this late moment, a patchwork-in-progress) that would as often as not prove to be missing. Whether these instructions were garbled by intermediaries or misinterpreted by me, I never knew.

During the interludes, I was ostensibly awaiting my next call, which frequently never reached me, but mainly I was sitting there feeling my energy and concentration leaking away. Sometimes when I reappeared on the set it seemed like hours, or days, since my last visit. When the show eventually aired, I actually appeared to have taped it at widely varying ages.

Encountering Liza Minnelli or Doug Henning during these comings and goings was, in my increasingly hallucinatory perception, like seeing them at a busy airport and having one of those jovially forced, truncated conversations that harried travelers have in passing. The only difference was that these encounters were going to be on national television.

(Later I sent notes of apology to Doug and Liza. Especially Liza, who was not only fighting a cold but rehearsing a Broadway musical at the time. My final line: "I will never forget how you soldiered through uncomplainingly, hours after Mother Teresa would have told us to go fuck ourselves.")

Why was the studio audience virtually ignored? During the excruciating delays, nobody ever explained to them what was going on—assuming that anybody knew—nor ever instructed the band to help pass the time with a few tunes.

And, making matters worse, not enough TV monitors had been provided for the audience to see what was being picked up by the cameras—that is, during our occasional spurts of performing. If you've ever been to a TV show you know that it's much easier to follow the proceedings on monitors than in the hubbub of the studio floor. For some reason the CBS studio contained only two monitors for the use of the audience *and* the cast and crew on the floor, an ideal number to insure that neither group was adequately served. Some members of the audience told me they could either hear or see but never both at the same time.

The same person who dealt with the monitors must have been in charge of hanging live mikes over the audience. When they laughed or applauded, which I could swear they did once or twice, scarcely anything registered on the sound track.

Screening the tape later, we discovered that all we had in the way of audience reaction—vital in enlivening the atmosphere of a show—was a sort of distant, dry rustle, like autumn leaves being blown across a tin roof. The sound track was going to require what is known in the trade as "sweetening."

Typing out these and dozens of similar questions made me feel an iota or two less miserable, even though I knew none of them would ever be satisfactorily answered. I went back to bed for a few hours.

Towards noon a colleague arrived at my apartment for a postmortem, and never was the term more apt.

"I wonder what the tape looks like," I said. "If there's anything airworthy on it we don't deserve it, and I have my doubts."

"Maybe this is where Bill and Mary's editing wizardry comes in," the colleague said. "As scheduled, they're over at the editing room looking at it right now."

"They're *what?*"

Suddenly I remembered a paranoid dream I'd had during the night. Chuckling malevolently over the tape, Mary had said to Bill, "We'll keep Cavett so busy with the second show he won't have *time* to stick his nose into the editing."

Blitzed by the previous day's events, I had apparently forgotten that editing had to start right away, and now I focused all my jangled anxiety and frustration on this imaginary scene. I saw various shades of crimson.

The next conscious memory I have is of putting the phone down after speaking to Bill. My colleague assured me that when I called I adopted a subtle psychological approach along the lines of, "If you touch one inch of that tape before I get there you'll be out on your ass so fast it'll make your head swim."

We tore over to the editing room in a taxi. I had blown off most of my steam on the phone, so I was able to greet the Lanes relatively calmly, although our eyes rarely met. Tense and bruised, we were like a group of people who had run into one another in the daylight after having survived a sado-masochistic orgy, which in a way we had.

For the rest of the afternoon what seemed like miles of tape unreeled before our glassy gaze. Occasionally someone would look up from jotting a note and, trying for a tone of cool professional assessment, would say, "You know, there really is a show in there somewhere."

Since none of these cool professional assessors had been to bed since the taping, I wasn't about to rush home and draft my Emmy Award speech.

The first show was scheduled for broadcast in slightly less than two weeks, and CBS would need to receive the final edited tape a few days before that. While that was being assembled there was also the second show to tape, as Mary had noted in my dream, and the third and fourth to plan and write.

Thus my cab ride that day was the first in what would be a month-long series of bumpy weavings through Manhattan traffic between my apartment and the editing room, the rehearsal hall and the editing room, the studio and the editing room.

And that afternoon's screening was the first in what would be a soul-killing—and, at $336 an hour, budget-busting—month of vigils over those whirring spools of tape.

In a movie this would all be superimposed over progressive closeups of my teeth being ground down to seedlings.

My physician has advised me not to undertake the strain of narrating the subsequent events in all their grimly numbing detail, so I'll spare both you and me the dreariest parts—the late hours in the editing room over congealed pizza and deli sandwiches, the chopping of the only sequences that I thought had any hint of spontaneous or relaxed appeal, the endless haggling over lines and timings and our old friend Logical Flo, the nervous bluffing with Alan Wagner and others at CBS over how things were shaping up, the contradictory chorus of suggestions from the writers on new directions to try, the bookings that fell through, the sketches that misfired and were cut out or, worse, left in.

To mention only a few.

Somewhere in midpassage, Imogene Coca made the wise decision to withdraw quietly from the whole shellshocked enterprise. I remember thinking, "Here is a woman who did hundreds of ninety-minute 'Show of Shows'—vastly more complicated than our modest endeavor—*live,* year after year with rarely a visible hitch, and now she finds herself in these marathon tapings that are like watching a spastic try to build a house of cards. Who can blame her?"

Oddly, the sole phase of editing that yielded a mite of amusement was the work of the "sweetener." Gray-haired and portly, conservatively dressed, he had the calm, smiling air of the specialist whose work flourishes regardless of the circumstances that occasion it, like an embalmer.

This gentleman and his black box were celebrated throughout the business. The box was a wooden contraption about three feet square with a sort of cash register keyboard attached to it. Its owner guarded it as a spy does his briefcase. It was said that he never let anybody see the mysterious interior of the box, that he never let it out of his sight, that when he traveled with it he booked an extra first-class seat so it could ride safely beside him.

Evidently the box contained a complicated battery of tape recordings comprising every variety of audience applause and laughter. The sweetener's method was to begin by watching whatever program segment he was going to work on. Then, after hooking up his box to the editing equipment, he played the segment again, this time clacking away at his keyboard after each joke, song or other bit, causing the sound track to blossom with clapping, whistling, chuckles or explosions of mirth.

Sometimes, hunching over the keyboard like a Horowitz, he tossed off virtuoso effects in which, for example, he caused the audience to murmur for a few seconds before getting a joke; or he made a laugh die away abruptly, leaving only the quavery giggle of what sounded like a woman in the balcony.

It was ingenious and fun to watch, especially during my monologue, when his ministrations brought forth big enough roars of hilarity to do belated justice to my jokes. Well, almost big enough.

In the end, of course, a laugh track is still a laugh track. The sweetener's high-priced skills, although impressive, should not have been necessary, and were only helping to make the show more synthetic and canned. But then, how many other high-priced skills had been working to the same effect?

Nearly everybody's, was the inescapable conclusion when I watched the final edited tape that was at last so laboriously constructed.

To be fair, I somehow came out looking merely ill at ease instead of trapped in an abyss of demoralization, as I knew I had been during the taping. And Liza and Doug and the others somehow appeared to be merely going through contrived paces instead of thrashing about in a miasma of muddle, as I knew they had been. These were triumphs of a sort.

Yet the overall effect was choppy and stiff; it didn't breathe. At best it looked like a moderately clever facsimile of a variety show. What's more, in my admittedly jaundiced view, I doubted if even a scan by an electron microscope would have detected a trace of a Concept in it.

The word that came back to me after Alan Wagner and his CBS crew had screened the tape was, "Very promising start . . . bound to shake down as you go along . . . excited at the prospect of the remaining three." They disliked it that much.

I felt that I ought to make it easier for them by saying something like, "Please fellows, don't go through contortions to say something optimistic on *my* account." A deep, numb sense of anticlimax had long since set in.

The show was broadcast in mid-August. According to the resident witch doctors at the A. C. Nielsen Company, it was seen by something like one-fourth of the total TV audience during its particular time slot, or approximately twenty to twenty-five million people.

This number is half again the circulation of TV Guide, the equivalent of the population of Canada, and more than probably saw all of the Barrymores put together during their entire stage careers. But as a prime time network number it's a yawn. It wouldn't buy you a third martini on Madison Avenue.

Could that be why I am still waiting for the phone call that the departed Fred Silverman promised to make to me after my first show?

The reviews were more or less what we deserved. To give you an idea, the Sunday New York *Times* carried a piece by John Leonard ("Cyclops") under the headline, "Cavett—Nice Guys Finish Last," and Leonard had always been one of my most sympathetic critics. He was perceptive, as usual: "The hour lacked conviction; it was not persuasive. Everybody seemed to be looking over his shoulder, as though expecting a karate chop."

He then took a broader look at where my career stood at the moment: "Engaging, intelligent, anxious to please, [Cavett] seems to have been caught in a revolving door, or, more accurately, to have been threshed by TV, to have been beaten as if with a flail. His seeds are scattered."

Amen, brother.

And yet no calamity is totally without its redeeming charms. As we slogged determinedly through the other three shows, there were occasional moments that turned out well. To put it more cynically, the distinction of total badness eluded us.

Peter Ustinov was one of my subsequent guest stars, and he demonstrated a lesson that should be a must in any TV course; namely, that when you have a talent who is a variety show in himself, the best production concept is a long, uninterrupted sequence of him sitting and doing whatever comes into his head. And Jean Stapleton showed herself to be a brick in a near-beguiling sketch with Ustinov.

The great master of closeup magic, Slydini, contributed a quietly dazzling segment using no other props but cigarettes, some coins and a few foam rubber balls. The interplay between him and a genuinely impressed and mystified Cher, who was one of the people seated around a green velvet table with him, was delightful.

Steve Allen clowned engagingly through a sketch about a radio serial in which he and I played all the voices, male and female, while Marshall Efron was a farcically overtaxed sound effects man.

Perhaps best of all, Jean Marsh and her co-stars on "Upstairs/Downstairs" flew over from London to talk about their enchanting show (after we overcame some nervousness at CBS about plugging a series that was then running on PBS) and to toss off some spoofs of such American institutions as baseball and cowboy and Indian movies. Jean's gang turned out to be as briskly cheerful and professional as I had fondly imagined. Under the lightness of their touch our format actually seemed airborne for a few days, and working with them did not resemble work. When their taping was done and it was time for them to move on, I felt a wistful urge to go with them, like a boy who is tempted to run off with an improbably sophisticated band of gypsies.

If only I could have.

September came, and the four broadcasts seemed over in an eyeblink. Naturally there was no discussion of CBS picking up the show for its regular schedule. Nobody had the poor taste to so much as mention the subject.

As for those four hours being rerun sometime—say, after the Late Late Show or on Sunday mornings—there was somewhat less than the proverbial chance of a Chinese gentleman. For all I know, CBS hauled the master tapes out into the Atlantic and dumped them somewhere on the ocean floor in lead containers.

By this time, after the turmoil of the previous few months, I would have thought that my capacity to be thunderstruck was depleted for life, along with most of the rest of my vital signs. But no, it rebounded with a vengeance when one more stunning revelation broke over me.

It was after the mop-up production work was finished and the extra staff had been let go. The offices began to resemble Fort Zindernoof again. The Xerox machine had fallen silent. Over this peaceful, if desolate, scene, snow began to fall.

Well, not snow exactly, but a thick flutter of little white slips—bills run up during the show.

They mounted and mounted until my accountant glumly informed me that, while the payments from CBS gave us income of $440,000, our outgo had surpassed that and was heading for something like a cool half mil. Somebody was going to have to come up with the difference

—which finally leveled off at about $50,000—and the nearest mirror revealed who the poor sap was.

This was the ultimate straw. Not only had I been in effect threshed and flailed in public, to use John Leonard's terms, but now I was going to have to pay handsomely for the privilege.

"Where were my financial watchdogs?" I shouted, tossing papers into the air and kicking wastebaskets the way they show you at the Harvard Business School. In the real world I might have looked to my producers to crack down on expenses; but here I had to rely on my own accountant and other advisors, who assured me they had no way of knowing what the totals were going to be until it was too late.

With the calm precision of the truly irrational person, I explored all the conceivable ways of making the Lanes themselves cough up the overrun, none of them legal and very few of them mentionable. (The Yellow Pages revealed no one who rented a medieval rack.)

In the end I realized that all I could hope for from them was an answer to another in my endless series of "whys?" Perhaps, as with all the other "whys," there would be no answer, but it seemed better to put the question to Bill and Mary than to go on waking up quivering in the middle of the night.

So we met once again. It was awkward, since we had already said our strained farewells a while earlier. At that time only Bill had been able to muster one of the polite insincerities of such occasions: "Well, Dick, we'll get 'em next time."

Now, as we sat in my office reviewing the show's expenses, I realized that we had quickly succeeded in putting vast distances between each other. Our conversation didn't seem to connect; my anger dematerialized in the remote atmosphere. The phrases they used seemed airy and faint, as if they—or I—were fading out. A budget is only a guideline . . . quality a consideration . . . do what seems necessary at the time . . . an investment that would be returned a hundredfold if the show were picked up. . . .

I started to say, "why didn't we recognize on square one that the things we had both been successful at were so different?" But I didn't.

There was no answer. There was nothing left but for the Lanes and me to say our farewells again, this time for real.

As I watched them walk toward the elevator I had to take what bleak, weary satisfaction I could from the thought that, together, we three were about as likely to see Bill's "next time" as I was the fifty grand. So far I remain right on both counts.

Excuse me a moment, I must get the phone. It may be Fred Silverman.

THE CAVETT ALBUM—III

OF THE MANY LIVES I wish I had lived in addition to my own—
and on some days instead of my own—my favorite is that of my Uncle
Paul. "A real hell for leather guy," my father calls him. Stricken with
wanderlust, bored with school, unable to get along with his sometimes
tyrannical father, he hopped a freight out of Grand Island, Nebraska,
one day when he was in his early teens and has made his own way ever
since.

His has been a roaming and rambling existence that sounds like a
boy's dream. There were years of riding freights from coast to coast and
in every state (back when there were still forty-eight). He has been a
barber, a cab driver, a fry cook, a field hand, a seaman in World War
II and has worked at about a hundred other odd jobs along the way.

I love listening to his tales of bumming around the country, working
for a while, finding adventure, then hopping a freight and moving on.
And now that he is virtually incapacitated by illness and laid up in a
small apartment in northern California, I deeply regret not knowing
him better when he was in his prime.

Paul Richards is my mother's brother, one of the several children of my formidable grandfather Richards, the Welsh Baptist preacher. "I didn't mind home as long as Dad wasn't there," Uncle Paul tells me. "He was frequently doin' evangelism work in South Dakota, but when he was home we didn't get along. Also, I just knew I didn't like goin' to school. Only got as far as ninth grade. I only liked football at school, so I waited till the middle of February, when football was over, and took off. Freight train come by, I got on. Rode up to Broken Bow. Got a job out in the Sand Hills puttin' up wild prairie hay."

From there he just kept on going, lighting out for the next town whenever things got dull or got to be too much in some way. Whenever I ask him how he happened to go some place that he mentions, the answer is simple: "Just dropped off a freight train there."

In telling me about it he frequently has to pause to define some of the bummer's lingo that he is surprised I don't understand, as when he says, "I was ridin' blind between Provo and . . ." Riding blind, for the unfortunately uninitiated, is short for riding as "blind baggage," a term derived from the fact that baggage cars had a dummy platform at one end without a door; thus, once you were on that platform you could not be seen from inside the car.

A variety of other accommodations was open to the bummer. The back of a coal car, for example, or—the most luxurious since it was indoors—the interior of a boxcar. "Sometimes you got to ride the reefer," Paul says. "The reefer was a little door where they put ice in a car, but when there was no ice you could get in there out of the wind and the cold."

The most uncomfortable way to go was to ride "the rods," which were metal braces under the cars. Paul laughs when I tell him that Robert Mitchum in his bumming days almost froze to death under there once. As a novice rail rider he had failed to calculate temperature and distance and the train was going too fast for him to get off.

Paul learned the way to make the bare rods more comfortable. "You'd take a door from a grain car—you'd find 'em stacked out in the lumber yard—and put it under there to lay on."

I tingle to think of that Huck Finn life, with a grain door across the rods corresponding to Huck's raft, watching the countryside roll by, periodically dropping onto the cinders of an unknown railroad yard and heading into town to find work or adventure or trouble, or all three.

Depending on the attitude of the conductors and the "yard bulls" (railroad cops), an unticketed stowaway who was caught could be simply heaved off unceremoniously or he might get sent to jail or to work on a road gang. So certain skills had to be developed. One of Paul's was getting back on the same train he had just been thrown off.

On one occasion getting caught saved his life. "That was my closest shave, when I missed the sheep. It was a hell of a thing. I got on the cow catcher of a passenger train one night at Flagstaff. [The cow catcher was the scoop-like device on the front of the engine designed to lift or push aside any obstruction that might derail the train.] They run me off and I got back on and they run me off again, so this time I got back on the rear. If I hadn't I'd a been dead. We got up to about sixty-five mile an hour outside Prescott and suddenly I seen stuff go flyin' by. Some damn sheep were crossin' or sleepin' on the track and we plowed into 'em. What a damn mess. Shit and blood all over the place. If I'd been sittin' on the cowcatcher I never would a known what hit me. Thirty, forty sheep were piled up. They had to send another engine out."

The toughest "bull" he knew of was in Yerma, California, an aggressive, vindictive man whom he went to great lengths to avoid. He and three companions once dropped off a train outside of Yerma and began walking in the desert, hoping to detour around the town and, more important, around the bull. "Damned if he didn't come out after us on a *horse*. He had about a six-foot blacksnake [whip] and he said we'd go to town. We said we wouldn't. He snapped that snake and we decided we'd go to town. They locked us in a big cage outside the depot, then later loaded us in a cattle truck and took us to Riverside. They took us in front of the judge for evading payment of railroad fare. The judge said, 'You're gonna do sixty days on the county road.' I said to myself, 'I'm not gonna work on the county road.' So I showed the

judge my barber tools and told him I had a brother in Los Angeles who
had a job waitin' for me. I didn't have a brother or a job there, but he
believed me and turned me loose. I guess the others went on the county
road."

A dependable refuge for riders of the rails was the "old jungle" beside
the tracks outside of Provo, Utah. It was more a grove of trees than
a jungle, apparently always populated with hobos, well known as a
stopping and resting point for members of that romantic breed. "They
had a big can always steamin' and they'd make up a mulligan stew by
gettin' vegetables, or somebody'd steal a chicken, anything you could
throw in. Liked that place. It was always there and you were always
welcome and could get a meal."

One of Paul's early trades was potato picking around Chadron,
Nebraska. "This guy found me in a pool hall and hired me. He had two
forty-fives he wore around his hips and he thought he was a hot-shot
gunman. Practiced by the hour to be a fast-draw artist. I was fourteen
or fifteen and he was thirty-five and he'd been married a coupla years.
His wife had the hots for me but I stayed away because of those guns."

Paul claims he lost his virginity at the age of twelve, on a windmill.
At first I pictured him and the girl somehow wheeling around and
around on one of the sails, which, knowing Paul, didn't seem too
outrageous, but he said no. "It was on the platform of the windmill.
We could see about a mile down the road from there, in case anyone
was comin'. She was a neighbor girl from Lomax, a few years older than
me. She started it. If Dad had caught us ther'da been hell to pay. He
never told me the facts of life. Course, farm boys don't have to be told;
you see the cows and horses and pigs."

Another early way station was Long Pine, Nebraska, where he
worked at the counter of the depot restaurant, part of the Harvey
House chain. His colleague at the counter was, as he says, "an old gal
who knew her way around and taught me a few things." Among them
was how to cheat the cash register now and then, by which means he
laid up a nest egg sufficient to learn the trade that has been his main
support, however intermittently, ever since.

What made the most sense, he reasoned, was providing a service that is constantly in demand. Observing that hair grew constantly and barber shops nearly always had waiting customers, he bade the Harvey House and his economics instructress goodbye and hopped the appropriate freights to Omaha, where he hunted up a barber college. He invested his savings in tonsorial tuition, but after three weeks his impatience got the best of him. He decided he knew enough to cut hair, and headed west.

In those days long hair was uncommon; people needed frequent haircuts. When all else failed, Paul would pull into any town, go to the barber shop and say, "Who wants a few days off?" Some barber could always be convinced that he needed a rest and a few days of fishing or loafing. Paul would stand in for him and line his pockets enough to be able to move on when he felt like it.

One day when he was working a stint in a barber shop in California a rather snippy, dandified fellow came in and asked, in all seriousness, for a haircut that would make him look like Rudolph Valentino. In that day's newspaper, by bizarre coincidence, Paul had noticed a picture of Valentino with his head shaved for his latest movie role. Paul decided to liven up the afternoon.

"He had all this carefully combed black hair, and I took hold of the front of his forehead with one hand and run the shears from the base of his neck straight over the top to his forehead. Well, he leaped outa that chair screamin' and yellin' with a bald strip down the middle of his head, and he was so damn mad I thought he would die. He went out and got a cop and brought him in and said, 'Look what he did to me!' I told the cop, 'This is an up-to-date barber shop and he wanted to look like Valentino. There's Valentino right there in the paper.' "

I guess many people would find this story unfunny and feel sorry for the victim (as I do, a bit), but I cherish it as an example of the true devil-may-care attitude that I've only seen genuinely embodied in Paul. In him it was never just boorishness or affected insouciance but the real thing.

"I never had any trouble finding work," he says. "My problem was not getting into trouble and losing it." By this he refers not only to capers like the Valentino haircut, but to his inability to take any guff combined with his propensity for "wading into" anyone who offended him.

His fistic skill occasionally earned him a few bucks, as when he would get $15 for boxing four rounds in small towns in Montana. "The only catch was, if you didn't last the four rounds you got nothin'. Whenever I got in over my head or wasn't boxing with a friend, so we wouldn't really hurt each other, I did a lot of runnin'." He always stayed the distance, but decided that barbering was an easier way to make money than having his salients rearranged in the ring.

He also knew when not to put up a fight. What he regards as the worst job he ever had was in Antioch, Nebraska, then a booming potash center but now a rusting ghost town. His chore was to go in among the giant cylindrical tanks of potash and hammer the sides to loosen the residue that stuck there. It may sound easy, but the temperature was inferno-like and there was a constant danger that you would pass out and cook yourself before being missed.

One night he had just collected his pay in bills and silver. "I rounded a corner and found myself lookin' down the barrel of a forty-five with a hole big enough to put your thumb in. I could see the guy was nervous and he sure was a greenhorn, because when I handed my fistful of change over to him he took off without waitin' for the bills. I guess he figured that was all I had." Paul took this as a signal to terminate his career as a potash hammerer and move on.

They say Thomas Carlyle couldn't remember a time when he didn't read Greek. Paul can't remember a time when he didn't know how to play poker. "Hell, that's how I made most of my money," he says. The first car he ever owned was won in a poker game in Casper, Wyoming. "The car was just a frame, really. Sort of a skeleton car with two seats on it. You'd call it a dune buggy today. This was about 1918 or '19. I and another guy drove out to a place called the Dew Drop Inn in the mountains about thirty mile outa Casper, and the brakes went out. We rolled outa the car and *it* rolled about fifteen times down the mountain-side. Still there, as far as I know."

Later, in the Navy, he ran a poker game aboard ship and managed to send home thousands of dollars from his winnings. He hates to think how much he spent in Honolulu as a young Turk on shore leave. "I'd usually win three or four hundred a night and blow half of it. We all did."

When he tells me this, I ask what sailors could spend all that on in Honolulu.

"You've been there. You know what's there," he says.

"When I was there it was mostly bars, nightclubs and hookers."

"Well, it hasn't changed."

My Uncle Paul. Yes, I know what the moralists and the responsibility mongers would say about him. The same thing the Widow Douglases and Miss Watsons always say about the Huck Finns of the world. Willful, undisciplined, hostile to authority and probably a great deal more besides. No doubt there is a certain amount of truth in these judgments. Yet I would gladly trade them all for a month of riding the rails with him.

And, in his favor, he was stable enough to get married in his early twenties and stay married. While barbering in Billings, Montana, he noticed an attractive young woman who frequently sat out in front of the shop with her married sister. He said to his boss, "I'm gonna get me some o' that." Five weeks later they were man and wife.

Her real name is Lela, but she has been called Bill ever since she was a toddler. Bill was her father's name, and because she followed him everywhere, people took to saying, "Here comes little Bill," and it stuck.

In the fifty-eight years since they were married, Paul and Bill have been "damn near everywhere," driving cabs, living in trailers, camping out, raising a son, fishing together. On their fiftieth anniversary he told her he "had decided to keep her." He credits her with keeping him out of fights, except for one or two that were "just too damn good to stay out of."

She is still with him, tending him in the apartment in California, hard of hearing but game as ever. "Bill says we had the good times, now we have to take what comes," says Paul. "She doesn't gripe like I do. Can't hear me half the time. Some she gets and some she doesn't. What she ain't supposed to get she gets."

The only time they were apart for long was when Paul went into the Navy. During those years he seems to have reverted to his old rambunctious ways.

In the classic service tradition, Paul was saddled with an officer who "rode his ass" at every opportunity. In one case, he was on gunnery duty and asked to go to the head. The officer, whose name was Hubbard, refused him permission even though nothing was going on. A few minutes later he asked again.

Hubbard said, "Richards, you'll go to the head when your duty ends."

Paul picked up a bucket, dumped out the shells and began to lower his trousers.

"Richards, what the hell do you think you're doing?"

Paul replied, "Hubbard, the Navy can tell me where to shit but it can't tell me when."

Another time he was exhausted in his bunk after a rough day's duty when a fellow seaman brought an order from Hubbard to report to Hubbard's quarters and cut his hair. Paul sent word that his day's work was done. The seaman came back with the same order. Paul told the seaman to tell Hubbard to "stick his hair up his ass," insisting that the message be delivered verbatim.

Shortly thereafter he found himself before a disciplinary officer, who asked, "Did you tell a seaman to tell Officer Hubbard words to the effect that he should stick his hair up his ass?"

"No, sir," Paul replied.

"You deny the report?"

"No, sir."

"I don't understand."

"It was not in words to that effect; it was exactly those words."

The amused officer meted out the mildest of punishments.

Paul's ship was the heavy cruiser *Louisville*, which saw its share of action in the Pacific. One day off Okinawa, Paul left a group of buddies to go below decks for cigarettes. That errand may have been as fateful as getting run off the cowcatcher at Flagstaff. While he was below, an airplane that had been misidentified as friendly proved to be a Japanese *kamikaze* and scored a direct hit on the *Louisville*, killing a score of Paul's fellow seamen. He came up to find, among others, "the body of a kid laid out on deck whose hair I had just cut that morning. That Jap musta been firin' as he came in 'cause the kid had a straight line of bullet holes across his belly."

Paul never thought he might end up that way. "Never occurred to me. I guess when you're young and full of piss 'n' vinegar, even seein' people get it right next to you you don't think it'll be you. I came pretty near goin' over the side a few times, though. Once, up in the Aleutians, the ship was rollin' in a storm and I was in a gun emplacement. Damn ship would roll fifty-five degrees. Nearly turn over. One wave hit and she rolled just as I was movin' to a different gun mount. I remember slidin' and rollin' and grabbin' at somethin'. When she came back up I was hangin' on the outside. I was so damn disgusted with myself I nearly jumped into the next damn wave on my own. We lost several good men that way."

The years just after the war brought Paul's first Nebraska visits that I can clearly remember. He and Bill drove me on a trip to Omaha when I was about ten years old. I rode up in the front seat with them, sitting on Bill's lap and entertaining them by calling out the answers to a quiz program that was on the radio.

Despite Paul's vagabond life, he stayed in his relatives' good graces and was welcomed at home whenever he blew through. I always assumed that after he left home his mother wondered where he was and saw him maybe once a year when he dropped off a passing freight. "No, no, I wrote to Maw nearly every week. Only time I didn't was when I was in jail for a while. I think she knew, but I told her the mail had got lost."

I ask how he got into the slammer. "Hit a cop." Paul had dropped off a train somewhere and at the station saw a cop standing over a derelict who had one leg amputated at the knee. The derelict was told to move, couldn't, and the cop kicked him in the ribs. Paul tapped the officer and, when he turned, laid him out on the concrete. For the next thirty days he was in the employ of the state. "They give me ten days at first. I was out on the road gang and took a sneak. Twice. Caught me both times. Ended up doing thirty days."

In this episode he was more like his father than he may have realized. He used to tell me admiringly of a childhood memory in which his father knocked a man "ass over teacup" with a single blow for making a slighting remark about his mother.

Now, although he can no longer see what he's typing, Paul keeps up a weekly correspondence with his brother Lloyd, a lifelong English teacher with a softer, jollier disposition than his. "Hard to believe we're from the same family," Paul says. "I love Lloyd's letters, but I keep tellin' him to stop usin' all those bullshit college words and talk English."

My father, another English teacher, has always liked Paul immensely and particularly admires his directness. They were downtown together once when they found they needed to relieve themselves. They walked into the first likely establishment they could find, a tea room. A well groomed hostess came forward, but before she could greet them Paul said, *"Where is it?"* She wordlessly pointed them in the right direction without missing a beat.

Now Paul tells me that after my mother died he and Bill talked about how they would have enjoyed adopting me. "You'da traveled with us all over from Texas to Canada to Florida, sleepin' in trailers or on a cot by the side of the car. God, we'd a had a lotta fun. You'da got a better education."

Certainly a different education from the one I got. Paul constantly chides me about the fundamental life experiences I've missed out on and know nothing about. "Didn't you ever cut pigs?" he'll say.

I tell him I know that cattle-cutting means separating one from the herd—but pigs?

It was one of his least favorite jobs when he was still a farm boy. He had to hold pigs by the hind legs while his father castrated them with a pocket knife.

"Why did they have to be castrated?" I ask.

"Hell, you'd have a three-ring circus otherwise. Nothin' but boars. What a question. I can't believe you never nutted pigs."

"What did you do with the . . . results?"

"Ate 'em. You never ate hang fries? Ask any chef about hang fries. Better than any steak you ever ate. Like fine fried oysters. Dad always threw 'em in the dirt for the chickens, but Aunt Belle, she used to fry 'em up and there's nothin' better."

"I *have* heard of prairie oysters—"

"That's it. Same thing. We called 'em hang fries. The way Belle fried 'em for supper they tasted like tenderloin. Surprised you never ate 'em."

Such delicacies are long gone for Paul. "I can't taste nothin' now. Don't know if I'm eatin' a pickle or a banana. Bill cuts stuff up for me and I just spoon it up." His failing eyesight has forced him to give up books too. He was always an enthusiastic reader, especially of his favorite writer, Zane Grey.

A chronic emphysema sufferer, he had a heart operation a few years ago, and more recently a stroke. Not to mention the countless more or less healed broken bones, scars and batterings of a lifetime.

His attitude toward all this is typical: "This 'golden age' business is a load o' crap. You can't see, you can't taste, you can't get around. Just sittin' here. Only thing I can do. Hell, I'm ready to see what's on the other side. Been tryin' to die for five years and can't do it."

When I call or visit, there invariably comes a point in the conversation when he says to me, "God *damn,* I wish we'd got to know each other better when I could still get around, before this golden age shit set in. I coulda come back East there when you got outa Yale. We

coulda pitched a bitch, couldn't we? Course I didn't have the money
to come back then, and I couldn't very well bring Bill on a freight."

And when I hang up or drive away, there is always the fear that I'll
never see him again. I'm filled with a deep melancholy yearning to turn
the clock back and have another chance at what feel like wasted years
when I could have spent more time with him.

As he says, we coulda pitched a bitch.

IF I WERE MAYOR OF NEW YORK

FROM TIME TO TIME I am asked whether I would be interested in running for office. In the post-Watergate era I have taken to answering that I don't see the point of bothering with politics; it seems so much simpler to go *directly* into crime.

But seriously, the question alarms me, because it implies that who —or what—I am automatically qualifies me to run for office. Around the time of the Kennedy administration we started turning our politicians into pop celebrities. Now we're turning our pop celebrities into politicians.

In any case, my feelings haven't changed since I told Jerry Rubin on my old ABC talk show, "Politics bores my ass off!"

That's politics; power is something else again. Everybody is interested in power, if only on a fantasy level. I do enjoy thinking about how I might use political power to change things, to make them run my way.

During one of New York's mayoral campaigns, when the New York *Times* got tired of printing the views of the real candidates (shortly after the public got tired of reading them), it asked me to write an article titled, "If I Were Mayor." I happily complied because it gave me a chance to fantasize about taking charge of the world's greatest city without undergoing any of the strain and tedium of the job.

Now I'm offering my platform again here as a public service, for the benefit of other cities and to remind New York's mayor, Ed Koch, that it's not too late to pick up a pointer or two.

My first official act as mayor of New York would be to admit defeat. The big problems of the city are clearly insoluble. Big questions, such as tax incentives to corporations to keep them from moving away, are beyond my ken and apparently beyond everybody's. I would confine myself, as mayor, to what might be called the little things. By this I mean the more tangible "quality of life" problems; the petty annoyances that drive people to drink or to New Jersey.

My first move would be to require all cab drivers to have at least a twenty-five-word vocabulary in English. I happen to enjoy foreign languages, and am grateful for the smatterings of the romance tongues that I have picked up from New York hacks of many nations. Only last week I had the pleasure of teaching a good-natured driver on his first day on the job the words "right" and "left." I tipped him fifty cents and his delighted face as he pronounced the words, "For me?" was a joy to behold. But the problem remains, as when your driver says, "Broadway Street?"

And what is the latest excuse for not replacing all New York taxis with London cabs? Everyone knows the latter are smaller, consume less fuel, are more comfortable, can turn on a dime and if they stop suddenly, your features are not flattened against a dirty lucite shield. I would, as mayor, import London cabs even if it meant depriving the Londoners of them.

I would, once and for all, ban the automobile from midtown Manhattan. Every other form of transportation would be available: flooded and frozen streets for skating and dogsledding in winter, and rickshas and rollerskates in summer. There would be sedan chairs for the status-conscious, and for those who cannot afford them there would be large men to carry you from place to place.

I have not yet devised a fitting punishment, but those who ride motorcycles in the wee hours with the throttle wide open would do so only once.

I might be laughed out of office, but I would adopt the novel notion of enforcing some of the existing anti-pollution laws. Several times, as a good citizen, I have reported flagrant violations of the incinerator law, and after losing several dimes in a pay phone while watching the black smoke curl heavenward, finally reached a city employee who was unequal to the task of copying down the address I was giving. Once the voice at the other end insisted that there is no East 74th Street.

I would encourage the development of more street eccentrics, the kind only New York seems to develop. They add color and spice to the city. The wonderful creature known as the Skating Pixie, who performs delightful arabesques while clad in taffeta gown and pillbox hat as he rollerskates through the city, would be subsidized. I once saw him tap a startled traffic policeman on the shoulder with his wand while executing a perfect figure eight at an intersection, then vanish airily down the avenue—a veritable Makarova on wheels.

I would similarly reward the marvelous man with the rubberoid hairpiece who bends at the waist and plays the street with drumsticks. These people would be declared human landmarks, exempt from local taxes.

I haven't come up, yet, with a punishment severe enough for landlords who fail to provide heat in winter, but it would be one of my first tasks as mayor. I would look into the possibility of reopening Devil's Island, or mandate compulsory attendance at a marathon production of the complete works of Eugene O'Neill. Or both.

And there are things that I would bring back. I would bring back the Roxy. I would bring back the Astor bar, if I could figure out how to do it without bringing back the Astor. And I would restore to the city the open-top, double-decker buses. I realize something would have to be done first about the city's air. At present, after a two-mile ride, the *al fresco* passengers would probably look like a minstrel float in Mardi Gras.

Then there are the city's sex problems. As for the controversy about legalized brothels like those in Europe, I would end it by establishing one. As host of the award-winning TV program "V.D. Blues" I would, of course, see to it that it was immaculately run. It would be for everyone. The tasteful front entrance would be for those who enjoy being seen entering a brothel, but there would also be a discreet entrance for the shy. In addition, there would be a reading room for those who want to be seen entering a brothel, but would rather not do anything.

I would line the Fifth Avenue side of Central Park with female hustlers, to balance the male ones on Central Park West. In spring, they would have a tug-of-war.

Finally, there would be three days a week when no one is allowed to say either "Have a nice day" or "What's your sign?" Violators would have their copies of Kahlil Gibran confiscated.

I have many more ideas, some of them equally as good as these, and will make them available to any interested party. After all, I have a vital stake in improving the city. I intend to live in New York until my sense of humor gives out or my lease expires, whichever comes first.

WAY DOWN YONDER

THERE ARE CERTAIN PLACES you can travel to that make you feel that you've *arrived* at home rather than left it. New Orleans does this for me. I feel more at home there than almost anywhere else, even though it feels like a foreign city to me, more foreign than, say, Paris.

Once, on the eve of a trip to Italy, I asked Ruth Gordon what city she thought I should visit.

"Florence," she said. "I never got the hang of Rome, but Florence speaks to ya."

I guess I never got the hang of a lot of those places, but New Orleans speaks to me. I discovered it about a dozen years ago in the only way you can truly discover it: in the company of a southerner who knows the place, in this case my wife. Our taxi crossed Rampart Street and glided into the French Quarter (Vieux Carré), and it was as if I were in another country and another time.

It was a beautiful sunny day, the air was balmy and the magnolias were in bloom. We stopped for a cocktail in a little patio that had a fountain and lush greenery. The sensuous lassitude of the place stole over me. I was in love.

I have returned to that patio many a time in the years since. It is behind a once grand private residence on Toulouse Street, now converted into a snugly elegant hotel called the Maison de Ville.

I always feel I could spend a blissful day just sitting there now in the warm sun, now in the cool shadows, mindlessly letting the hours drift by, with everything quiet except for the distant sounds of Dixieland that filter through the foliage (New Orleans is the only place where overheard music is not an irritant).

As with any famous city, everything that can be said about New Orleans has been said. That it is rich in history, tradition and beauty. That at the right time of year (and this is all-important) it is relaxed, dreamlike, illicit, carefree. Also that it is cheesy, tasteless, being exploited and eroded, and, like all American cities, sometimes dangerous.

People who say they didn't like New Orleans probably saw this latter side of it. They approached it wrong. They probably stayed at a high-rise modern hotel, for example, instead of the Maison de Ville. And they probably hung out on Bourbon Street.

Bourbon Street: where witless T-shirts and plastic novelties are hawked among blaring tourist traps, Takee Outees (fast "Chinese" food) and topless-bottomless bars with doormen providing the rubes a tantalizing peek between gulps from a bottle in a paper bag; where people of all sexes rub shoulders with double-knit couples with Instamatics from Des Moines; where stray dogs and burnouts lie in the gutter and black urchins tap dance (brilliantly) for silver while Moonies with zombie smiles push flowers and others push worse.

I once saw a grubby leather boy having a convulsive drug seizure on the sidewalk of Bourbon Street while friends tried to hold him, and a nearby derelict with a sense of rhythm snapped his fingers in time with the violent spasms.

But enough of old New Orleans remains to make you realize that there was once a wonderfully different way of life in America, at least in the Old South—a way of life slower yet more intense than our bland cosmopolitanism, more physical yet more esthetic, earthier yet more sophisticated.

My friend Mary Scales, a doctor in the Quarter, once took a longtime resident in her car to see a colleague outside the Quarter. Her passenger was old man Brocato, owner of the turn-of-the-century ice cream parlor that bears his family's name. He expressed astonishment at all the new buildings on St. Charles Avenue, by which he meant not only the Hilton and other towers that violate the city's skyline but structures that had gone up thirty and forty years earlier. These astonishments were only some dozen blocks from his shop. He hadn't ventured out of the Quarter in decades.

Another local friend told me about a woman who had lived in the city's Garden District for seventy-three years. When asked if she had been to the Quarter lately, she said, "I have never been there. I know very well what sort of things go on there." Although they are only a few miles apart in the same city, I guess that woman and Signore Brocato are as safe from meeting as a polar bear and a crocodile.

The visitor who has only two hours to see New Orleans would do well—after strolling the Quarter, of course—to ride the city's sole remaining streetcar along Charles Street, starting in the modern business district and moving through the transitional neighborhoods, where tract housing and glass-box office buildings are replacing well-worn, venerable frame structures, and ending up in the Garden District, where ante-bellum mansions of every conceivable architectural style and eccentricity are set amid majestic oaks festooned with Spanish moss. The Garden District has an unearthly quiet majesty and beauty that I doubt is matched anywhere.

Having friends who live in New Orleans naturally makes all the difference in penetrating the inner life of the place. The tourist who goes to a pseudo-folk banjo parlor and makes a quick circuit of Jackson Square may well wonder what all the fuss is about. He is never called by Mary Scales to "go get some crawfish," which with Mary can mean being taken to a private home, the second oldest house in the Quarter, where amid splendid antiques heaping trays of crawfish and potatoes boiled in pepper water are consumed; and our hostess, Miss Dixie, gorgeous in her seventies with flaming red hair, gets out the clarinet she hasn't played in twenty years and accompanies herself on a record she made when she ran a club in the Quarter and was part of an act called something like "The Sizzlers."

Nor is he taken by Mary Scales to meet Bobbie, a man in his eighties with a pink, cherubic face who lives in an exquisite apartment, makes superb lampshades and plays precisely twenty-three songs on the piano. Bobbie learned them by rote years ago—mostly Cole Porter and other pop standards—and keeps a list on the piano to remind him of the titles. He does not know another note or scale or exercise.

I love early Sunday mornings in the Quarter, when you can have it to yourself. Nearly everyone is hung over and still behind shutters (why do shuttered windows suggest illicitness as nothing else does?) and you can walk the sunny, quiet old streets like Barracks and St. Ann and be in a realm apart.

The houses and all the trees and shrubbery appear to have grown up together. You can see the same kind of lush foliage elsewhere; Beverly Hills, for instance, has it in subtropical profusion. But there the houses seem like giant decorated cakes that have been baked and delivered that morning.

Here, as in the Garden District, you can be drifting along, half conscious, and be stopped in your tracks by a sudden glimpse of an idyllic courtyard, or of some fading eminence rising against the sky with its ornate grillwork, sagging balconies and overgrowth of ferns and vines stretched across ancient cracked plaster, which has fallen away in places to reveal a variety of hues of weather-smoothed brick.

Each house is worth stopping to look at, from the most romantically squalid all the way up to the Beauregard House, the former residence of the writer Frances Parkinson Keyes, whose high-ceilinged splendor and richly brocaded furniture are now preserved as a museum. All emanate an almost palpable aura of bygone human lives. Some have legends attached to them, or are said to be haunted. I once met a woman who lived on the top floor of a building at the end of Pirate's

Alley who informed me matter of factly that she had a ghost, in much the same way that someone might describe something as mundane as a plumbing problem.

It seemed that someone had met a violent end in the house about a hundred years before, and the victim's restless shade often cut up around eventide, pushing the furniture around in the woman's sitting room or violently rocking her rocking chair, sometimes until it fell over. She was a nicely dressed, attractive woman who worked in the advertising department of a local department store and there seemed no reason to disbelieve her.

Many of the Quarter's streets run down to the Mississippi River, which curves sinuously along the city's edge. Sometimes, looking toward the river end of one of these streets, you will see the upper part of a huge metal structure pass smoothly by, almost as though it were gliding across an intersection. It is a freighter or tanker from some exotic port, but only the upper part is visible because the city is *below* the water level. If the levee ever broke the Quarter would be an Aquacade.

One morning I strolled to the levee behind the vast white shell of the old Jax Brewery, now abandoned, and saw a Soviet freighter, the *Sebastopol,* moored there. The immediate area was roped off. A dock-hand told me that the crew was not allowed ashore because of some petty bureaucratic squabble.

A sailor was leaning on the rail of the ship and I started a disjointed, yelled conversation with him in Berlitz-book Russian (mine, that is; his was excellent). He gestured for me to wait and disappeared.

When he reappeared a few moments later he beckoned me as close to the rope as possible, then winged a package of Russian cigarettes (Pyno) to me. Not sure what to do, and unable to think of the word for thank you *(spasibo),* I waved back and we grinned foolishly at each other.

Suddenly I had an inspiration. Returning the wait-there gesture, I ran a few blocks to the Cafe du Monde, bought a pound of their special chicory coffee and hurried back to the dock. The sailor was gone.

In some unaccountable way I felt I had lost a dear friend. I was also

acutely aware that two people, tourists clearly, had seen Dick Cavett
run exuberantly to a rope barricade with a can of coffee, look up at an
empty ship and stand there confused. Blushing slightly, I began tossing
the can in the air stiffly, trying to look as if I had always meant to play
catch with it, and wondering why at my advanced age I was still subject
to self-consciousness of that kind.

Mercifully my friend reappeared. With a small book in his hand he
put a finger on the page and yelled, "Gude marneeng!"

When I nodded my understanding he was elated. Obviously, disappointed at being unable to come ashore, he was seizing his only chance
to try his English. There was something so cheerful and guileless about
him with his language book and his big grin that I felt an instant warm
bond between us.

Apparently he was ordered away by someone I couldn't see. He
waved while looking for a word, found it and yelled, "Gude by!"

As he turned to go I remembered my coffee and yelled, "Hey, wait!"
(in English). He paused. He was nearly two stories above me and at an
angle. If it fell short it would go into the drink. I wound up and flung
it hard. It arced upwards end over end and he caught it at chest level.

He made a triumphant gesture and two other sailors who had appeared on a higher deck applauded. It apparently would be their only
souvenir of New Orleans.

Now they were all called to duty of some kind. The sailor and I waved
again and I turned back to the Quarter, full of good fellowship and the
ironic, trite thought that his country and mine had missiles pointed at
each other.

Jackson Square, hard by the river, is another favorite haunt of mine.
I'm fond of the statue of Andrew Jackson, holding his hat aloft and
rearing back—i.e., mounted on a horse that is rearing on its hind legs
(obviously not its *side* legs). Old Hickory is usually populated with
pigeons, one of them atop his head, which reduces his dignity considerably. The impression is that he has just done a magic trick and removed
his hat to reveal a pigeon on his head.

Looming over the square is the near-white facade of St. Louis Cathedral, which is washed with subtly changing pastel colors as the light alters from morning through dusk. Watching this shifting spectrum can be a rewarding day's occupation.

Next to the cathedral is the Cabildo, the seat of the provincial government during the Spanish occupation of the city. My wife remembers a childhood visit to it when it was still cobwebby and dungeony and Edgar Allan Poe–like, before it was cleaned up and restored.

She and a friend held hands and ventured through creaky doors and down black stairwells seemingly unexplored since the place was a Spanish fort, until a rat turned them back. I envy her that escapade.

Thanks to an architect friend, I did get to see the defunct New Orleans Mint a few blocks away, a vast, brooding structure where millions of U.S. silver dollars were once struck and in front of which a public hangings once took place. From a bright sunny day I stepped into a gloomy world of shadows and sudden chills and rusty old gates that clanged reverberatingly and inexplicable piles of dusty antique furniture: rocking chairs, harpsichords, wicker cradles.

I've been back since the mint was replastered and freshened up with new paint that is too bright but will soften quickly in that climate, and the restorers are to be commended for having saved the old place from becoming a site for condominiums.

But I saw it best before, of course, and wish it could have stayed that way. I even find myself thinking the heretical thought of a friend who loves Venice so much that her response to the preservation efforts is, "Let it sink." The idea being that the city's beauty is incompatible with newness and can't be dragged into modern times. I tend to feel the same way about the Old Mint, about the Quarter, about all of the New Orleans that I love: rather than corrupt and adulterate it, let it go, peaceful and unaltered.

* * *

I cherish everything that is *old* about New Orleans and resent the new. I actually avert my eyes to avoid seeing certain things, like some of the cheesy motels the city fathers have allowed in the Quarter. Any change in the Quarter I first knew, whether the ugly handiwork of "developers" or the depredations of nature, I feel as an intrusion on my own flesh.

This intense and intimate attachment once led me to raise a very big and public stink in New Orleans, one of the biggest I've ever been involved in.

While making one of our fairly regular visits several years ago, my wife and I kept stumbling across appalling evidence of a colossally misguided program by then mayor Moon Landrieu to spruce up the place. He seemed to be trying to give the Quarter at best the synthetic flavor of Williamsburg, or at worst the prissy boutique atmosphere of San Francisco's Ghirardelli Square, which I heard he had just seen and been entranced with.

First there was the renovation of the French Market. The great open-air sheds of this venerable institution offer a feast for all five senses, with their jumbled stalls of colorful fruits and vegetables and the colorful people who sell them, like the old black man who appears on Saturdays chanting. "Hot sweet potato pie, hot sweet potato pie . . ." I had always enjoyed sitting there in the mornings over chicory coffee and hot, fresh beignets, which are sort of square doughnuts with an indescribable and induplicable flavor.

But Mayor Landrieu had "improved" one end of it, an end that now featured wretched candle shops and boutiques and places who names ended with ". . . 'n' Stuff."

Then one of the leading local *boîtes,* the Cafe du Monde, had its long-familiar green awning removed and its indoor coffee room refurbished. Jackson Square was newly flagstoned and bedecked with the ever-popular crepe myrtle trees in characterless concrete tubs; and the mayor announced a ghastly scheme to install a sound-and-light show in the square and charge admission.

Beyond the Quarter's boundaries, a perfect emblem of what was happening in the city was the virtually simultaneous opening of that

Brobdingnagian concrete igloo, the Superdome, and the demolition of the venerable St. Charles Hotel.

My wife and I were hardly the first to feel outraged by this dismal trend. Among others, Calvin Trillin of The New Yorker and Ada Louise Huxtable of the New York *Times* had raised the alarm about the erosion of New Orleans' architectural past. But they were writing for a generally national audience, detached and objective. I wanted to stir up the hometown folks. So one day I had lunch at a Quarter hangout called Mena's Palace with Jim Amoss, a young reporter for the New Orleans *States-Item.*

"Any town that would put up the Dome and the Marriott and take down the St. Charles Hotel deserves what it gets," I told him.

As for the argument that the Quarter was being restored in the spirit of Williamsburg, I went on (making sure that Jim was writing all this down), "The greatest thing New Orleans has to offer is a step into the past, not a cheesy replica of it.

"Doesn't Moon Landrieu feel a difference between sitting in the Napoleon House and the new Cafe du Monde? Or is it all the same to him? People who live here all the time maybe don't notice it, but it's heartbreaking each time you come back to this place and find something else gone.

"Don't they understand they're destroying an international landmark? It's like putting arms back on the Venus de Milo, like fixing up the Colosseum in Rome and staging phony gladiator events, or like wallpapering the Grand Canyon and putting up a patio and serving dinosaur burgers."

All this and more duly appeared in the *States-Item* and touched off a furor. I heard from preservationists and concerned citizens. I was urged to do a TV show on the subject. One man wrote suggesting that I move to New Orleans and run for mayor. I was also labeled a Yankee busybody and exhorted to put my money where my mouth was. And predictably, I was accused by a local columnist of merely making a play for personal publicity.

But the most vehement reaction came from Moon Landrieu himself. At his next press conference he was steaming about my remarks. "I suppose Mr. Cavett on his rare visits here finds it interesting to come gaze upon a certain historical decadence and would like us to preserve that for his personal use," Mr. Mayor said to the assembled reporters. "Well, I don't intend to do that."

He complained that I had been allowed to get away with cheap shots at the city, that Jim Amoss had failed to grill me with the kind of tough questions with which the City Hall reporters grilled him all the time —the sort of paranoid semi-sequitur that politicians are so adept at.

Had he been the reporter, Landrieu said, "I would have asked Mr. Cavett if he ever stayed in the Sheraton Charles Hotel in all the times he visited this city. Did he ever stay as a paying guest, not as a freebie?

"I would have asked him how he would have saved the St. Charles Hotel, whose passing I also lament. Would the city have bought it if he were mayor? Would he simply have passed a law that the man who owned it must save it and operate it even at a loss?

"I would have asked Mr. Cavett if he had been behind the French Market and seen the trash and the stench and the dirt and the filth that existed between the floodwall and the buildings. I think that is a magnificent area today.

"I would have asked him what is wrong with Williamsburg, which before they restored it in a museum kind of setting was a completely destroyed community."

When, the mayor wanted to know, had I become an expert on urban affairs?

There are few things I enjoy more than a brisk battle of words in public. Since the mayor was standing his ground and spiritedly countering my charges, and since the brouhaha was now being picked up by newspapers around the country, I decided it was time to get off my best salvo. I wrote a letter to the editor of the *States-Item*.

I had no idea my remarks about your city would cause
such a flap locally and get picked up by the national press

[I began, a trifle disingenuously]. I hear the mayor is sore as a crab. And since so many of your citizens have written to me, perhaps you will permit me to reply at some length.

First, I did not mean to hurt Mayor Landrieu's feelings. I had been told that he is sensitive to criticism (who isn't?) and although he has a national reputation as an enlightened mayor, in this case I think he has a lot to be sensitive about.

Obviously, he hears a chorus of praise for what he has been doing with (and to) New Orleans. A mayor's office is an insular place—like the White House—where one is told by one's aides what one wants to hear. He may be genuinely unaware that there is another chorus to be heard, saying, "Isn't it a tragedy what is happening to this place?"

The night before I left there, I stood outside the "renovated" room of the Cafe du Monde, and a well dressed but forlorn looking man said to me, "Isn't it a shame? . . . I brought a dozen boys from Kansas City to see this place I'd been raving about and had loved so much, and when they saw *this* they thought I was crazy. They thought they were back in Kansas City."

I guess that little anecdote says it all. (Cross my heart, I didn't invent it.) A depressed waiter came out and said to a group of melancholy fans of the old cafe, "How do you like our new Burger King room?"

If the mayor misses the point of this, I suppose there is no use going on, but politeness dictates that I respond to at least *some* of the questions he indignantly chided a reporter for not asking me.

No, I never stayed at the Sheraton Charles. The mayor's got me there. Now perhaps he will reveal what this has to do with anything. If I had, would he have it put back up? (He complains that he never escapes tough questions, but since no one asked him to explain the relevance of this, I guess the boys were going easy on him for a change.) I have never stayed at the Parthenon either, but I'm glad the Greeks have managed to preserve it nonetheless.

Charity prevents me from commenting on his speculations that if I did stay there, it was probably "a freebie." A mayor accusing a *citizen* of payoffs? I assume that it was hot in the press room that day. (A Xerox of my New Orleans hotel bills will be forwarded to his honor on request.)

No, I am not sorry that the stench and filth behind the French Market are gone. But, as someone pointed out in your letter columns . . . isn't that the business of the sanitation department, rather than the concrete pourers mayors love so much?

Was the only alternative to filth a concrete fountain and plaza whose style could only be described as Late Hollywood Mortuary, circa 1974? (I was told the much-loved awning of the Cafe du Monde had to come down because it was historically inaccurate. How many electric-lighted concrete fountains were there in the 18th and 19th centuries?)

The mayor scores one in asking if I am an urban expert. I confess I am not, and all those who assumed I was were wrong. And I genuinely sympathize with him that there may have been just no way to save the hotel if the owners didn't want to. I am encouraged to hear he laments its passing. . . .

The mayor defends Williamsburg as if I had insulted the flag. For his information, there is a school of thought that views Williamsburg's restored cuteness as on a par with Disneyland more than with history. But I have never stayed there, so I make no further comment.

My only hope for the "improvement" of Jackson Square that is apparently irreversibly underway is that, if we are lucky, perhaps it will *not* resemble the plans displayed prominently near the work site . . . [They] must have Old Hickory himself doing 78 rpm in his grave.

When I tell people that a sound-and-light show has been seriously proposed for Jackson Square, they laugh and tell me I am hallucinating. I hear the mayor has pronounced this a dandy money making scheme. I hadn't realized that the *raison d'être* of Jackson Square is to hustle tourist bucks, but it explains much. The thought of the haunting beauty of that square at night being violated by the installation of that noisy, vulgar tourist gimmick dreamed up by the French to turn a buck on their surplus castles is sick-making.

I assume anyone not actually bedridden or jake-legged will make the necessary trek to City Hall or wherever to protest this lunacy. . . .

Turning the square into a hockey rink would make money even quicker and would provide an excuse to pour even more concrete. Or the square could be turned into a drive-in, with movies projected onto the white walls of the cathedral. No X-rated films, of course; no one wants to be accused of bad taste.

But enough. The point is not to trade insults, nor is it Landrieu's feelings or my urban expertise. The point is that a great historic city of the South, unique in all the world, is rapidly being turned into a combination of downtown Cleveland and the plastic, boutique atmosphere of San Francisco's Ghirardelli Square. What it *had* is so vastly superior to both. It is like trading Paris for Pittsburgh.

Any city administration concerned with tourist dollars should know there is a growing army of potential tourists who love(d) New Orleans, and who are given pause by what made a resident say to me on my last trip: "I'm surprised there's still enough left of this place to attract you here."

Politicians care about their place in history. If I were mayor of your wonderful city, I would toss in my sleep at the thought of being remembered as the man who presided over trading the romantic grandeur of a great city of the South for the very things people come here to get away from.

Aux armes, citoyens!

Reading this letter over today I'm struck by how relevant these issues are in cities all over the country and in Europe. They must be relevant even in Cleveland and Pittsburgh, to which I guess I owe an apology. Fortunately, they're *slightly* less urgent in New Orleans today than when I wrote the letter. Not that any of the "improvements" have been undone, and apparently nothing can stop the fungus-like spread of garish fast food shops and motels. But at least the transformation of Jackson Square got toned down and the sound-and-light scheme permanently shelved.

Whether my sounding off had a direct influence on this, or even an indirect one by giving a boost to local preservationists and helping them to be more effective, I can't say. But sometimes, when I'm walking through the square nowadays and I'm sure no one is looking, I do allow myself a quick, conspiratorial wink at the statue of Andy Jackson.

*   *   *

One of the only drawbacks to seeing *A Streetcar Named Desire* in the theater is that you don't get to read this haunting passage from its stage directions:

> The section is poor but, unlike corresponding sections in other American cities, it has a raffish charm . . . The sky that shows around the dim white building is a peculiarly tender blue, almost a turquoise, which invests the scene with a kind of lyricism and gracefully attenuates the atmosphere of decay. You can almost feel the warm breath of the brown river beyond the river warehouses with their faint redolences of bananas and coffee. A corresponding air is evoked by the music of Negro entertainers at a barroom around the corner. In this part of New Orleans you are practically always just around the corner, or a few doors down the street, from a tinny piano being played with the infatuated fluency of brown fingers.

Many writers have lived, and do live, in New Orleans, but for me Tennessee Williams was the true poet of the place, and especially of the Quarter. Not only did he capture its atmosphere of squalid glamor in his work, but Tennessee himself seemed its perfect inhabitant— gifted, colorful, moody, with a kind of mellow decadence about him.

He roomed in the Quarter as a hungry young writer, and in his later years he kept one of his two houses there (the other was in Key West). It was as close to being a home to him as any place. Nobody made much fuss over him there and that was the way he liked it. He could subside into its languid rhythms and find a haven from his own celebrity, not to say notoriety.

One of the few times he allowed his privacy in the Quarter to be invaded was when he good-naturedly agreed to do a ninety-minute late-night TV show with me on location there. It was a spur-of-the-moment scheme. My wife and I had been in town on vacation, and while having dinner with Tennessee had suddenly conceived of a show built around the theme of Tennessee Williams' New Orleans. The whole structure was sketched out by the three of us between the crawfish bisque and the pecan pie.

Within forty-eight hours my production staff had flown down from New York, a film crew had been hired, local technicians had been rounded up and electrical cable had been laid at one or two of the locations we planned to use.

Among various interview segments, we planned to intersperse a film of Tennessee and me riding around in one of the horse-drawn tourist carriages that clatter through the Quarter's streets. The idea was that I would be the outsider getting a kind of behind-the-scenes insider's view of the place. And what better guide could I have than Mr. French Quarter himself, pointing out places of interest, relating little-known bits of lore and giving mini-histories of locales along the way? A touch of voodoo folklore here, a bit of historic scandal there, all adding up to a unique glimpse through the eyes of the best cicerone obtainable.

My first hint that there was an unsuspected fallacy in this ideal notion came shortly after we got underway. I asked Tennessee what street we were on. (There aren't many.) He wasn't sure.

We passed an old house that is on every tourist map of the Quarter. A grisly history is attached to it, concerning the discovery in the attic of the bodies of tortured slaves, the arrival of the authorities to investigate and the escape of the doubtless insane occupant, who leaped into a carriage and disappeared up the River Road. It is a familiar tale to anyone who knows anything about the area, and since I felt presumptuous telling it myself I asked Tennessee if he had any historic details to add to my version.

His surprising answer was that he had nothing to add, having never heard the story.

As we approached the brooding, ghostly old New Orleans Mint, I described having seen the interior in its pre-restored state, when it would have made a splendid setting for a horror movie. I then suggested that Tennessee tell the story of the man who was hanged from one of the trees out front during the last century.

He said he would be glad to tell it if he knew it, but that somehow the story had escaped him. He added, "I always wondered just what that old building was."

After one or two more similar episodes in which he confessed to hearing a rather well-known piece of local color for the first time, he allowed as how this was quite an educational trip for him. He told me how happy he was to be picking up these bits of information.

I began to find it increasingly funny that I was informing him of things I had assumed *he* would be telling *me.* It was rather like exploring London with Charles Dickens and having him ask me the name of the big clock striking in the tower over Parliament. Was this a wicked game of Tennessee's? Was the man beside me, in fact, the real Tennessee—or a lookalike prankster?

The answer, I realized later, was quite simple. Although Tennessee's feeling for the Quarter was unparalleled, it was visceral and empathetic, not "worked up." He knew all that he needed to know about it at something below a conscious level, and had simply never bothered with the guidebooks and their exportable souvenirs of its history.

It was the same with his writing, as Gore Vidal and others have pointed out. He had—intermittently, anyway—the perceptions and instincts of genius, as well as an almost mystical capacity to get inside the thoughts and feelings of his characters. But he was not very good at talking about all this. He had no conscious theory of playwrighting, and very little literary or intellectual shoptalk of any kind. Someone who met him without knowing his work might easily underestimate his gifts.

The one local attraction he had no trouble identifying left him with little to say about it for this very reason. We pulled up in front of the famous streetcar with the destination sign "Desire." That line had long since been discontinued, but the one streetcar had been put on permanent exhibit in a public square.

"Well, there it is," I said.

"Yes. The last one," Tennessee said. There was a goodly pause, during which the rich flood of expected reminiscence about the old streetcars or the romantic neighborhood names or the play whose title one of them had inspired did not come.

Finally I asked, "Does it embarrass you, having that thing sitting out in public like that?"

"Oh, Dick," he said, chortling, "I don't think anything could embarrass me anymore."

That was all right. I was embarrassed enough for both of us.

There was something ludicrous about this whole tour anyway, quite apart from the assumption that my companion would be a master guide. Remember that we were filming as we went along. The viewers at home would see only Tennessee and me, lounging in our summer whites in the back of an open carriage. But people on the street saw what looked like the flight of a band of eccentric refugees, or some amateur acrobatic stunt in progress.

A few feet in front of Tennessee and me, a jumble of humanity was piled precariously on the swaying carriage. There were, in addition to a camera, recording equipment, wires and microphones, a cameraman, a sound engineer, a director and—hanging off the sides so that they were occasionally goosed by the rear-view mirrors of parked cars along the narrow streets—a producer and an associate producer.

If the horse, which was fortunately wearing blinders, had been able to turn and see what it was attached to, it would have jumped six feet straight up and expired on the spot.

The ride ended in a near-tie between farce and tragedy. The carriage had a sort of fixed pedal that you put your foot on in either stepping down out of it or hoisting yourself up into it. When we deposited Tennessee at his house, he put his foot on the pedal without holding on to anything, then stepped again for the curb. His weight left the pedal at what appeared to be one-thousandth of a second before the horse, stung by a bee perhaps, jerked forward violently.

Had he still been on the pedal he would have been flipped onto his head on the pavement. Since he was blind in one eye, however, he never saw the carriage move. The effect was like a silent movie in which a safe lands with a crash behind a deaf man who remains blissfully unaware.

The interview segments of the show went much better, especially the one at his house, which I found intriguing and at times moving.

We taped a portion out back beside his swimming pool, which was shadowed by huge overhanging willow trees. Tennessee swam religiously every day. Whenever he traveled he had to hunt up a pool the way a junkie locates a source. He declined to demonstrate for us on camera, but on other occasions I did join him for a dip. He cut the water like a competitor, lap after lap, the only faintly comic aspect being his bathing cap, one of those squarish rubber caps with peaked corners that men wore decades ago.

Despite the physical and psychic rigors of his often tormented life —the nightmarish emotional breakdown, the psychological pressure of not living up to his early masterpieces—perhaps it was the swimming that kept him looking a good fifteen years younger than he was. Had it not been for that fatal plastic bottle cap, who knows? He might have lived past the century mark.

While the crew set up for the next shot, I watched Tennessee sit in front of a blaring TV set and slug down several vodkas, and I reflected that, with or without the swimming, he must have had the physical constitution of an ox to withstand all the booze and pills he ingested on top of everything else.

His left hand drummed idly on a table. That is the hand, I thought, that typed on a sheet of blank paper the words *A Streetcar Named Desire*, or at least that is the hand that typed all but three of the letters. This was followed by the thought that the hand was flesh and bone and the play was an airy nothing, but the hand would perish and the play would live.

This was followed by the thought that I was starving and wished I had some oysters from Felix's Oyster Bar. 'Twas ever thus when I ventured upon profundity.

Tennessee had that too—a saving streak of humor and a sense of the absurd. There is more of it in his plays than is usually recognized, and in private it bubbled out of him constantly.

My wife and I ran into him once in the San Juan airport, where he confessed, unnecessarily, that he had been whiling away the time between planes with about five margaritas. Sitting down with us in the waiting lounge, he lowered himself first onto the arm of the chair, realigned himself, then sank into the chair proper, spilling only a drop or two of number six.

As his young male traveling companion excused himself to check on something and strode crisply and efficiently from the room, Tennessee gestured after him with his glass and said with rheumy-eyed sadness, "Look at that poor young man—a hopeless alcoholic."

Time and again during our interview he punctured some solemn moment with a joke, followed by the *hyuk-hyuk-hyuk* of his wonderful throaty chuckle. Our taping had moved into his front room, which contained an old-fashioned brass bed and a small, neat desk with a typewriter and a pile of manuscript pages. In keeping with his non-literary surface, there was little in the room other than the typewriter to indicate a writer's presence. Books were sparse, and the only thing on his night table was a copy of Gentlemen's Quarterly.

It was his writer's sanctum, though. He wrote there every morning, with the somnolent streets and buildings of the Quarter catching the early morning sunlight outside his window.

He told me he wrote for the same reason other people eat and breathe: if he stopped he would die. I asked whether, locked in a cell without food or water but left with a typewriter, he thought he would survive. "I know I would," he said. Then, characteristically, he broke into a grin and added, "I might have to cheat a little and eat some of the typing paper."

Across the street from his house was a little restaurant where he ate most of his meals. As a writer, he said, he was accustomed to loneliness, and had learned to do just about everything in life on his own except for eating. He felt so strongly about this that when in a strange town and seated alone in a restaurant, he would ask the nearest single person to join him.

He said, "If I had to choose, and thank heavens I don't, between sleeping alone for the rest of my life and eating alone, I would have to opt for the former. So now you know, Dick. I am totally and indisputably crazy." Again, the infectious chuckle.

After Tennessee died, I got out a cassette of that show we did in New Orleans and replayed it on my tape machine. It was comforting to see him back in the Quarter, where he seemed to belong, and to hear him laugh once more.

I had to agree with Elia Kazan, who had brilliantly directed so many of Tennessee's plays, when I ran into him at the theater a few days later and he complained that the obituaries were excessively gloomy. "I think they're all wrong about Tennessee," Kazan said. "I don't think he had an unhappy life at all. All that talent—wouldn't it be wonderful to have all that talent? And to laugh as much as he did?"

* * *

For many people New Orleans is synonymous with Mardi Gras. Whether that is a good thing or a bad is the question.

It always looks like fun on film or TV, with the festive floats and merry revelers, the zany and sexy costumes and the promise of naughtiness and sin. Some of the getups look as if they were constructed by MGM's wardrobe department. Then there are the simpler statements, like the sailor in immaculate whites with a perfect square cut away netherwards to reveal his bare hindquarters.

The conflicting opinions of Carnival (as the locals call it, since Mardi obviously refers only to Tuesday) are mystifying. Some Orleanians observe the annual rite by pointedly getting out of town; others can't wait for it. The former say it's mostly grotesque and sleazy, and about as much fun as a day trip through an abattoir. Many of the latter view it as a heartwarming festival of love and sweetness and colorful social events with only a fringe element of the tawdry.

A local lady of the evening said to me, "I recommend it. Believe me, there's sumpn' out there on the street for everybody—and I mean *everybody*. Live out your fantasy!"

Other adherents extol it as a three-day escape from reality into never-never land, or because "you can stay drunk for three days and only remember getting laid standing up in a doorway." I suppose there is something to be said for an event in which a respected businessman can prance down the street dressed only in a diaper and incur no shame or ill consequences professionally or socially. Can you imagine that in New York, or Omaha, or San Diego?

I recall that in eighth grade a friend of mine had somehow attended the festivities, and he reported seeing a couple screw on a balcony in the French Quarter while an appreciative crowd of onlookers applauded the finer points of virtuosity. Never having, myself, screwed or seen anyone do so (I'm not sure I even believed anyone ever did), I pondered this for days. My friend *saw* that sight, and presumably had I been standing beside him I would have too. Awesome.

A compromise view on Mardi Gras is that you should go once, as with Las Vegas, because you won't believe it. I have only seen part of it, and I only partially believed it.

Certainly no one with half a mind goes *for* the final night, but I happened to be passing through town and despite a fine, misty rain decided to gather a few images and impressions.

My first hint of anything unusual was glimpsing from my cab a man with a briefcase walking along the street with his girlfriend, holding a newspaper up to shield them from the rain. She looked normal, but he was wearing a maroon jumpsuit with a jockstrap on the *out*side.

In the French Quarter my cab had to slow down when it encountered some listlessly surging semi-throngs, but they could have been
college kids milling about with beer cans on the night of a frat party
except for the occasional feathered wand, wilted Day-Glo wig or fantastic face paint.

On foot I checked out Bourbon Street. Things were swinging along
sloppily. The great sport seemed to be to tempt the folks on the
simulated iron balconies of a motel to throw down the strings of
worthless glass beads that are the prized souvenirs of Mardi Gras.

An overweight chap—bloated would be more accurate—with his
wet Levi jacket suit unbuttoned to reveal a white, flaccid belly was
competing with a band of similarly elegant worthies for necklaces
dangled tantalizingly by two college girls from a third floor balcony.
Having failed to get the ersatz bijoux by entertaining the girls with a
chorus of superloud belches, they decided, to a man, to lower their
trousers and moon the damsels, which unappealing array produced the
desired results. Down came the frippery.

Two of the flung necklaces landed in the gutter at the feet of a
stoned teenage female junkie, who bent down and fished the tangled
strands from the two inches of flowing God-knows-what they had
splashed into and held one in her mouth while untangling the other.

I decided to skip dinner.

A commotion burst out behind me. I turned in time to see two
mounted policemen, off their horses, swinging vehemently and wildly
at a sort of aged hippie type who was saying, "I'm sorry, I'm sorry."
They hustled him with excessive zeal behind some barricades and
frisked him for weapons.

When they became aware that they were being observed, one of the
cops turned to me and said with incongruous politeness, "Please don't
stand here."

"Afraid I'll frighten your horses?" I asked angrily.

"Yes, that's right," he said with the same glazed, chilly politeness.

As I was leaving, a third cop, not having seen what the guy had done
any more than I had, leaped into the fray to land a few blows on the

human punching bag before they turned him loose.

I recalled my cab driver, an old black man, saying on the way in from the airport, "I don't care for Carnival any more. Any more seems like the fun is not what it was. I saw some po-lice beat a fella—a white fella —the other day for no reason I could see. Just take their clubs and jam 'em in his stomach like to kill him. There's no call for that."

Mardi Grim. This had to be the true dregs of the occasion. I started walking toward Jackson Square.

The gutters were ankle deep with plastic beer cups, confetti, sodden streamers and broken glass. The rain was coming down harder. I went by a macho male in jeans and T-shirt who was comforting his pallid young beau on a wet stoop; both looked forlorn.

A couple of chaps in animated conversation passed me going in the opposite direction. Just as they drew opposite me, one of them attempted a broad gesture and his beer cup slipped from his grasp, spanned the six feet between us and got me on the left shoulder, dousing my left side with suds. Anywhere else I would've been furious, but they were so totally amused and apologetic that I enjoyed it too.

Jackson Square was deserted and nearly *knee*-deep in refuse. The cathedral loomed up shadowy and spooky, and I got a slight *frisson*. I had to whistle as I made my way past ominous dark doorways in Pirate's Alley back to where the crowds were.

My favorite hangout, the Napoleon House, was sensibly closed up tight with the chairs stashed on top of the tables.

For a while I watched the colorful comings and goings from the entranceway to a corner bar. Next to me stood a very pretty black lady of the evening wearing a black dress and a turban formed from a long white fur piece that also hung down her front. Her high-heeled shoes were damp and she was chilled but on duty.

Making conversation, I told her she was very pretty. She said she was a teacher in a nearby town and hoped she wouldn't be recognized. Her ambition was to enter the Miss America contest, she told me, but as a teacher she didn't have the money for all the necessary expenses.

Just then a passerby said to his girlfriend, "Now there's a guy dressed as a gal."

"I am *not* a guy," my new friend yelled after them.

A handsome black wearing an Army camouflage suit and smoking a giant bejeweled cigar came up and engaged her in some mildly amusing repartee, ending with, "Honey, have you and I ever slept together?"

"I doubt it, baby," she replied. "I never forget my *little* tricks."

Feigning pained insult, he mock-staggered away.

My mind was still on the passerby. "Why did that man think you were a guy?" I asked.

"What do you mean? I *am* a guy." She hadn't recognized me, and now took it that she had a hopeless bumpkin on her hands. She quickly guessed the source of some of my confusion, explaining, "I thought you realized I was talking about Miss Gay America."

I must have still looked perplexed, for she said, "Here—gimme your hand," and shamelessly placed it on her crotch, moving it around so that I could get an idea of how things were arranged.

She was a guy.

Although it *was* the Wicked City, I blushed slightly, and to cover my embarrassment I said, "Do I owe you anything for that?"

I felt like I was fourteen (i.e., fourteen in *my* day—about seven by today's standards) and was being told to run along and come back when my beard started growing. She excused herself to pursue a live one.

By now it was about two A.M. I wandered by Mallusco's, a notorious lowlife bar, and if anything I detoured slightly around the entrance as I passed under the hanging wooden sign with the carved letters. I was remembering something my wife's Mississippi friend Polly said about the place. She recalled that she had gone there once during a youthful night of pub crawling.

"Polly!" my wife said to her. "You've been inside Mallusco's? I know *men* who are afraid to go in there."

"I know," Polly said. "It was after a debutante party and we decided to see *everything*. If Mama knew I'd been in Mallusco's she would disinherit me."

"Did you see anything unusual?"

"I guess you could call it unusual."

"What?"

"A man screwed a dog."

I came upon a bunch of bedraggled singles standing under the dripping awning of a gay bar. They looked like wet birds under an eave. They took no particular notice of a young fellow who tripped by in a white toga, green glitter eye makeup and gold sandals, arms hugged across his chest, shivering against the chill air.

In my head I either composed or partially recalled some line like, "It is late and we are all cold and wet and have not yet made a liaison for the night."

I was curious to see what was going on inside the bar. Although it was nearly the hue of pitch in there, I kept my dark glasses on, and my stocking cap too. I had bought a Lone Ranger–style mask, but it had battery-powered blinking lights and I didn't have the guts to wear it.

The crowd included people of both sexes (I assume both; apparently I am not a reliable witness) squeezing out the last drops of strenuous fun.

Atop the rectangular bar a languid young man, painfully pale, was bopping to the music, naked except for what I think is called a "posing pouch," a sort of G-string two sizes too small. Occasionally an admirer would reach up and insert a bill into this micro-jock, for which he would be blown (or given) a kiss. Then the dancer, whose mind was miles away (if in fact in existence), would undulate to another part of the bar, hoping to add more protruding bills to his minimal habillement.

Two men standing next to me, who looked like they might be Con Edison hardhat types in New York City, were kissing and fondling passionately. Suddenly one of them paid the bill and left, and I realized they had just met.

The other one sidled over to me and said, in a voice a bit light for his build, "Having a nice time?"

"Yes. And no, I don't have a match."

"That's okay. I just hoped you were having fun," he said with harmless-seeming friendliness, leaving me ashamed of my curtness as he moved onto the dance floor.

Back out on the street, the last outlandish human flotsam was drifting homeward. I saw a woman in scanty black panties and bra, brandishing a long bullwhip. Two men were necking under a streetlight and a municipal streetcleaner picked up around them without a glance or nasty remark.

I heard someone say, "Aren't you sorry it's nearly over?" My feet were wet and I was chilled and suddenly the question seemed about as appropriate as if someone clinging to a life raft had said it as help arrived. I had an overwhelming urge to get between clean crisp sheets and read Donne's sermons.

Then, like a parting gift, what was to become my favorite overheard fragment of Mardi Gras conversation floated across the wet pavement from two men who were strolling together.

". . . and he won the Gay Rights Float costume award for his butterfly costume."

"Who did?"

"My psychiatrist."

As I headed for my hotel, I wondered what Dr. Freud would think of a disciple who spent his off-hours sewing sequins and spangles on his butterfly suit.

I decided if I ever gave Mardi Gras another chance it would at least be in daylight.

*   *   *

Not even Mardi Gras, however, ranks as my most bizarre experience in New Orleans. That dubious distinction belongs to an evening I spent at the Post Office in the Quarter. I don't mean the government agency, but a nightclub of the same name.

I'll try to bring it all into focus, or perhaps I should say into a still position on the kaleidoscope.

I think it all began, as so many adventures begin in the Quarter, with a chance meeting on a street corner. Ruby was her name.

Ruby had large breasts clearly visible through a tight T-shirt, black fingernail polish, lush black hair and dark flashing eyes befitting her surname, Rodriquez. Ruby recognized me from TV, pronounced me "much cuter in person" and asked for my autograph.

"What do you do, Ruby?"

"Me? I'm just a queen."

Even in New Orleans I retain some capacity to be surprised. Could this creature, like my friend outside the bar at Mardi Gras, be a transvestite, a drag queen? "You mean . . . you mean those aren't real?" I asked, glancing poitrine-wards.

Ruby's accented pronunciation of "you" came out "djou." "Djou like my breasts? They preteee? Djou feel my breasts." She took my hand. "See? Not hard like silicone. They make from salt water. Djou see? Feel nice like real."

She was right. (I realize I should say *he* was right, but for all so-called practical purposes I still felt I was talking to a woman.) She explained earnestly that the salt water technique was the latest thing and a vast improvement on silicone, which was now widely outlawed because of its tendency to wander and cause other health problems.

Grotesque images occurred to me, and I wondered aloud if silicone's tendency to migrate was gradual or if one awoke one morning to find a breast in the middle of one's back or forehead. Ruby found this hilarious.

She said she had worked hard and saved to be able to afford her twin alterations, and that numerous "johns" had unwittingly contributed to the cause. She hoped to have enough within a few months to complete her gender transformation from Rudy, her given name, to a true, new Ruby.

One obstacle was that The Johns Hopkins Medical Center was phasing out its sex-change practice and would no longer be performing several thousand such surgical procedures annually. That was where she and several of her friends had hoped to go.

As we chatted on, she let drop that she had been married for a time to a sailor who departed one day after a severe quarrel. I asked if it was over her having been a man.

"Oh, no. He never found out about that."

I reeled a bit, wondering how the average man would handle such a discovery. Ruby assured me that there are "plenty men not know what they are married to."

Before I could pursue that, she was seized with an idea. The Quarter's queens performed a show on Saturday nights at the Post Office, which was also slyly known as the Male Box (get it?).

"Djou bring your wife and friends to our show?"

Alas, we would be leaving town Saturday afternoon. Undeterred, Ruby offered to get all the queens to put on a special show Friday night just for us. I demurred, but Ruby was adamant and a few hours later, as we had discussed, left a note at my hotel that it was all set.

Later that same day I stopped in at a small corner grocery near the hotel. The man behind the cash register, with whom I'd struck up a casual acquaintance, told me he had heard via the grapevine about the special midnight matinee on Friday. He said that he was actually a plainclothes cop, and since the Post Office was a rough place he and his wife would accompany us.

I am not making this up. He didn't ask if we would like some company, he simply announced that they were coming along. Although he showed me some identification he became evasive when I began asking questions. Like why he knew all the queens, and why he worked in a grocery. I decided he was gathering drug information but didn't press him further.

Since we were making a party of it, my wife and I decided to recruit further moral support from a Quarter-dwelling friend called simply Beazer, a part of his full real name. You would cast Beazer as a handsome, affable con man who is immediately liked and comfortable anywhere and who seems to have a variety of professions, including, in

Beazer's case, those of antique dealer, part-time assistant surgeon and organist in a church.

The Quarter abounds with such people leading mysteriously multiple lives, and it accommodates them so thoroughly that you wonder how or where they could live if it didn't exist. Sometimes they do none of the things they say they do, but some other equally odd combination of things. I know Beazer did at least the three I mentioned. Where but in New Orleans would you meet someone who when he wasn't playing organs was suturing them?

On Friday I saw my corner grocery man again. He warned me that I was in for a long and unforgettable experience, that every queen in the Quarter wanted to be in the special show for Dick Cavett and that I might want to take a nap in the afternoon to rest up for a demanding night.

I took his advice, after which I also went along with my wife's urging that we dress up nicely to acknowledge the honor we were receiving. We rendezvoused with Beazer and the plainclothesman and his wife, and our unlikely but well-attired quintet set off.

The Post Office was, as described, a dark and sinister looking joint in the part of the Quarter that the police advise tourists not to wander in. Before we went in, my cop friend urged us to stick close to him, to get against a wall if trouble broke out and to make sure that our guests-of-honor table put us in dorsal proximity to one. Throughout what followed, I noticed that he kept his eyes largely on the crowd.

There was a burst of applause as we stepped through the door. The bar area, towards the front, was jammed with every type of homosexual, from motorcycle to pansy. From the number of times I caught some variation of "Well, he came" in the crowd murmur, I gathered that there had been widespread anxiety that we would be reluctant or afraid to show.

Squeezing past the bar to a chorus of greetings and remarks like "Hey, he *is* cute," we made our way to the table of honor (yes, against the wall) at stage left.

Everyone was exceedingly concerned that we have a good time and order anything we wanted on the house. We were assured that Ginger Snap—a queen I had been told it was not wise for *anyone* to cross— had decreed that there would be good behavior tonight or her to reckon with. Ginger had passed some time in the slammer and was about as effeminate as the late William Bendix. I made it a point to pay homage to Ginger on the way in.

The lights soon went down. A begowned "mistress" of ceremonies mounted the small but pretty stage and announced that she had both good and solemn news. Her good news was about us, the guests of honor, and she took this opportunity to deliver another caution about good behavior.

The bad news had just flashed over the wires: Joan Crawford had died. There was a flurry of shocked comments and outcries around the room, then the emcee asked for a moment of silence. The evening's show was dedicated to Crawford's memory.

With that began about three hours of entertainment. I remember it as a night of singing but of course no one really sang; the queens silently mouthed the lyrics to recordings by Judy Garland, Barbra Streisand, Dionne Warwick, whomever they admired and could get themselves up most closely to resemble.

It was funny, sad, rousing and poignant by turns. The deep desire to be female, and the effort that had gone into attempting to be so, was touching. The results ranged from ludicrous to totally convincing. Some came close, but were betrayed by a prominent Adam's apple or hands and feet of a size rarely encountered in the fair sex.

Each queen had her particular fans—I almost said supporters—and in the main the lip-synching and mike-handling were so skillful that they appeared to be singing live. Many of them moved better in their gowns and high heels than all but a few women do. With the melancholy exceptions, the illusion that they were women was complete.

The most spectacular success hit me with what I can only describe as love-at-first-sight impact. This was Paulette, a bewitchingly attractive creature who had charisma, the emotional power of a major actress and, despite her nearly six-foot stature, total femininity without a trace of flounce or fagginess. She registered not male effeminacy but woman-liness. She was simply a lovely and appealing woman from head to toe.

I later got to know Paulette and found her to be intelligent as well. Unlike many of the queens she was not a hooker. The last job she had before I lost track of her was doing something at a computer terminal for a newspaper.

Once I was in New Orleans on a TV project and took Paulette along to dinner with the all-male crew. Playing it cool, I said nothing until two days later, when I asked if they saw anything unusual about her.

"You mean aside from her height?" one guy asked. Other comments ranged from how ladylike she was to more lecherous remarks.

"She's a man," I said casually. To this day they don't believe me.

The evening at the Post Office rolled on—four Streisands, three Garlands, a Liza Minnelli or two, a Diahann Carroll and many more. During the applause after one of the acts, a queen at a neighboring table leaned over and whispered in my ear with a kind of hopeful expectancy: "Honey, are you gay?"

The query was polite and without malice. In an effort neither to disappoint the sweet-faced questioner nor to take a superior tone, I heard myself say, "No, but I've thought about it." My answer startled me momentarily but seemed to please her.

There were occasional interludes between songs during which various queens came by our table. Their most frequent questions were whether I had met Judy Garland (yes), whether I was uncomfortable with them (no) and whether Robert Redford was gay (ditto). On the last point one of them said, "Honey, I want you to give him my phone number in case he ever changes his mind." (Shrieks of laughter.)

Then there was this overheard exchange between two black queens at a nearby table. ". . . and then a float came by with none other than Mr. Paul Newman, and when he saw me he raised his hand and stopped the float and leaned down and pulled me up to him and gave me a big long soul kiss and I like to melted and died right on the spot."

"Paul Newman kissed you?"

"I said I'm talkin' 'bout in my dream."

"Honey, 'til you get those teeth of yours fixed, Paul Newman ain't gonna kiss you even in a *dream.*"

I was amazed when I looked at my watch and saw that three hours had gone by. The show was (forgive me) dragging to a close. But the adventure was not over.

Following another thank you to us, the special guests, there was a grand finale with a chorus line, during which one of the stageful of beauties came down and took my hand to lead me and my party to the stage. My cop friend looked alarmed, as if this might unleash the pandemonium he had been fearing. My wife turned to Beazer and asked, "What are we going to *do?*"

Beazer replied, "Darlin', we're gonna *dance.*"

It was a chance for me to be inconsistent with my so-called image, and besides, there was obviously no choice. So I leaped onstage into center position amidst a garrison of high-kicking queens.

The cheering was deafening. But suddenly the rows of grinning faces out front lurched and swam. I experienced an odd surging shock in the crotch area and a sensation of sudden levitation. Had someone dropped acid in my drink?

I felt I was up among the colored lights on the ceiling. This was not entirely illusory. I was.

Overcome with exuberance at how democratically I had joined in, one of the prettiest of their majesties—a Dionne Warwick ringer, but with biceps—had stooped behind me, placed the back of her neck firmly in my crotch and straightened up suddenly, whooshing me aloft until my head was within an inch of the gaily colored Mazdas.

This touched off even louder screams of delight and approval. As I swayed precariously up there I pictured headlines saying, CAVETT SUFFERS FATAL FALL IN DRAG SHOW. But after a few moments I was lowered to terra somewhat infirma.

No sooner was I down than a queen who looked like Sophie Tucker gave my hoister a sharp smack across the face, followed by the dulcet words, "You stupid bitch, I oughta rip your tits off. You coulda broke his neck!"

The tension dissolved in the general din and euphoria, and the show was over.

My group and I payed our respects all around, and after edging through the throng with many waves and smiles to congratulate the performers in the dressing room, wended our ways home.

It was hard to sort out the jumble of the evening's impressions, which ranged from charming to lurid and included surprise, humor, puzzlement, socko entertainment, grotesquerie and, the longer I thought about it, a kind of pervading sadness.

The queens fascinated me as exotics, though I could also recognize what it was about them that a "normal" person would find repellent. But my strongest impression was of a certain bravery and pathos in them. Because of their sexual compulsions they led a perpetual sticks-and-stones existence, cut off from much of life, usually alienated from their families, constantly taunted and ridiculed, despised even by many homosexuals, always on the run.

There was no possible happy denouement to their scenarios, because time and age would inevitably rob them of their all-important looks, and then where would they go? Circumstances forced them to make their lives into what must have been a fatiguing act of defiance, yet underneath they seemed fragile and vulnerable.

I kept thinking of one performer in the dressing room, wide-eyed behind her garish stage makeup, demurely holding her dressing gown closed over her synthetic bosom. "This has been the biggest night of my life," she said to me with utter sincerity. "I wish I could write home about it but my parents throw away my letters without reading them."

*   *   *

Going to church had always bored me to idiocy. I agreed with Mark Twain that the other six days of the week were for recovering from the suffering of Sunday.

As a kid I was told that going to church was good for you, and I suppose maybe it was, in the same sense that not asking for a drink of water when you're thirsty, as German children were taught, allegedly builds character. Through discomfort we learn that life is not a bed of American Beauty blossoms.

The wearying sameness of the service—the processional and all the rest—had me fighting sleep from the first moments. Even though I was the grandson of a Welsh Baptist minister, the sermon always sounded like a replay of the week before. The only antidote I discovered was to see how many anagrams I could form out of the words *The Pilgrim Hymnal* and to mentally undress the handful of attractive young women in the choir, who despite the drab gray robes stood out with a lusty salience from their plain colleagues.

It was in New Orleans that I realized for the first time, in my thirties, what a memorable experience church could be.

I was out walking on another of those peaceful, sunny Sunday mornings when the remote streets of the Quarter are like a timeless Mediterranean village. No one was abroad except for a few people returning from God knows what.

I ventured across Esplanade, the live oak-lined boulevard that separates the Quarter from the largely black area known as the Fifth Ward. I found myself in a lovely neighborhood of cottagelike houses with the quiet of an abandoned but well-kept cemetery. As I passed a small corner building a door opened and for a moment I heard the rich sounds of gospel music.

A plump black woman by the door who had on an immaculate white outfit, like a nurse—the sort of woman with strong, warm hands and a soothing voice who you hope will take care of you when you are *in extremis*—wished me a good morning. I told her the music sounded wonderful, and she asked if I would like to come in.

I assumed she was joking. I gestured at my attire—faded blue T-shirt, white Levi's and sneakers.

She closed her eyes sweetly and said, "Everyone is welcome here."

It was clear that she didn't recognize me. The invitation was obviously sincere, and the music was soulful and appealing. "If you're sure it's okay," I said, "perhaps I could sit in the back."

"Certainly. We are happy to welcome you to our church."

Before I could go in, a cab pulled up and a man who looked like an ancient and dapper black tap dancer got out somewhat shakily, stumbled a bit on the curb, then righted himself to have a go at making a steady entrance. He was impeccable in light blue trousers, orange jacket, pink shirt, yellow tie and a maroon homburg, but he was redolent of the grape from Saturday night's indulgence and a bit abashed at his unsteadiness and tardiness.

The woman closed her eyes again and said, "Come in, Lenard."

He passed gingerly between the two of us, a wiry seventy if he was a day. "How you people?" he asked, tipping his homburg.

While Lenard took a seat on the aisle, the woman led me to the bench along the back wall as I had requested. I felt ludicrously conspicuous in my crude clothes and lily white skin amidst the sharply dressed all-black congregation. The choir was wailing out a spiritual and I was almost dazed by the highly charged emotional atmosphere in the room.

I squeezed into the only space on the bench, between two large women, and almost immediately I could feel their body heat through my thin Levi's. Wedged there, I began to get my bearings, but lost them again because of what happened next.

The woman to my left rose abruptly, threw her head back and let out a shriek. "Oh, sweet Jeeeeesus!" she screamed, and began to crumple.

I thought her outburst must have something to do with me. I expected all eyes to turn and someone to yell, "Who let that honky in here?" followed by a melee and the forcible ejection of the disrespectfully clad intruder.

Several women dressed in the same nurselike outfit as my greeter (they are called deaconesses, I learned later) hurried toward our bench. Oh God, I thought, they're coming for me. Instead they went to my neighbor's side and with accustomed skill, like a team of paramedics, lifted her up and fanned her and helped her into a side room.

In a few moments the same thing happened again down front, with the deaconesses moving in efficiently to administer smelling salts, patting of the forearms, fanning and support. I soon realized that this was hardly an unusual occurrence. In fact, a certain suspense was created by not knowing when the next eruption of ecstasy would take place.

Fascinated and still somewhat shaken, I realized that, far from being conspicuous, I might have been invisible. No one paid the slightest attention to my presence; everyone seemed caught up in the general enthusiasm and the music. As my pulse returned to normal I too began to feel the wondrous spirit and fervor of the proceedings.

The choir was a far cry from the gray-robed and gray-faced zombies of my youthful Sunday sufferings. White-robed, all female, they sang together with disciplined unity but each member moved in her own distinct way. Some women, generally the older ones, were almost immobile but somehow vibrant from within; others swayed and trucked like Tina Turner's backup singers.

Their soaring voices and undulations, their rocking and finger-snapping and interspersed "Hallelujah!"'s were marvelous to behold and infectious in their enthusiasm. My throat constricted and tears welled up, and I suppose only decades of Anglo-Saxon inhibition kept me from swaying and clapping and singing out as I wanted to.

A few minutes earlier I had been ambling along a placid neighborhood street with only an occasional bird song to break the silence, and now I was caught up in a throbbing and exhilarating communal experience like nothing I had ever felt or seen.

The minister began reading Bible verses. Instead of the monotonous droning response I associated with church, the congregation chimed in with "Yes, Lord"'s and "Bless his name!"'s, following some uncanny collective instinct for gradually building the rhythm and intensity to successive peaks of jubilation.

Next, things quieted down as the minister introduced a "speaker," another large woman in a flowered dress and wide hat with blossoms covering it. Her topic was the role of women in the church. She started in quietly, and the mood was that of a P.T.A. meeting.

As she went along, however, her voice rose and she became more animated. Her hat came loose and she laid it aside, then began to let rip. The congregation started punctuating her assertions with "Yes, sister!" Then at intervals she would suddenly subside to a calm and quiet level, until she started gathering steam all over again.

During one of the quiet spells she quoted St. Paul to the effect that women had no place in the running of a church. She took polite issue with this, apologizing for seeming less than reverent toward the saint but suggesting that he had erred in this instance.

But as she gathered conviction her tone became more annoyed and her vocabulary modulated noticeably toward down-home. The carefully enunciated phrase "the women" became "the womens" and eventually "de womens," as she reeled off all the things women should be praised for.

She was really revving up now and carrying the congregation with her. "Saint Paul was *wrong!*" ("Yes, sister!") "Saint Paul was wrong and if he was here today I would tell him so!" ("Tell it, sister!") "I would tell him so and I would tell him so to his face! I would look him in the eye and say, 'Saint Paul, you is wrong!' " ("Tell it, sister!")

She gestured broadly at the choir. "And look at this glorious choir! Where would this choir be . . . where, O Lord, would this church be . . . without de womens? God bless de womens! God bless you all!"

As if by prearranged cue the choir and organ and (yes) drums launched into a song that made all the music that had gone before seem tame. During this, people went forward with offerings. I scrounged some wadded bills from my pocket and went forward with them unhesitatingly, all inhibition having been swept away by the emotional currents that had surged through my system.

Afterward, on the street, as members of the congregation lingered in chatty and friendly clusters, I ceased to be invisible. The TV viewers among them recognized me, and one group that was going on to a wedding produced Instamatics and began snapping my picture.

A pretty young girl invited me home with her to meet her mother, who was a fan. Partly to preserve my sense of communion with these total strangers a little longer—a communion I have always been able to achieve more easily with black people than with anyone else—I went.

In their neat, modest house, her mother gave me cake and coffee while her brother lounged in the corner and eyed me suspiciously. After some more picture taking, I thanked them and left, feeling contented, gratified and glad to be alive.

I was feeling something else as well: envious. As I went to sit by the river and savor the morning's experience, I thought how good it must be for all those people in the congregation to have such a wonderful catharsis every week and I was sorry I couldn't have it too. That, I decided, is what Sunday ought to be, and I suspected that Mark Twain would have agreed.

In any case, I knew he would have enjoyed that service.

THE CAVETT ALBUM—IV

OF ALL THE PEOPLE who lived well into my lifetime that I wish
I had met, George S. Kaufman heads the list.

Groucho Marx unashamedly referred to Kaufman as "my personal
god" and the fact that I got to be friends with Groucho eased some
of my frustration. But nowadays, bumping into someone who worked
with Kaufman, hearing one of the legendary anecdotes or rereading
something he wrote, redoubles my sense of loss.

I became an ardent fan of Kaufman's through his appearances on the
long-gone TV show "This Is Show Business." The premise of the show,
which was live, was that an entertainer came on and, before singing,
dancing or whatever, laid some personal "problem" before a panel
emceed by Clifton Fadiman. After the entertainer performed, his or
her problem was humorously discussed.

Kaufman was a regular on the panel, and as so often in his public
appearances he filled the role of the delightfully amusing sourpuss, the
mordant skeptic, the debunker.

Another regular was Jacqueline Susann, who in those days was trading aggressively on a not very successful career as an actress. (Her husband, Irving Mansfield, was the producer of the program.)

I cherish the memory of one moment when Susann tried to embarrass Kaufman by telling a story of being turned down by him for a role in one of his plays. Kaufman—chin down, eyebrows raised, gazing over the tops of his glasses—stopped her cold by saying, "That's a very amusing story, but completely apocryphal."

The future novelist all too obviously wasn't certain what the word "apocryphal" meant.

Another hapless soul who foolishly tried to score off Kaufman was the comedian Joey Adams, who appeared on the show to plug his latest book. When Kaufman referred to something in it, Adams quipped, "Oh, you *know* my book, Mr. Kaufman? Who read it to you?"

Kaufman shot back, "The same person who wrote it for you."

But the incident that endeared Kaufman to me for life occurred when the very young Eddie Fisher was a guest. His problem, Fisher earnestly confided, was that because of his youth the chorus girls at the Latin Quarter, where he was then appearing, would not go out with him. Then he sang his song.

When it came Kaufman's turn to discuss and advise, he took a long moment, his head leaning wearily against his hand, and finally spoke.

"Mr. Fisher," he began, "on Mount Wilson there is a telescope that can magnify the most distant stars to twenty-four times the magnification of any previous telescope. This remarkable instrument was unsurpassed in the world of astronomy until the development and construction of the Mount. Palomar telescope.

"The Mount Palomar telescope," he went on, as I recall, "is an even more remarkable instrument of magnification. Owing to advances and improvements in optical technology, it is capable of magnifying the stars to four times the magnification and resolution of the Mount Wilson telescope."

Here Kaufman paused, while tension built in the studio as to whether he had lost his mind.

"Mr. Fisher, if you could somehow put the Mount Wilson telescope *inside* the Mount Palomar telescope, you *still* wouldn't be able to see my interest in your problem."

The laughter continued almost into the following program.

Alas, Kaufman was later bounced from the show by the network cowards-that-be because a few boobs complained when he made an offhand remark about the excessive playing of "Silent Night" at Christmastime. I went into angry mourning.

Fred Allen's comment was, "There were only two wits on television, Grouch Marx and George S. Kaufman. Without Kaufman, television has reverted to being half-witted."

A few years later, while walking past a Broadway opening, I got my first in-person glimpse of "the gloomy dean of comedy" as he entered the theater. I was a young out-of-work actor at the time, and although I wasn't shy about introducing myself to the famous the gulf between me and Kaufman seemed unbridgeable.

I stood rooted to the spot for a time. I had laid eyes on the man who said, when a play of his got tepid reviews, "All we have to worry about now is word of mouth"; and who, while shopping with his wife in a drapery department, asked a clerk, "Have you got any good second-act curtains?"

I resumed walking up Broadway, turning my favorite sayings of his over and over in my mind. Like the one prompted by a stage doorman who failed to recognize the famous forlorn countenance when Kaufman arrived for a rehearsal. "Are you with the show?" the doorman asked.

Kaufman replied, "Let's just say I'm not against it."

Or the one that was Groucho's favorite, occasioned by a Broadway-bound comedy that was trying out in New Haven. Kaufman's invaluable services as a play doctor were solicited for the show by its producer, who was the owner of Bloomingdale's department store in New York. As Kaufman emerged after watching a performance, Mr. Bloomingdale was waiting eagerly in the lobby. "Well, Mr. Kaufman, any advice?"

"Yes," said Kaufman without pausing in his forward motion, "close the show and keep the store open nights."

Years later, the fates conspired to tantalize me even further about him. My wife and Leueen MacGrath, who was once married to Kaufman, became close friends while acting together. At occasional heady moments Leueen would say to me, "George would've enjoyed you so much." Oh, the pangs, the pangs.

But enough of this self-pity. I suppose the "This Is Show Business" kinescopes have been lost or dumped in the East River. The appearances that Kaufman made with Jack Paar on "The Tonight Show" are probably gone. But Kaufman's writings and remembered witticisms remain.

The plays that he created with his various collaborators—*You Can't Take It with You, The Man Who Came to Dinner, Of Thee I Sing, Dinner at Eight,* among many others—still hold the stage wonderfully. They are a legacy for the American theater and an annuity for his immediate heirs.

But he was also a superb writer of short comic sketches and essays, many of which originally appeared in The New Yorker. One described a waiters' school where the students were trained, among other things, to interrupt Kaufman anecdotes just before the punch line. Another was a devastating parody of Gilbert and Sullivan. His "If Men Played Cards As Women Do" was a wicked burlesque of a kind we see too little of in these days of raised consciousness.

Among my mentally noted pet projects that never got done was a plan to go to the New York Public Library and track down all those magazine pieces and other miscellaneous writings. Recently, though, someone did the job for me. Donald Oliver put together a vintage anthology called *By George!* To borrow from an unknown blurb writer on a book of old Jewish folk songs, the collection filled "a long-needed want."

Kaufman once said plays are not written, they're rewritten. And rewriting, for him, meant shortening. Because of his well known obsession with cutting, reading his surviving prose makes me wonder what gems he may have committed to the dustbin.

Even his letters were terse. (And prompt, I might add. His daughter,

Anne Kaufman Schneider, once told me that he went from bed to his writing table in pajamas in the morning and would do no other work until he had answered all his mail. I would love to emulate this, but I would have to begin with mail from eight or ten years ago.) Once, in a New York autograph dealer's shop, I ran across a letter Kaufman had written on the stationery of Boston's Ritz Hotel. It was a model of epistolary succinctness: "Dear Sir, I don't want any German plays. George S. Kaufman."

When asked to write an appreciation of S. J. Perelman for a dust jacket, he wrote, "I appreciate S. J. Perelman—George S. Kaufman."

Despite the master's edict about brevity, the only way I could appreciate his shelf of works more would be if it were longer.

* * *

Groucho Marx the wit and comic was a masterpiece of nature, a performer equipped with perhaps the most formidable array of gifts ever bestowed on an individual funnyman.

He could also be a generous mentor, a warm friend and an endlessly amusing companion. This was the Groucho I knew and had undiluted affection for.

But in the years since his death I have had to adjust to the fact that there were other Grouchos, some of whom I had heard about but never encountered firsthand. As I suppose is only natural, a stream of books, reminiscences and even court testimony has offered them to public view, in unsparing and sometimes pathetic detail: Groucho the impossible husband, the wounding father, the lonely depressive who walked his dog past a neighbor's house repeatedly in hopes of being invited inside for dinner and company.

Relatives, in-laws and some erstwhile friends have all taken opportunities to bad-mouth Groucho—not always unjustifiably, I fear. The apparently irreconcilable feelings he inspired, ranging from devotion (in my case) to loathing (at least one former writer), force us to broaden our picture of a genius-neurotic comic giant and, I hope, to broaden our sympathies too.

If, as Diana Trilling once speculated in an essay on Marilyn Monroe, there is a law of negative compensation at work in the world—a law that the greatly gifted must suffer agonies proportionate to their talents —then Groucho was its victim. Whatever finely tuned mechanism made possible his lightning wit, his extraordinarily intelligent and complex verbal play, and his genius selection of instant wording, phrasing and inflection, it went along, as if the gods were jealous, with an incapacity to find any sort of long-term emotional contentment with his wives and children.

If he did love them, and I am convinced he did, then something prevented him from doing them more good than harm. There is a story of his first wife, Kay, trying to give a party for Groucho's fancy friends and having her little games and favors brutally scorned and ridiculed. The incident, almost unbearably poignant, may well be a fair sample of their life together, which could probably be done justice only in a Dorothy Parker short story.

The late Hector Arce, a Hollywood archivist who wrote the best of the latter-day warts-and-all portraits (titled simply *Groucho*), has a harrowing passage about Groucho's sexual problems with premature ejaculation, but also cites his ability to write hilariously about it to close friends—a paradigm for the twin-mask quality of his hectic personal life.

Much of Groucho's destiny had to do with the predatory mother who launched her sons willy-nilly into show biz. Groucho was the first of her babies to be clearly and displeasingly Jewish looking; too much so for the hair-bleaching jobs done on Harpo and Chico. I've been told that she referred to her bookish, brooding Julius, as Groucho was named, as "Der Dunkler"—the Dark One. Thus he failed to please the first woman in his life.

Apparently he failed to please a good many others—and they him —as he rose through Broadway shows to movies and TV. Probably someone has already written a heavy and unnecessary analysis of his cinematic treatment of the noble and put-upon Margaret Dumont as a projection of his attitudes toward women.

His older daughter Miriam, who reportedly suffered bouts with booze and mental illness, once put her finger on the problem astutely, if chillingly. "I do everything to fulfill my father's feelings about women," Miriam said. "He hates them, and I prove him right."

One's heart goes out to Miriam, whose early life glimmered with some of her father's individualism and wit but never brought her any of the rewards. The Arce book tells of a time the ever fractious Miriam was asked why she couldn't behave more like one of her school friends (who happened to stammer). Miriam replied: "I'll s-s-s-s-start r-r-r-r-right n-n-n-n-now!" Wherever you are, Miriam, I love you for that.

Perhaps the nature-nurture controversy could be settled for all time if the gifted and nerve-wracked Miriam could somehow miraculously be raised all over again in the loving atmosphere of Harpo's home. Unlike Groucho (and for that matter unlike the feckless Chico, with his ruinous gambling), the saintly Harpo inspired nothing but affection in even the most casual acquaintance.

Groucho's work remained curiously unaffected by the strife at home. Perhaps the desire to escape into work sharpened his performances and took his mind off the custody fights and his ability to drive wives to the bottle and turn children into enemies.

His wit certainly remained lethal, on camera or off. He and a director named Sam Wood were not mutual admirers. One day on the set, an exasperated Wood snapped at him: "You can't make an actor out of clay." Groucho: "Nor a director out of Wood."

He had the wisdom to age publicly, whereas his brothers' attempts to preserve their elfin screen personalities ill became their advancing years. Still, the fact that Groucho's brilliant career more than once flickered and nearly guttered out gives me pause.

Luckily, the TV quiz show "You Bet Your Life" brought him back from a brush with obscurity to dazzling popularity and wealth. Another dip, and then the campus throngs that lined up in the 1960s to see the brothers' films brought a third wave of adulation.

These younger discoverers, however enthusiastic, cannot imagine the impact the films had when they first came out. Derivative "wild" comedy makes them seem less revolutionary today, but my father confirms that when "Coconuts" first landed on Grand Island, Nebraska, those who found themselves rolling in the aisles hardly knew what hit them.

By contrast, I first saw Groucho on the quiz show, *then* discovered the films, which, by the time I met Groucho, had a cult following about which he wanted constant reassurance. He particularly needed this adoration of the young. He once said to me, "I get along with *these* kids . . ." and left the rest unspoken.

The last woman in his life was Erin Fleming, the vivacious and ambitious former actress who lived with him and took care of him in his final years. Erin recently had to go to court to defend her disputed share of the estate against a suit by Groucho's son Arthur and the executors. The jury ruled against her in a complicated and confusing verdict. More generally and figuratively speaking, the jury on her will probably be out indefinitely.

She lined up a series of concert appearances for Groucho, to the dismay of many of his old friends who felt he lacked the stamina and perhaps the desire for them, and who suspected that the purpose was less to get Groucho back into the limelight as to get herself into it with him. There was not only the worry that he might not be able to get through the appearances, enfeebled as he was on most days, but also that only a handful of people would come to them. Could he stand that?

Fears on the last point, at least, proved unfounded. The first concert was at Carnegie Hall in New York. I agreed, with trepidation, to introduce Groucho. When I arrived tuxedo-clad a half hour early, having asked the cab driver to drop me at the front entrance specifically so I could check the crowd, I found a huge and excited throng. Many seemed to be college kids, several dressed as Groucho; I made a mental note to tell him about that. Their mood was infectious and a song that I had once sung on the air with Groucho, a song from one of the brothers' movies, began going through my head:

Everyone says I love you,
The cop on the corner and the burglar too . . .

When I went inside to the dressing room, however, I was horrified. Groucho was slumped on a couch looking more frail and papery than I had ever seen him. His voice was a hoarse whisper. Those kids were in a near frenzy outside to see "the one, the only," and here he sat before me looking like moribundity warmed over. Clearly it would be a miracle if we could get him downstairs and onstage, let alone through a two-hour "concert."

"How do you feel, Grouch?" I asked with ersatz brightness.

"Tired," he said. And then, "Did I ever tell you about the time that Kaufman . . ." It was an anecdote he had told me at least four times. A bad sign.

I went over to Erin, who was finishing her makeup at the dressing table, and said, out of Groucho's earshot, "What are we going to do?"

"He'll be fine," she said cheerily. Then, undaunted, she proceeded with last-minute preparations. It reminded me of one of those performances that heroic mothers of dying children are able to summon, bustling about with a chipper air and saying with a smile, "Today we're going to read a *lovely* story . . ."

I couldn't decide whether Erin was crazy or I was. The music in my head had switched to the theme from "The Blue Angel." It crossed my mind to thwart her by taking Groucho out a side exit and putting him to bed. But I decided that she and the audience would hunt me down and lynch me. Instead, the show went on.

After my introduction, Groucho shuffled out to a truly moving hero's welcome. The rafters seemed in danger of falling from the shrieks, whistles and prolonged, unbridled stamping, cheering and clapping. His performance consisted mostly of an unenergetic reading of his favorite anecdotes from three-by-five cards, which I feared would turn even that audience to stone. But they were so presold to have the time of their lives that they barely seemed to notice any difference between the all-but-drained Groucho on stage and the capering madman of the movies. And he did "come up" a bit.

Having held my breath through the first half, I went backstage and suggested cutting the second-half musical number between Groucho and Erin in order to conserve the old man's energy. Erin, already in costume for the number, flared up and came as close as she ever did to harsh words with me. I backed off, thinking maybe she knew best and deciding to trust the gods who had gotten us all that far. They— or she—got us through the evening and many more besides.

I still don't know what I feel about all this. I am so close to the forest as to be almost one of the trees. Yet it seems that whatever manipulations and self-promotions and hectoring Erin may have been guilty of, she did bring some light and cheer into Groucho's last days.

At his house in Beverly Hills, she frequently stage-managed dinner parties with his cronies and admirers. She fed him straight lines; she set up anecdotes by bringing out awards and mementoes and letters from the famous; and around dessert time, when he became restless, she got him to the piano to regale everybody with Harry Ruby songs or the Gilbert and Sullivan numbers for which he had such a passion, doubtless overtaxing him at times but also putting him where he wanted to be: at the center of attention.

Many of the adjectives applied to her, beginning with "exasperating" and ending with "impossible," could also, I now know, be applied to him. For better or worse, she brought a near-dead man back to life repeatedly, even if she seemed to risk killing him in the process.

He brought his own light and cheer too, of course. Visiting a friend in the hospital, an exhausting chore at his age, he was still able to say as the elevator door closed, "Men's tonsils, please."

Steve Stoliar, a young writer who worked for Groucho as an archivist near the end, told me that at one point when vital signs were low, a nurse appeared with a thermometer.

"What do you want?"

"We have to see if you have a temperature, Mr. Marx."

"Don't be silly," said the barely audible figure in bed. "Everybody has a temperature."

It may have been his last joke.

Despite everything, I hope some kind of eternal peace is being enjoyed by the man who merits our eternal gratitude for having lived in our time; who imagined the Stamp Act of 1765 as two fellows who came onstage, stamped their feet and finished with a song; or who could say to an operator, as I heard him do, "Extension 4-8-2, eh? 4-8-2. Sounds like a cannibal story."

Such a man deserved flights of angels to sing him to his rest. For his sake, I hope they sang "The Mikado."

SECOND BANANA TO A HORSE

SOMETIMES I WONDER WHATEVER became of Ed Steib. Perhaps you remember him as he billed himself: "The Mysterious Mr. X and His Mind-Reading Horse"? I guess not.

Ed offered me what seemed like the first big break in my performing career when I was about to enter tenth grade. The phone rang one summer evening and a voice said, "Dick Cavett?"

"Yes."

"This is Ed Steib. Are you the young magician I've been hearing so much about?"

Since I was the only fourteen-year-old magician with that name in Lincoln, Nebraska, it seemed safe to assume he had the right party. To my astonishment, he not only wanted me to appear with him at some sort of fair in Omaha but offered me $100, about four times my highest fee to date.

At fourteen, when someone calls and offers you $100 to play not Fairbury, not Broken Bow or Central City, but *Omaha,* it's big stuff. The performance was to be in an outdoor stadium, which brought to mind a huge stadium show I had seen a few months earlier in Omaha featuring Milton Berle. That's the way I pictured myself with Ed— standing in the convergence of long spotlight beams, smiling and bowing to the multitudes like Uncle Miltie.

Ed said he had heard that I was good, and added that he had also heard I was "a nice-looking kid." It may have been the latter that prompted my father to accompany me on this particular gig.

Since it was to be outdoors and on a stage I decided to do my rabbit-vanish. In this astounding illusion, I placed a rabbit in a break-away box sitting atop an Egyptian folding screen. Then I took the box completely apart, showing each piece on both sides as I disassembled it. The rabbit was gone.

When I set aside the Egyptian screen, however, a bit of fluff could be seen sticking out from one side. I waited until members of the audience repeatedly yelled "Turn the screen around!" before I took notice of the fluff, feigning embarrassment. This made them yell all the louder. I would then rotate the screen, on the back of which was no rabbit but only the words "Ha Ha!"

It was the biggest moment in my act. I rehearsed it daily in preparation for what would be the largest audience ever to see it.

My father and I drove to Omaha the night before, since the first performance of the show was scheduled in the afternoon. Another was to follow in the evening. We stayed at the Rome Hotel, an establishment that thoroughly lived up to a joke I would use, years later, in my nightclub act: "It's the kind of hotel where they change the sheets every day—from one room to another."

The momentous day dawned and we reported to the fairgrounds. Behind the stadium we found a horse van and a man who might have been a Nebraska farmer of peasant German stock. He proved to be Mr. X himself, Ed Steib. The mind-reading horse was grazing nearby, looking a little bored and decidedly untheatrical.

I was a Fred Allen fan, and even at that moment I could muster enough detachment to smile inwardly at the thought of the famous nasal voice saying, "Tell me, Mr. Steib, how long have you and this equine clairvoyant been wowing the populace?"

Ed showed me the stage, a wooden platform set up inside the race track just across from the grandstand. Because it was windy, I used some tire chains to secure the legs of my aluminum magic table. I had the rest of my apparatus laid out and checked and doublechecked by an hour before showtime.

From behind the platform I nervously scanned the vast stadium. Then I sat back to await the throngs that would soon flow through the turnstiles and scramble for seats.

By showtime it was clear that something had gone wrong. Either the throng got its directions confused or to a man had misread the date and hour on the Mr. X posters tacked up along the busier avenues of the fair. To put it at its simplest, nobody showed up.

The clock ticked past showtime—two minutes, three minutes, five minutes. Still nobody.

There was something awesome about the sight of that stadium. For sheer emptiness I have never seen anything to match it. I've seen empty cupboards, empty streets, even empty wheatfields; but for blank, unparalleled vacuity nothing holds a candle to an empty stadium in Nebraska on a sleepy summer afternoon. Pompeii when the ashes cooled was more populous than that grinning expanse of geometrically segmented concrete void.

I take it back. There *is* something emptier: the same void with three people in it. About seven minutes after showtime, a forlorn trio of figures wandered into the upper level, sat down for a moment, looked around, then got up and wandered out.

Ed had a miraculous resilience. He appeared undismayed, merely muttering something about poor placement of his "paper" (posters). As I unchained my magic table he reminded me in businesslike fashion to be on time for the evening show.

The horse, too, appeared unfazed. But then, being psychic, it had doubtless foreseen the whole thing.

My father and I had lunch and drove around Omaha for a while. He joked and tried to keep my spirits up, pointing out that I was getting good experience at unpacking and packing my act. I was woefully crestfallen but did my best to keep it hidden.

That night we packed them in. By eight P.M. the stadium was jammed and roaring with eager spectators. I should mention that they were probably not all Ed Steib fans. The SRO crowd may have had something to do with the fact that we were the *entr'acte* for a stock car race.

Obviously the addition of the race was just what the public needed to remind them of their keen desire to see Ed and the nag and me. Whatever the explanation, my spirits soared.

The only hitch was that the management, not wanting to prolong the intermission unduly, decided to dispense with the kid and his conjuring trumpery.

It was a bitter blow. Nervous as I was, I desperately wanted to play to that huge crowd.

My disappointment was abated somewhat when Ed remembered that he needed someone on the public address system to narrate his turn with his spavined partner, and I got the assignment. It seemed glamorous sitting up in the booth with the track announcer and reading the faded, worn "copy" that Ed had given me. I thrilled to hear my voice boom over the loudspeakers as I exclaimed that the blindfolded horse was stomping out the number of fingers held up by Ed, and other wonders.

For the life of me I can't recall any of the horse's other showstoppers, except for walking up a teeter-totter blindfolded, tipping it and proceeding down the other side, while I, with dramatic inflections, impressed upon the spectators that this stunt would be extremely difficult even for an un-blindfolded horse. (The fact that not even a horse would be dumb enough to try it *unless* blindfolded didn't occur to any of us until later.)

Afterwards I was filled with the heady glow of having given a performance. It had been a large and enthusiastic audience, there was the excitement of the car race and I was getting $100 to boot. Could Broadway be far off?

It wasn't until my father and I were halfway back to Lincoln that I realized I hadn't done what I had come for. I hadn't stood in bright spotlights before cheering thousands as I had seen Milton Berle do. I hadn't brought off my rabbit-vanish.

Moreover, Ed hadn't so much paid me my $100 as told me he *would* do so (carefully noting my address). Still, I had no reason to doubt his word. He had never not paid me before.

I think we were almost back to Lincoln before my father managed to include me in his vast amusement over the whole thing and we got to laughing so hard we could hardly see the road ahead. He advised me with knowing glee not to spend the entire hundred all at once. I laughed at that too, but I guess I wasn't suspicious or cynical enough to be certain that my check wouldn't arrive in the mail.

"Aw hell," my father said, "we had a thousand dollars' worth of fun out of it."

That was more than thirty years ago. Have I become jaded and hardened by the intervening years? I think not. Because when the money does come, I plan to give it to charity.

MY NAME GOES UP IN PLASTIC

HAD I STOPPED TO think about it, there were several good reasons for me *not* to step into the starring role of *Otherwise Engaged* on Broadway.

The play was a highly civilized British comedy and I, the last time I looked, was a midwestern American. Even though Anthony Burgess had once said that a Nebraska accent like mine was one of the most attractive American accents—persuasive, homey and somewhat witty —it was still a long way from Bloomsbury.

I would be following an established, consummate actor in Tom Courtenay, who had played the role throughout the show's six-month Broadway run—and for that matter, in Alan Bates, who had originated it in London.

Although I was trained as an actor and had done some plays in the early years of my career, it was a long time since I had attempted anything of this sort. The last serious acting I had done was appearing interested during a TV interview with Elliott Roosevelt.

As a TV personality all too obviously being brought in to boost the box office as the play approached the end of its run, I would be open to the charge of crass hustling, heedless dabbling or a compulsion toward public humiliation—or a tidy combination of all three—by critics and those who thought of themselves as *real* actors.

I feared that the strain of eight performances a week would cause me to lose my voice, a trauma of psychogenic origin that had plagued me off and on since my amateur acting days.

Besides, at that time I was already in the midst of preparing for my five-times-a-week interview series on PBS, a task that if not overwhelming was at least whelming.

The point is, however, that I didn't really stop to think about it. With me, decisions are not a methodical, deliberate process but, at best, a sudden urge that comes over me while swimming or lacing my shoes. My manager had told me about the offer. I didn't take it seriously, but carried the script along on a trip to New Orleans (I hadn't seen the play). One rainy afternoon in the French Quarter I opened the script at random and liked the first page I read. I got that tingling feeling that it would be fun to say those lines.

That was it. A tingle. After a few pages I called my manager to see if the offer was serious and still open. The answer was yes to both. "Take it," I told him, without even reading any more pages of the script. They were, I assumed, written by the same author.

Part of the offer was that Harold Pinter, who had directed the production, would fly over from London to rehearse me in it. That alone ought to be an experience worth risking one's professional neck for. Perhaps I was having what Walter Kerr once called delusions of adequacy, but my instinct was to stretch myself in a new direction, find out how hard it was, see if I could do it.

One of the things I already knew about the play was that it contained a slightly shocking scene in which an attractive young woman takes off her blouse and displays herself bare breasted to "my" character, attempting to seduce him. This too appealed to me, not only for the salient reasons but because I always like the idea of doing something that conflicts with my image.

I imagined indignant matinee ladies writing in, "I never thought Dick Cavett would consent to be a party to such proceedings, and as he has seen fit to do so I shall never watch his television show again. I am certain, Mr. Cavett, that you are not deigning to read this letter yourself. Good-bye forever!" (I love letter writers who speak to you even though you are not there.)

I had once revealed the same amount of my own anatomy on one of my late night shows, and the hate mail I got would fill a slim volume, most of it containing the favorite final line, "Goodbye, Mr. Cavett, forever." One good lady from the Bible Belt asked, "How could your *wife* let you do it?" Presumably my wife stood in the wings and gave me hand signals when it was okay to do something that might raise eyebrows in the nation's sewing circles.

Another factor contributing to my urge to do the play was a single word that had held a lifelong allure for me: Broadway.

Perhaps only if you've been a child growing up in the provinces, daydreaming to the sound of train whistles, listening to radio shows like "Mr. First-Nighter" and seeing movies like "All About Eve," can you imagine what a special aura Broadway used to have. Broadway was romance, sophistication, dressing-room mirrors wreathed in caged light-bulbs and good luck telegrams, curtain calls and bouquets, white silk scarves, penthouse parties and the *sine qua non,* your name in lights.

It didn't matter that as a dominant entertainment medium Broadway had been outstripped by movies, television, pop music and in fact just about everything including old National Geographics. It retained some of its aura for me even after I saw that The Great White Way was actually a tawdry honky-tonk and sex shop district and became aware of what a grinding and often cruel business it was behind the scenes, and how mediocre and meretricious its glittering opening nights often turned out to be.

Besides, hadn't I been there before? As a young actor I had appeared on several Broadway stages during Actors' Fund week, delivering solicitation speeches at intermissions. I invented some gags and little bits of comic business to lighten my spiel, and I went over pretty well. I thought, "Someone will surely discover me doing this. I'm on my way, I'm on Broadway and I'm getting laughs." But no one noticed.

Wait, I take that back. Once I did my pitch between acts of Mike Nichols' and Elaine May's smash show, and before going on asked Nichols if he would watch from the wings. I got big laughs and glowed at the thought that one of my heroes was seeing it all. Except that when I glanced into the wings, he wasn't there.

Deflated, I pressed on. Then he *was* there. More big laughs, and when I came off he was most friendly and told me I had "great aplomb."

Recently, to my horror, I found a copy of the stuff I had sketched out for that appearance (". . . and in the third row, ladies and gentlemen, your friend and mine, Mr. Boris Karloff. [shading eyes] Oh, pardon me, lady."). That this got a laugh as big as those Mike and Elaine were getting indicates that audiences can appreciate more than one level of humor (he said, still wincing).

Anyway, Nichols had not said that I was funny, I noted much later, but that I had aplomb. That was something. And there the matter rested for some years.

Now I had my chance to return as a star and I was going to take it, with trepidation perhaps, but without apology. I would mount the boards and, in Shakespeare's phrase, "cleave the general ear." And if they didn't like me, that's where they could stick it.

In other words, this was one time when cooler heads were not going to prevail, nor hotter ones either. When I got back to New York I encountered plenty of both. There were the predictable "Bravos," pitted against an equally predictable chorus of "Why take the risk?— think of what you have to lose," with each side sometimes throwing in for good measure, "Yes, but can you act?" (I wanted to say, "Can I *act?* You think I like you, don't you?")

When word reached the press, Frank Milton, one of the play's three producers, was quoted as saying, "I'm not worried. Acting is really not acting, if you know what I mean." I've always meant to ask Frank about that.

Robert Redford encouraged me, saying wistfully that he wished *he* had a play to do. That was a powerful incentive: to have something that Redford wanted.

Woody Allen, my frequent mentor, said: "Not a bad idea."

My wife's view was exactly the same as Woody's except without the "not." She never said so in so many words, but I suspect she thought I was a loon to do it.

Years earlier, she had told Life Magazine that we had a standing arrangement for avoiding professional rivalries in our household. As she described it, "I don't try to be a talk show host and he doesn't try to be an actress." Now I was coming perilously close to violating that treaty. (I half expected to see her trying on Dinah Shore hand-me-downs to get even.)

But I think what really disturbed my wife was that, being a brilliant professional herself and knowing as much about the theater as she did, she had a far more realistic idea than I of the pitfalls that lay ahead of me. Ignorance *is* bliss. She probably pictured the opening night crowd unhitching the horses from my carriage and pulling me through the streets and straight into the East River.

Short of something like that, I was determined to assume that nothing bad could come of it. What were they going to do? Haul me off my TV show, saying, "You stank up Broadway, so wash up and go home—we don't want you here either!"?

As for the reviews, the worst things that could be said about me had already been said in print somewhere or other, and I was still standing. Besides, I could write the reviews in advance, and often did in my imagination. One was headlined "Cavett Scores in Broadway Debut"; another, "Cavett Lays Egg Bigger Than Superdome." Somehow the latter was always more vivid, going on to speculate on what sort of hubris had led a genial talk show host to assume he could take his place among professional thespians, considering that he moved like an arthritic robot and had the emotional range of an avocado.

As I assured the public in a TV commercial—a split screen self-interview—that I later made to promote my appearance in the play,

"The audience wins either way, whether it sees a great performance or a big star making a fool of himself."

*   *   *

I lost no time in undertaking speech instruction. My one genuine fear in taking the part remained the vocal burden. I went to the legendary Alfred Dixon clinic, where the widow of the founder put me through some mysterious exercises.

Alfred Dixon had saved the voices and careers of many an illustrious theatrical personage and thereby achieved the status of a saint in the business. The centerpiece of his method involved a certain kind of mooing. I had read that Noel Coward went to Dixon, who in turn had taken the Lunts, so that subsequently when the three of them acted together it sounded like a dairy barn backstage.

I mooed diligently for weeks. That, plus perhaps the placebo effect of having an expert say, "There is nothing wrong with your voice if you use it correctly, and you will; you should be able to give twenty performances a week instead of eight without even getting vocal fatigue," was wonderfully bracing, even though I still couldn't notice much resemblance between myself and Coward and the Lunts.

Meanwhile I began studying the play. The plot concerned an urbane forty-year-old London publisher named Simon Hench who spends an entire Sunday afternoon trying to listen to a cherished new recording of "Parsifal," all the while being interrupted by a succession of unpleasant, boring and miserable relatives and acquaintances who parade through his house and eventually leave his life in a shambles.

I recall the strangeness of seeing a performance and thinking, "I am going to sit in *that* beige chair and wear those clothes and say those words that Tom Courtenay is saying? Impossible." It was like trying to imagine yourself in a painting you are looking at.

I did feel an affinity with Simon, though. He was certain things I was at least alleged to be. Articulate, for instance. Also cool and emotionally detached. Like me he tended to use language as a mask, a weapon and a distraction, subtly switching subjects, pointing out little surface ambiguities and constantly playing on words. Perhaps the producers had these similarities in mind when they thought of me for the part.

Making too much of them, however, could be dangerous. In an interview on the "Today" show, I said that there were real parallels between Simon and me—startling ones, in fact. Then, thoughtlessly, without any transition I happened to mention that Simon had a failed marriage. Until that moment, my own had been fine.

In the play, the characters who fail to get the satisfaction they want from Simon come to see his ironic reserve as a form of contempt. He is described, during a painful scene with his wife, as somebody who only lets little bits of life get through to him, whose serenity stems from moral rot, whose very sanity causes people to go quietly mad around him.

That was a bit unfair, I decided as I began to get sympathetically inside the character. Along with Simon, I'd suffered an awful lot of bores willingly and sometimes not so willingly. I could understand why he got upset when he felt threatened. He denied and shut out a great deal but I didn't see him as a bloodless character. He was a man who deeply craved an ordered life, and had settled for certain rituals and comforting arrangements that he didn't want violated.

It was the ritualistic side of him that accounted for those pages upon pages of formal and meticulous language that I was going to have to memorize. Normally when I do scripted performing of any kind, I drive my colleagues bonkers by never learning my lines with certainty until the dress rehearsal, or sometimes after. Even when I do know them I often rephrase them as I go along, to sharpen the sense or get a better rhythm.

In this case I was put on notice that the playwright, Simon Gray, and of course Mr. Pinter, would insist that I be word perfect in my lines. This was like insisting that Dizzy Gillespie just stick to the melody, but it proved to be no problem at all. The play was so crisply and perfectly worded that it would've been silly to change a syllable. (Would Gillespie mess around with a Stravinsky melody?)

In general, the better a line is written, the easier it comes. You hear it right the first time, it has an inevitability about it, it stays with you. Playwrights, take note.

My only real difficulty was to pitch it all in the right English accent. I had to soften my *R*s (a special problem for midwesterners), watch my final *Y*s, broaden my vowels and rise and swoop with a new inflection on all those "look heres," "reallys" and "actuallys."

Still, long and intricate as the part was, by the time Harold Pinter arrived I *was* word perfect in it, if nothing else perfect.

I had wondered for weeks what Pinter would be like. A moody eccentric? (One had heard, after all, that he spent day after day lying on a sitting room couch reading about cricket.) Full of ambiguous silences, like his plays? Speaking with an oblique, Pinteresque menace?

"None of the above," would be a better description. His manner was frank and genial, and with his dark suits and hornrimmed glasses he could have passed for an insurance man or barrister. Over lunch or drinks he told elaborately amusing anecdotes, and even when he expressed anger or frustration about the bungling of some of his own productions he was always wry and witty in the process.

He was genuinely friendly, not phony theater-friendly. I liked him from the start and felt instinctively that he was a director whom an actor would earnestly wish to please, not placate out of fear or awe, nor merely tolerate or bypass. I very much wanted to please and tried hard to remember to pronounce his first name less Amurrican. (It should be h-a as in "hat," not as in the first syllable of "herring.")

Working with me in rehearsals, he never said anything literary or theoretical. He never began a sentence with the words, "This is a play about . . ." or, "Simon is a character who . . ." Invariably he confined himself to the practical, specific and concrete—where to sit, when to vary the pace, how to manage a crossover. He would say, "I think you need just a slight pause there," or, "Perhaps it would go better if you stay upstage, then come down on the second line."

It all showed a fine tact and consideration for an actor's problems, and reminded me that Pinter had started as an actor himself. He had a true colleague's ability to impart confidence and security, two items of which I was in decreasing supply. (He was also actor enough not to show his doubts if he had them.)

In contrast to more subjective American theater folk with their agonizings over motivations, "values" and "subtexts," he held to the brisk British professional's belief that if you knew your business and avoided bumping into the furniture, inspiration would take care of itself.

Tom Courtenay was the same way. When I sought his advice over dinner in some dingy *boîte* in the theater district, he kept speaking of how tiring the role was. He reminded me that Simon is onstage—and mostly on his feet—throughout the entire play, except for six seconds or so when he dashes off to answer a doorbell.

Courtenay passed the torch to me with these words: "Be sure and get yourself a comfortable pair of shoes."

Gradually the rehearsals incorporated more and more of the regular cast members, who had to put in extra time with me while continuing to do eight performances a week with Courtenay. They responded to these demands in the way actors usually do when someone joins a long-running production; i.e., as if helping a drowning man into a lifeboat.

It was touching, the extraordinary lengths they went to in coaching me, passing on lessons they'd learned over the months, offering to spend extra time running lines with me. Particularly Nicholas Coster, who undoubtedly itched to play my part. If there was any under-the-breath muttering about the gall of this glossy TV celebrity presuming to take his place among *serious* actors, it probably came from me.

One member of the cast, Michael Lombard, had been a fellow apprentice with me at the Stratford, Connecticut, Shakespeare Festival nearly twenty years earlier. It was an odd feeling being back onstage with him—both closing a circle with my youthful acting aspirations and reminding me how time and chance happeneth to us all.

I persuaded Michael and several of the actors to say their lines into a tape recorder, leaving silent gaps where my speeches would fall. This gave me a sort of Music Minus One recording with which I could rehearse at home, getting used to their tones and rhythms and drilling myself at the same time. Purists would undoubtedly disdain this as too mechanical, but it was a help to me and spared them the tedium of additional rehearsals.

I felt I was beginning to get into the play. Which is not to say I didn't still have stabs of panicky uncertainty: What if I get my hand in the air in a gesture and can't get it down? How the hell do you *walk* onstage? Whenever you return to acting after a hiatus you discover again that simple actions like opening a door, never a problem in real life, feel weird. And although you never miss the holes on the telephone dial at home, finding them on a stage prop is suddenly a feat of marksmanship.

In all I had three weeks of preparation before the first public performance. To someone who had done ad lib talk and variety shows on TV for years, the idea of rehearsing at all had seemed adequate. (Silly boy.)

In fact, it was as if I had no sooner completed my first walk-through than I was suddenly saying to myself, "Jesus! There's going to be an audience out there tonight."

And there was. Oh Lord, there was.

When my fateful moment came, my Broadway debut—or my return to Broadway, if you count the Actors' Fund speeches—I got through it by switching into one of the two time-honored psychological states: numb terror. (The other being, I suppose, alcoholic trance.)

Of course, I employed all the classic techniques for not appearing nervous. Trying to remain vertical on both feet, for example, or keeping my hands in my pockets so as to avoid stuffing them simultaneously into my mouth—little tricks of the trade like that.

Somewhere late in the second act (there were only two acts), respiration returned and I began to get the sense of security I should have started with. I said to myself, "I'm better than I thought I would be," which, I grant you, was not necessarily saying much. I let my thoughts drift ahead to the moments after the final curtain when everybody would crowd around and congratulate me for the way I brought off the performance.

Afterwards everybody did crowd around, but paradoxically it was disappointing because they over-congratulated me and went too far in their compliments. Even I knew I wasn't *that* good.

I now had ten days until the critics came and I faced, in effect, another opening night. Again, that seemed like plenty of time at first. I had been in summer stock productions that opened, played their whole run and closed within that interval. But again, it melted away with alarming suddenness. Although I was reasonably calm when the night arrived, I had an unsettling sense that I had not done whatever it was I was going to do to get ready.

Unlike the cast and crew, the critics did not over-congratulate me. Or so I gathered. I had long since adopted Woody Allen's philosophy that if you don't read the reviews they somehow don't exist, and a very helpful philosophy it is.

I knew there were at least two good reviews because blowups of them were promptly mounted in the lobby. At a glance I noticed that Rex Reed of the New York *Daily News* had said I took the stage "with surprising grace." I didn't want to know any more.

As for the other reviews, well, I could have predicted that the *Times* would be judiciously disappointed, that Clive Barnes of the *Post* (himself an Englishman) would fault my accent, that John Simon of New York magazine would say I wasn't pretty enough, and so on.

Intimations that most of the reactions were less than hosannas came from well-meaning people who said things like, "I don't care what Mr. X says, *I* liked it," or from self-consciously provocative interviewers who would ask, "How did it feel to get pasted by the critics?" To the latter, I could at least truthfully reply that I didn't know I *had* been.

Except in one instance.

One evening, while happily mooing and wishing the clock would run faster so it would be time to go to the theater, I was flipping the channels on my TV set and I heard my name. It was a local news show and Pia

Lindstrom, their resident critic, was saying, "—vett's English accent sounds like he has an English muffin in his mouth and he can't be heard beyond the eighth row. Cavett should leave Broadway to the—"

Click. I could imagine the rest.

Apparently Pia's especially fine-tuned auditory apparatus told her that I did cleave the general ear, all right, but as the Bard went on to say, "with horrid speech."

At such moments, one tries calmly to remind oneself that countless brilliant performers have gotten bad reviews, that in the 1890s the New York *Times* called *The Importance of Being Earnest* and its author "trifles to be quickly forgotten," that people and even critics are entitled to their own opinions, that one man's meat, etc. Regardless of how many of these talismans (talismen?) of reassurance one fondles mentally, the net result is that one's true feelings override them unimpeded.

And one's true feelings are of shock and devastation, of wounded rage that eloquently cries out, "What are this woman's credentials and why can't she be drowned in Tabasco?" (I'm softening my actual attitude toward the lady at the time for fear of offending the gentle reader.)

If only I hadn't turned on the frigging TV I would still be feeling swell and looking forward to curtain time. Instead I wanted to bury myself in bed. A scalding sweat had bloomed on my brow when Pia's words zinged into my brain. She had taken all the fun out of my adventure and clearly I would never be able to face another audience.

Suddenly I remembered that Pia's mother, Ingrid Bergman, had also seen my opening night performance. Did this mean that she hated me too? She had come backstage afterwards very graciously but, come to think of it, had not actually said anything directly about the performance.

On the other hand, maybe Ingrid had raved about me, and Pia, who of course loved me too, was going through a burst of daughterly defiance toward Mommie (dearest?) and merely used me as the convenient whipping stick. Yes, that must be it.

Leaning heavily on such self-protective rationalizations, I somehow got myself to the theater, whistling an abnormal amount on the way and toying with the idea of having a black friend pick up a six-pack of conjure candles in Harlem and fashion a wax effigy of Pia for me.

I already had a ritual for propelling myself into the performances. As I stood on the darkened stage at curtain rise each night, waiting for the lights to go up and the obligatory applause for the TV face to wash over me, I would alternately tighten and relax my arm muscles, breathe deeply and think of Bob Hope striding onstage with that fabulous assurance.

Tonight, without planning it, I added a fourth element. After the stage manager's order to "take it up," I said aloud (covered by the whirr of the rising curtain), "Fuck you, Pia Lindstrom."

Miraculously, I was freed. The words made me laugh to myself; my confidence was restored as if a fairy wand had touched me and a crystal "ping" had sounded. I was brimming with invincible enthusiasm.

From that time on, for the next three months, "F.Y.P.L." was an indispensable part of my ritual, and its magic never failed to do so much for me that I wondered if ethically I ought to pay her royalties. One night I think I said it a little too loudly and a few front row spectators may have thought their ears were deceiving them.

* * *

As my wife once described it, the miracle of (real) acting is that you can be standing onstage in a tragedy, genuinely feeling total grief and at the same moment be calculatingly conscious of keeping your feet, hands, head and *hair* in just the right position.

While onstage, actors are separated from the audience by an invisible wall. Although every detail of their performance is calculated with the audience in mind, part of their discipline is to remain oblivious, to behave as if the audience weren't there at all.

For me this is both a stimulating challenge and a frustration, because my natural instinct as a performer is to break through that wall and establish some kind of direct give-and-take with an audience.

One summer I appeared in *Room Service* at the Williamstown,

Massachusetts, Festival Theater. While an actress and I were playing
a quiet, sentimental scene, a stage light blew out. There was an explo-
sive pop! followed by the tinkle of shattered glass. Although out of
sight, it could be heard to the back of the house.

The actress looked startled at first, then blank. I could see that she'd
"dried up." The audience, murmuring, was well aware that something
had occurred that wasn't in the script, and it seemed silly not to
acknowledge the fact with an ad lib.

I said, "I *told* them not to leave the champagne on the radiator."

It got the biggest laugh of the evening. If the fragile make-believe
of *Room Service* was shattered just as thoroughly as the stage light, it
seemed worthwhile, partly for the bond that was struck with the audience.

In *Otherwise Engaged* I didn't have that kind of amiable latitude.
The play was much more tightly scripted and, for all its wicked humor,
much more serious (leaving aside the obvious difference that Broadway
isn't summer stock, except sometimes inadvertently).

During one performance there was a horrific downpour. As the rain
pelted that venerable theater, the Plymouth, it created a racket that
sounded as though a thousand tiny flamenco dancers were rehearsing
on the roof. Even when the other actors and I doubled our volume we
could scarcely hear each other, let alone get through to the balcony.

Late in the play the rain finally let up, but in the blessed quiet that
ensued we realized we had another problem—seemingly smaller but
actually more serious, because more distracting. The leaky roof was
dripping right onto our play.

In one spot in particular, the drops were falling with a hypnotic
rhythm—plink, plink—onto the sofa where Carolyn Lagerfelt, as
Simon Hench's wife, was about to sit for a tense, climactic scene with
me.

Carolyn took her place. Plink! A drop fell on her arm. She kept on
talking, but edged sideways. The audience tittered. Plink! Plink! The
drops seemed to be getting louder. I couldn't concentrate on anything

else, and I assumed that Carolyn and everyone in the theater couldn't either.

"Damn!" I thought. "I can't ad lib." But by thinking ahead a few lines I did form a plan.

At a break in the dialogue I got up, much to Carolyn's surprise and somewhat to mine. It's an eerie feeling to make an unrehearsed move onstage; your muscles resist you. Carrying on with my lines, I walked to a coffee table, picked up an ashtray and placed it under the drip.

The audience erupted with a tumult that, to my ears, sounded like a presidential nominating convention in full cry. The tension evaporated: we could all go back to concentrating on the play, though now with an extra feeling of exhilaration and oneness between actors and spectators.

The ashtray move won me points from the rest of the cast for presence of mind, and took a prominent place in the lore that every theater company builds up during a long run. My colleagues were more dubious, however, about my next escapade in oneness.

It came as we were all taking our final curtain call one night. On an impulse, I held up my hands to stop the applause and said to the audience, "You probably didn't notice it, but I left out four lines tonight. So I owe each of you a refund of eight and half cents."

The laughter and applause were encouraging, so I went on. I asked them how they had liked the play and offered to answer any questions they might have.

I guess I only half noticed out of the corner of my eye that the other actors standing up there with me were thunderstruck. Talking directly to the audience is something you just don't *do* except in the rarest of circumstances—if you're an aged tragedian making a farewell appearance, for instance. Some actors consider it unprofessional to break out of character on a curtain call with so much as a smile or gesture, let alone a speech.

Thus, while I bantered on, they stood there at a loss, smiles frozen on their faces, wondering how on earth they were ever going to get off the stage now that the customary routine of applause and bows had been disrupted.

The next day the stage manager handed me a note in which I was rather stiffly requested to have the consideration to warn my fellow actors the next time I intended to talk to the audience, so that they could at least brace themselves psychologically.

I did intend to do it again. I felt impelled to do it. I wanted to test the differences, while the evening's performance was still fresh in my mind, between talking to an audience and playing for one.

Each process had its special gratifications. In the play, I was learning all over again what fun it was to work on an effective scene, to anticipate it during the performance, then to come to it and get your instant reward from its impact on the audience.

By comparison, going off the cuff, taking questions, hoping people would try to embarrass me or whatever, was something I knew I thrived on; I had always wished I could do more of it on TV. I loved the thrill, the danger of it. It took me back to my days in nightclubs, when my favorite part of my act was the hecklers. I could scarcely wait to be heckled.

Eventually we settled on a plan to limit the curtain speeches to particular nights of the week. I offered to do them alone, but I wasn't about to get six other actors, even shy actors, to yield the stage to me just like that.

Besides, most of them were beginning to enjoy the sessions. Once they got over their original mortification, they took a wary pleasure in appearing before the audience as themselves. They were flattered when people recognized them from other roles, which happened especially with those who were working in TV soap operas. They were fascinated by the audience's questions, which sometimes reflected a view of the play and of their characters that had never been dreamed of in rehearsals.

It was fun to see them pick up techniques of free-form performing that were almost second nature to me but represented breakthroughs to them. They learned to save and reuse a good ad lib—looking blank, for instance, when asked the meaning of a particular line, then asking, "Do I say that?" The first time it happened the actor genuinely didn't recognize the line, as actors often don't when they hear a portion of their role out of context; but after that, they cunningly played it for a laugh.

I did my best, in my capacity as informal emcee, to keep them all involved by bouncing questions to them. That way I got credit for generously sharing the limelight, and at the same time was often able to deflect some or all of the three most tiresome questions that were invariably directed to me: 1) my favorite TV guest, 2) my most embarrassing TV experience and 3) my views on public vs. commercial TV.

The audience seemed to enjoy these little forums too, and except for the suburbanites who had trains to catch or long drives ahead of them, they stayed in surprising numbers to take part. One night I apologized for keeping them so long and a well-dressed man down front assured me, "No, no, we've got no place to go."

We even had a memorable moment or two. Once the comedian Andy Kaufman was in the audience and called out a rambling question in the guise of his foreign character—strictly deadpan, of course, and nearly incomprehensible.

"I'm sorry," I said, knowing full well who he was, "but you speak English so badly that I can't answer that." I turned as if to recognize another questioner, muttering about "these foreigners who come over and don't bother to learn the language."

A half-whispered "oooo" sound rose from the audience at this apparent rudeness on my part.

Kaufman persisted with his question, his voice almost pleading, and I persisted in cutting him off. Finally I barked at him, "Let somebody else talk, will you? If you can't behave I'll have you ejected."

There was a shocked silence. Much as I relished and wanted to prolong the drama that only Andy and I were really in on, I finally said, "Ladies and gentlemen, I'm sure you'll recognize the very talented Andy Kaufman," and Andy stood up as the audience, with palpable relief, gave him a round of applause.

It was a Pirandello vignette in which what the audience assumed was post-performance "reality" (actually a performance of another sort) was overlaid with a more mysterious performance (which the audience took for a heightened "reality").

The ghost of Pirandello had his revenge, however. Not much later it was our turn in the cast to have reality intrude on a performance in a bewildering fashion—this time right in the midst of the play. We came to refer to it as the incident of The Talker. At first it might've seemed that Andy Kaufman was back, but this was weirder, more pathological.

It began near the end of the first act. A man's voice from out of nowhere suddenly muttered something indistinguishable, but clearly audible. The other actors and I froze momentarily, then went on.

A few minutes later it happened again. An ominous muttering baritone, now detectably coming from somewhere near the back of the orchestra, overrode our lines. This time, irritated, I dried up for a few seconds.

At intermission we all talked about it backstage. We assumed that whatever it was, whatever was wrong, the man's friends or seatmates would help or the ushers would do something about it.

But twenty minutes into the second act, there it was again. The voice was louder if anything, saying quite clearly, "Murnle lat creely bitch will the crawbra!"

The other people in the audience could no longer ignore the demented rumblings. They began shifting in their seats and murmuring, craning their necks to try to see the offender. The actor who was onstage with me at the time looked thoroughly rattled, and rightly so.

By about the fifth audible outburst I was enraged. Why the fuck wasn't somebody doing something? A usually funny scene went by without getting a laugh, probably because the actors and I were on automatic pilot and the audience was on edge, and this made me even angrier.

Just before the play's final scene, the script called for me to have a nice moment alone onstage in which I mixed a drink and cogitated sensitively. Just as I turned upstage toward the drink cart for this interlude—you guessed it. Loud and clear. A few nonsense syllables from what was clearly a fevered brain, followed by, "You oughtta kill that brother of yours!"

That did it. For once during my stint on Broadway I broke out of character completely and crashed through that invisible wall during a performance.

I wish I had a videotape of what followed. If it were true to memory, it would show me vanishing from the vicinity of the drink cart and reappearing instantaneously at the front of the stage, saying into the wings, "Would you bring the house lights up? . . . Just bring the goddamn house lights up, okay? Up! Now, not later!"

The lights came up and, shading my eyes, I peered up the aisle. "I just want to see what you look like, you bastard!" I could dimly make out what a policeman would call a "white male individual" being removed or "helped" from a rear row. An usher was fatuously giving me the high sign. Where had he been for the past hour and a half?

To the audience, I said, "I apologize. It was impossible to go on and I don't know why no one had the brains to do anything before this."

They burst into wild cheers and applause. I stood there feeling ten feet tall and triumphant, fully energized with adrenaline and bile.

Now the question was where to go from there. After you squelch a heckler in a nightclub, the exhilaration quickly gives way to the awkwardness of getting back to your prepared material. There is always a risk that it will seem drab after the giddy spontaneity of a clash.

"I guess we could either give you your money back or go on," I said. "There's only about twenty minutes left. Although it's going to be rough on us all, we'll backtrack a few moments and see this through." More cheers and applause.

Meteorologically speaking, it was as if a high pressure system had passed from the theater. The tension had been removed, the mysterious had been revealed, anger and fear had been assuaged. Backstage, the actors who had seen my exploit were describing it to the unfortunates who missed it, and everyone was vibrating with excitement.

That final scene played as never before or since.

* * *

In his recent autobiography, Laurence Olivier somewhat surprisingly asserted that acting was not a profession to be enjoyed. But he granted one exception: playing light comedy to an appreciative audience.

Otherwise Engaged may not have been all that light a comedy, but the audiences were appreciative and God, yes, it was fun. When it really clicked it was like sex. I asked myself, "Why does anyone ever do anything *but* this?"

The closing date had been set since before I went into the play, so I knew I had just so many weeks to make the most of it. Some nights I wished I could slow up the performance so it wouldn't be over so quickly. And I came to regret my chickenshit decision—based on my old bugaboo of voice strain—not to play the midweek matinee.

The producers were unhappy about this as well, because I insisted that the newspaper ads and listings stipulate it and the boxoffice went down accordingly. One day I sneaked into the matinee to see my part played by the splendid but unknown young actor who was understudying me and there were about eight rows of people in the theater.

I felt guilty, too, about disappointing all the nice matinee ladies who came to see me. The usual practice when a substitute is going to appear is to have a less than prominently placed sign that reads, "At this performance the role of Henry Higgins will be played by Lemworth Scruggins." The unwary still may not realize, of course, that Henry Higgins is the role Rex Harrison usually plays, i.e., the lead.

So it was in this case. Since nowhere did it say, "Dick Cavett will not be here today," many members of the audience didn't fully take in the bad news until the curtain rose. And although they were entitled to a refund, by that time it was too late to see anything else.

For these and other reasons, when midweek matinee time rolled around I found myself yearning to be up there onstage as I was for the other seven performances.

It wasn't the sort of play you could get entirely right in any given performance, but in each outing I felt I got five or six things right that I hadn't the time before. I may not have made anybody forget about Alfred Lunt, or even Tom Courtenay (no slight intended), but I didn't get tarred and feathered and ridden out of town on a rail either; and I know I ended the run a better actor than I began.

One advantage I had from the start was that I knew comedy. Once I discovered where the laughs were in the play, I could step into them and make them count. Other elements were more elusive or intractable. Sometimes it was only after six or eight weeks that a scene would finally work for me and I'd see why, and then I felt I owed a kind of recall to all the people who had seen it too soon.

The semi-nude scene, I'm happy to report, yielded every bit as much naughty satisfaction as I had hoped it would.

It was written so that I had my back turned when the actress whipped off her blouse, and I measured the impact of her sudden revelation by the variety of gasps and ejaculations that came from out front. On weekend matinee days I could hear startled mini-shrieks from older ladies, as if they'd stepped into a urinal by mistake; and unless I was having aural hallucinations there would be a quartet or so of "mercys," and here and there a few "my stars."

A few lines later, the character blatantly spelled out her come-on to Simon Hench just in case he had missed the point. (Or should I say the points? No, I shouldn't.) I relished the moment when I leaned forward slightly, slowly raised my hand as if I might be about to reach out and touch her, then, after an ever so tantalizing pause, got up and handed her her blouse, spurning her offer.

Her line was, "Fidelity means so much to you?"

And mine, an icy stiletto, "Let's say rather more to me than a suck and a fuck with the likes of you."

The brutality of this, however well deserved, usually caused the audience to draw in its collective breath as if a wound had been inflicted.

As I recall, the only other occurrence in the play of our language's

most potent monosyllable was earlier in the same scene, when the
young lady reeled off a venomous recitation of her boyfriend's short-
comings, bad habits and intellectual pretensions, and capped off the
crescendo of abuse with, "on top of which he's a fourth-rate fuck."

The guaranteed laugh on this line usually lasted about six to eight
seconds, during which I could savor the blockbuster that would follow
when I mused, "Oh well, perhaps he's kind to animals."

The thunderbolt of hilarity released by this masterly retort brought
the house down and kept it down sometimes for a good half minute,
a long but pleasant time to bathe in cachinnation.

Two "fucks," then, carefully placed for maximum impact, appropriate to the characters and situations but nonetheless sufficient to cause
an occasional up-trouping of the aisle by one or two cases of outraged
sensibilities bent on refund. The box office staff could always tell which
scene had just played when confronted by an incensed septuagenarian,
dewlaps aquiver, protesting that she had not expected to see Dick
Cavett a party to such filth. Her money was cheerlessly refunded.

One performance inadvertently added a fillip of sado-masochism to
this mildly scandalous scene. When Lynne Milgrim, in the role of the
girl, pulled her blouse over her head it snagged on her earring and tore
her earlobe. She felt some pain but didn't realize that she'd injured
herself. I, with my back turned, was completely oblivious.

So it came as a disconcerting surprise to both of us, a little further
into the scene, when I noticed a rivulet of blood running down the side
of her neck but had no idea where or what it was coming from, and
she saw my eyes widen with alarm but had no idea what I was reacting
to. My instinct told me just to proceed with the scene, hoping that
nothing serious was wrong and that under the strong stage lighting the
audience wouldn't see the glistening scarlet on Lynne's neck. Fortunately I did, it wasn't and they didn't.

But more than any single scene, it was the whole process, the whole
idea of doing a play that made *Otherwise Engaged* a memorable experience for me.

It was a kick to glide toward the theater in a limousine among

Broadway's bustle and bright lights. (I never did see my name in lights, exactly; that's an anachronism. I saw it in opaque plastic.)

It was pleasant to go through the ritual of making up, hearing the buzz of a full house (thanks to my TV fame, we were sold out most of the time) and knowing that in the next two hours there would be bursts of applause, rapt silences, exclamations of delight and, best of all, surefire lines that would rock the house.

It was buoying and flattering to receive burbling visitors in my room afterwards, to have all the hugs and jokes and invitations, to see bobbing up among the faces the Walter Cronkites, Carly Simon or Jean Simmons, or not to see Woody Allen and Robert Redford but to know they had slipped in and out of the theater while the house lights were down and would "see me later."

The happy hubbub was marred only by an occasional, troubling, "What did they *really* think?"

Dressing rooms are at the heart of the theater experience. Though usually windowless and bare, they have a warm coziness about them, a prenatal feeling. They should be called dressing wombs.

I remember a time in London when I was visiting Robert Morley backstage and happened to peek into the dressing room of an elderly character actress. The play was a long-running hit, and my visit was between a matinee and evening performance. The actress was nestled with a thriller on a wicker chaise, killing time between shows. Around her were her knitting, a teapot wearing its cozy, a photograph of her cat and a couple of plants she had brought to brighten the otherwise unadorned cubicle. She had gotten into a worn and comfortable looking dressing gown and had brewed a cup of tea.

There was something arresting about this glimpse into the temporary little nest she had made, something at once cheery and sad—sad because it was temporary and made me think of the remark of another British actress, a single lady: "I love being in a long run; you have somewhere to go at night."

To an actor a cast is family—and a dressing room is home.

When you're in an established play you always know you can count on those two hours of your day. For a while everything is clear, mapped out, predictable and familiar. There is an order and clarity that everything else in life lacks. You *know* what will happen, what you and others will say and do, and—with minor and pleasing variations—what the reactions and consequences will be. For two hours, away from the nerve-jangling senselessness of life's random events, the stage is a place, as Yeats put it in another context, "where all's accustomed, ceremonious."

This may explain what to me is a perpetual marvel: the mysterious way in which neurotic, troubled performing artists whose lives are in a shambles and unraveling disastrously, whose minds and spirits are all but unhinged by drink, drugs or despair, can step from the wings into the limelight and be instantly transformed—confident, radiant, reliable and marble-firm.

I've seen actors who, thanks to booze, could scarcely navigate to the wings spring out onstage with the sureness of a sober athlete and give faultless, bang-up performances. The structure of the play seemed to organize their talents temporarily, even if afterwards they had to be assisted to their dressing rooms or poured into a taxi.

I think this is one of the great lures of the performing life. One escapes *into* performing and while exercising that mysterious gift from the gods is secure, in charge and fully at home. Troubles recede. For the duration one's scattered faculties are gathered—presto!—into smooth-working stability and all is controlled.

Unhappily, it can all vanish with the descending curtain. It is always disillusioning to go backstage to congratulate some great legend who has just commanded the stage and dominated, thrilled and hushed a sea of spellbound onlookers, and to see the transformation that has taken place. The god in whose presence you sat enthralled moments before is suddenly a shrunken thing, slightly enfeebled in a wornout bathrobe, unsure and eager for assurance that "it was all right?"

Mixed with a certain relief that a hard job is nearly over, I think most performers would admit to a feeling of sadness toward the end of a performance, when they realize that only a few minutes of this wonderful, secure unreality remain and then it's back to the chill of real life again.

There is a feeling after a performance of being sent out into the cold and I'm sure it's why the majority of actors can't go straight home. Not only is it hard to unwind right away, but it's great fun to talk over with colleagues what happened that night, to guffaw over mistakes or mishaps, and in general to keep the family together a little longer before returning, in some cases, to the single flat or hotel room with the gin bottle on the dresser.

My own disorder and unsettledness, though of a very mundane and unalcoholic variety, welcomed all the organizing and bolstering that *Otherwise Engaged* could provide. The three-month run went by in a twinkling; the following year I played it again in summer theaters; and suddenly it was over.

I wish I could find something like it again. I know I never had a better time in my life.

BESIDE THE NIOBRARA

ONE DAY A FEW years ago, I got into a car in Lincoln, Nebraska, and drove 532 miles westward. At the end of the day I was still in Nebraska and I had seen a total of maybe six other cars. Obviously, I avoided the sterile interstate and took back highways and out-of-the-way routes now scorned by the supertraveler.

The farther west I went the more I penetrated into a land of majestic cottonwoods and lone windmills and seemingly endless prairie that makes you realize that unless you've been in that part of the country, what you think of as a far horizon isn't even close (or is).

My destination was a rolling green region at the prairie's edge called the Sand Hills. I was going to film some segments of a documentary for Nebraska public television about the Sandoz family, whose famous member Mari wrote the western classic *Old Jules,* a memoir of her tyrannical Swiss immigrant father and his struggles to settle on a farm out there. The documentary was not only about Mari and her literary career but about the land that had formed her, and about the surviving

247

brothers and sisters who still lived there—a vigorous, independent, indomitable clan.

Business, then, was taking me to the Sand Hills; but it was a sentimental journey too. I had been making occasional trips there since childhood. It is the most peacefully beautiful area I've ever seen, and something in me seems to have its center of gravity there.

I arrived about dusk. I realized as I stepped out of the car to look around, a thousand miles from nowhere, that it had been years since I had heard quiet. In the vast evening calm I felt that I could detect the footfall of an ant.

In a field beside the road a mean-looking bull was giving himself a dust bath, pawing the powdery loose earth with a front hoof and throwing it up over his back. He was shiny black and heavily muscled and was giving me the evil eye. I was careful to keep the fence between us. I had been chased by my German uncle's dyspeptic bull in Colorado once and was not eager to repeat the experience.

I hopped up on the trunk of the car and leaned against the rear window, contemplating the scene. The sun had almost set and there was a kind of purplish haze near the horizon. Some sort of great bird glided overhead, probably a red-tailed hawk hunting for its supper. Adam before Eve came on the scene could not have felt more solitude.

The low rolling grassland seemed to stretch away endlessly toward the setting sun, and it occurred to me that the bull thought this was the whole world. He didn't know, for example, that there was a New York City, or that within it there was a Madison Square Garden where, thirty-six hours earlier, amid lights, cameras, a roaring throng and nerve-wracking chaos, I had served as one of the four hosts of an overblown live TV fiasco called "The Big Event." Sitting in this realm of quiet and cool evening air and rolling distances I could scarcely believe it myself. It was as improbable as *this* would've seemed from the lights and smoke and jangled hysteria of the TV special.

Which was preferable and more fit for human beings? I asked myself, and then mentally changed the subject in order to avoid facing up to the obvious answer. Why would anybody be there who could be here?

I realize there's an element of self-deception in all this; that what makes such moments so poignant is that they are a contrast; that too much of the one as a steady diet could be as wearing as too much of the other, and to think "I could live on *only* this" is a delusion to be wary of.

I know people in ulcer-inducing professions who have chucked them for a totally opposite life—a little patch of paradise in the Caribbean, perhaps—and found themselves climbing their thatched walls after a month or two, longing for a lurching taxi ride and a corned beef sandwich from a rude waiter in a noisy restaurant.

Over the next few days I did my work with the TV crew on the Sandoz documentary, traveling from farm to farm, meeting and interviewing Mari's relatives, trying to capture a bit of their way of life on film.

Soon, too soon, it was time to head back east. But not before communing once more with the spirit of the Sand Hills.

I had chosen my spot while we were still shooting the documentary. It was a grove near the sleepy Niobrara River, a low place with soft sounds of winds in the trees. "Young Jules" Sandoz, who was then seventy-four, had shown it to me and told me the old-timers used to have an annual picnic there and reminisce by the hour.

Now, early on my last day, I returned to it alone. The last of the sparkling dew was evaporating in the morning sun. It was going to be a clear, golden day. I found an old wooden chair lying on its side, a relic, perhaps, of those bygone picnics. I brushed some cobwebs off it, pulled it upright and settled myself in it.

Sitting there, I calculated how many of my supposedly enviable experiences I would trade for one day of hearing men and women who *to Jules* were old-timers sit and swap tales of the early days. I tried to imagine hearing their voices but heard only the occasional ripple in the river and the wind in the cottonwood trees. What a priceless thing a day of their memories would be, now lost forever.

I pushed my Stetson forward and stretched out my legs, watching an ant busily explore the toe of one of my boots. I felt the warming sun coming through the trees and listened to the rippling stream and the murmuring cottonwoods.

How delightful it would be, I thought, just to spend the rest of the day in that peaceful spot, without a book or a radio or anything but the splendid quiet. What would go through my mind after an hour? Or two? Or six?

If I could just sit there all day until the sun went down I could say that I had had one perfect day. Just sit there in the warmth of that pleasant grove where the view in any direction was a harmonious combination of earth and trees and sky and river and grass. Sit absolutely still and engrave it on my memory and not even stir for fear of somehow disturbing the composition.

Someday, I told myself, I would definitely do just that. And then whenever I found myself in angst or turmoil, I could always summon a measure of peace by mentally placing myself back in that one cloudless day in that beatific setting beside the Niobrara in the Sand Hills.

I got up with a sigh and said good-bye to the old chair. I placed it carefully back in its imprint in the grass the way it had been, and walked toward my car. After all, I was an adult living in the modern world and had important obligations and things to do.

What in hell could they possibly have been?